rules of the game:

global business protocol

NAN LEAPTROTT

Global Business Consultants

To John,
a professional with astute
business acumen!

Best regards,
Nan Leaptrott

THOMSON EXECUTIVE PRESS
A Division of South-Western College Publishing

Sponsoring Editor: James L. Sitlington
Development Editor: Betsy Newberry (Custom Editorial Productions)
Production Editor: Holly Terry
Production House: Trejo Production
Internal Design: Tom Hubbard
Cover Design: Michael Lindsay Design
Marketing Manager: Stephen E. Momper

I(T)P
International Thomson Publishing
Thomson Executive Press, a Division of South-Western College Publishing,
is an ITP Company. The ITP trademark is used under license.

Library of Congress Cataloging-in-Publication Data

Leaptrott, Nan
   Rules of the game: global business protocol / Nan Leaptrott.
       p. cm.
   Includes bibliographical references and index.
   ISBN: 0-538-85455-3
   1. Business etiquette I. Title.
HF5389.L43 1996
395'.52--dc20   95-38856
                                                     CIP

1 2 3 4 5 MT 9 8 7 6 5
Printed in the United States of America

Rules of the Game: Global Business Protocol is an essential tool for any businessperson in today's global business environment. Author Nan Leaptrott has applied her years of global experience to present a simple, practical methodology for understanding cultural interaction today.

Rules of the Game takes you beyond the "do's" and "don'ts" of international business customs to the rationale and reasoning behind these actions. You'll examine the fundamental motivating factors for each culture, and the rules for behavior that stem from them.

With this understanding of protocol and etiquette, you'll have the confidence to approach any culture and act consistently and effectively in all areas of business transactions.

Only *Rules of the Game examines:*

- ○ Points of protocol for specific countries and regions, and what purposes they serve.
- ○ How to deduce the proper protocol when you encounter a new situation.
- ○ How to develop an effective game plan for any multi-national business interaction.
- ○ The three fundamental world cultures and how to recognize them.
- ○ The basic motivating factors for each culture.
- ○ How to develop a character profile for the person with whom you will meet.

Depend on *Rules of the Game's* unique model of world cultures for success in all of your cross-cultural business relationships - both abroad and in the United States.

Author Nan Leaptrott, President of Global Business Consultants, is a recognized authority, consultant, and author on global business practices. During the past 25 years, she has led numerous seminars and coached top international corporate executives and thousands of business people throughout the world. Her writings have appeared in numerous publications including *Worldwide Business Practice Report, Success Magazine, Washington Business Journal, and Carolina Business Journal.* Ms. Leaptrott resides in Pinehurst, North Carolina and can be reached at 910-295-5991 or nleap@pinehurst.net - www.pinehurst.net/~gbc.

DEDICATION

Everyone we meet leaves a mark on our lives. A few people we meet have an especially significant impact. Lavinia Jensen is an impressive person to all she encounters. She has been my friend, my mentor, and a sustaining influence for a very long time. Without her unconditional love, respect, and generosity, this book never could have happened. Thus I lovingly dedicate this book to her.

ACKNOWLEDGMENTS

Special gratitude—

A manuscript of this magnitude is impossible to do alone. Phyllis Nordstrom has been there with me from the inception of the idea until the last word was written. She organized my research, gave me technical support, and shared her creative talent in words, thoughts, and research from her own professional international experience.

Phyllis and I have become both a team and friends, and it is my desire that she continue to be a consequential part of all my writing endeavors.

Thank you, Phyllis! You are one of a kind.

In memory—

David and Alleen Shearer, my parents, instilled in me the motivation to use my talents in unique ways. I learned from them to appreciate people's differences, for they lived their lives with the highest regard for all mankind.

Dr. David Shearer, my brother, tackled new endeavors at a very young age. He urged me to be true to myself and to go after the desires of my heart.

Jo Northrop, author and dear friend, taught me to see beauty in simple pleasures. Her way with the written word supersedes most others'. Her wit shed light on dark days, and her last words to me were, "Nan, never forget your dream of writing your book." She must be smiling down on me today.

Family is important—

Richard (Dick) has demonstrated immeasurable staying power through the long days and nights that went into this project. He corrected my punctuation and gave me his opinion on what read well and didn't. His love of detail helped me focus in a linear way when my diffuse personality went in too many directions. Dick, your uniqueness has been my staying power. Thanks for being there.

My three sons—Ben, Tim, and Jeff—represent for me a combination of depth, spiritual grounding, insight, creative thinking, practical guidelines, humor, and great love. And they give me great joy. I am truly blessed.

My daughters-in-law—Susan and Karol—through their inner beauty, have given me strength. They cheered me on every single day. They are a delight to be around and to observe, and they mean more to me than they can ever imagine. They touch my heart every day.

My seven grandchildren—David, Elizabeth, Russ, John, Zach, Anna, and James— are the serendipity in my life. I would rather be with them than just about anyone else. The mere sound of their voices always gives me the gravity to keep life in the right order. They are wonderful.

Nina Bard, my sister, is my sounding board. She has listened to me discuss every aspect of this book and she never looked bored. She and her husband, Bill, have given me much support. Thank you.

Professional thanks—
To all my clients and the readers of my articles who have added so much to my resource material, I am most grateful.

Hilka Klinkenberg, my colleague, friend, writer, author, and professional in this field of expertise, applauded, listened, and guided me in many ways. She is a first-class act.

Mary Elizabeth Nordstrom spent many hours reading and correcting this manuscript. She made sure that inappropriate words were deleted and corrected a host of other mistakes. Mary Elizabeth, mother of Phyllis Nordstrom, encouraged us, gave us worthy praise, and took care of us. Many thanks.

Pat Watson filed my research over and over again. She kept me organized and my office running smoothly. When the days were long and laborious, she made me walk away and go hit tennis balls. Thanks, Pat, for being a friend, colleague, and a part of my family.

Bob Linsenman, my agent, connected me to International Thomson Publishing. I will be forever grateful.

Jim Sitlington Jr., vice president/publisher, is the best there is. He always took my phone calls, and he brought out the best in me so I could create the best book possible.

Betsy Newberry, Holly Terry, and Margaret Trejo—Thomson support staff, added an innovative approach to the book. They are marvelous.

Dr. Lonnell Johnson reviewed the book and made valuable suggestions. He is a talented writer and human being. Thanks, Lonnell.

Bill Lambie, an expert in Japanese protocol, recalled and shared with me many days from his memory bank. He added much in practicality and humor.

Don and Joan Marshall, experts in Spanish culture, speaking from their own international experience, supplied me with a wealth of information. They are warm, giving friends.

Wes and Mil Weston, experts in South American and Japanese culture, are friends who spent a lot of time with me telling of their observations and experiences. Mil is the best clipping service there is, making sure that I received the latest article on my business.

Don McKenzie, a talented photographer, captured the essence of dining around the world in a most professional way. He captured my essence as well.

Marion Johnson taught me how to celebrate the best in me.

Brenda Parker, proprietor of the River Kwai, graciously let me use her dishes and artifacts for the Thai place settings. She also gave of her time to make sure the photographs were perfect.

Caroline Rhorer helped in many ways, especially by sharing her expertise on wines around the world.

Jean Ely, interior designer, offered me the use of her Japanese place settings. She is artistic in all she does.

Ed Ely, landscape artist, grew for the dining pictures the beautiful Star Rose, which has magnificent beauty and fragrance.

Belk Department Store, of Pinehurst, N.C., loaned me exquisite place settings for the other dining photographs. The store was helpful in every way possible.

Linda Cox, proprietor of Grounds and Pounds, made sure her delicious coffee kept me alert.

Theodosia Thomas, who kept my household running smoothly and whose friendship I value.

And the thanks go on—
My good friends have encouraged me in all aspects of my life. There are too many to list, they know who they are, and they know they are loved and appreciated.

FOREWORD

How fundamental is protocol to business? I'll answer this with another question: Have you ever tried to play a game without rules? Every business transaction involves two or more people. They know the end result they aim to achieve and the technical steps required to achieve it. But, as in a game, do they know the rules that govern each move? To many businesspeople, these rules are invisible. We all are accustomed to certain behavior and don't question why or how. Remove businesspeople from their own culture and the rules of interaction become enormously visible—often incomprehensible.

Protocol does not evolve randomly. There are both logic and purpose behind it. When the purpose of protocol is understood, the use of protocol becomes much more clear and dynamic. The ritual exchange of business cards in Japan, for instance, has baffled many Americans who casually hand out their business cards as though they were playing cards. If Americans understood that the Japanese hold their entire identity in that small card, they would not belittle the ceremony. They would not stuff the card into their pocket until they have admired every letter. They would know that the Japanese, in turn, perceive Americans' casual presentation as a display of low self-esteem. The purpose *Rules of the Game* is not only to inform you about international business customs but also to give you an understanding of the reasons behind those customs. The resulting knowledge will be a powerful tool for successful cross-cultural business interaction.

I prefer to view the subject of protocol in a global context. This book presents a *unified global approach* to the understanding and use of protocol and etiquette anywhere in the world. Most books offer lists of dos and don'ts, but no rationale behind the rules. The difference between the approach taken in this book and the approach in more standard texts on the subject is similar to the difference between studying a foreign language instead of buying a traveler's phrase book. You may be able to pronounce the phrases from the phonetic pronunciation guide, but if anyone asks you a question that isn't in that book, you're lost. You have no true command of the language. You might be able to find your way around, but you certainly don't seem to be in command. It is the same with protocol. Reading a list of dos and don'ts for a country does not give you sufficient information to develop the ability to act consistently or effectively. In cross-cultural business transactions, such ability is crucial.

When a company decides to expand into global markets, management usually targets specific countries. Too often, the target country is looked at without regard for its relative position in a much larger regional sphere of influence. For example, a company may target Thailand without understanding the enormous influence of ethnic Chinese Thais in that country. The chief executive of a Belgian company may be French by birth, and the company's chief engineer may be a native Pakistani. Few nations are immune to foreign cultural influences at their borders.

In the world today, economic interdependence has caused cultures to both overlap and interact. Almost every culture has been influenced in some way—positively or negatively—by Western—and mostly American—culture. Television, movies, computer technology, and consumer goods carry U.S. culture around the world. As countries become more westernized, we come to believe that they think and act more like us, and that they understand and accept those of us in America because they are familiar with our culture. This is an illusion. Although those of the younger generations may wear denim and listen to Western music, such customs do not change the fundamental beliefs that underlie their culture. Other cultures are in the process of adapting to Western technology and consumer goods, but they have a difficult time adapting our values to their culture. You will see why as you read this book.

Rules of the Game gives the businessperson a simplified, practical methodology for understanding cultural interaction. The methodology is based on a unique model of world cultures that examines the fundamental motivating factors within each culture, as well as the rules for behavior that grow out of basic beliefs. This model allows us to develop the principle of *global business protocol*—an approach to interaction that is applicable anywhere in the world. It is offered as a solution to the problem of developing a unified policy for conducting business relationships abroad. It will also enable the reader to interact effectively with people from different cultural backgrounds who live and work in the United States.

As you play this game, you will learn:

- Points of protocol for specific countries and what purpose they serve.
- How to deduce the proper protocol when you encounter a new situation.

- How to develop a game plan for any business interaction.
- The three fundamental cultures and how to recognize them.
- The basic motivating factors for each culture.
- How to develop a character profile for the person with whom you will meet.

Chapter 1 introduces the basic concepts of the rules of the game. In that chapter you will learn the basic method to follow in an approach to any culture for the purpose of doing business. If you are extremely short on time, you may want to skip to Chapter 10 for specific data on the country you are targeting. Following is an outline of the rest of the book.

Chapter 2 discusses in detail the concept of the three fundamental world cultures. Even an experienced international traveler will find the information fresh and informative. You will come away with an understanding of why those of certain cultures behave as they do. The difference between protocol and etiquette is explained, and the connection between protocol and culture is demonstrated.

Chapter 3 extends the three-culture concept to look specifically at the people with whom you will be interacting. Culture-based perceptions will be discussed and used to develop player portraits. The chapter concludes with a hypothetical example showing how these concepts are put to use. You will understand how to approach any culture by way of the information given in Chapters 1 through 3.

Chapters 4 and 5 present detailed information about major regions of the world. A game analogy is used for business to help illustrate the value of protocol. It is also more entertaining than digesting a multitude of facts. Chapter 3 describes how the game is played—that is, how to deduce correct protocol from a known cultural identity and how to develop an appropriate game plan. Chapters 4 and 5 show how the game is played in most areas of the world where Americans are likely to do business. As each game progresses, right and wrong answers to questions are explained. You are told not merely what to do but also why a behavior is appropriate and necessary in that cultural setting.

Chapter 6 is not only for women. Many men have found the concept of the so-called third sex to be enlightening. Gender issues are discussed and a successful approach to behavior is offered.

Chapter 7 is indispensable for anyone doing business overseas. When working cross-culturally, the words *right* and *wrong* may lose something in the translation.

Chapter 8 will be valuable to you whenever you host foreign visitors here in the United States. It discusses not only what you yourself should know, but also what your staff should know.

Chapter 9 is more important than you might think. "I know how to use a knife and fork," you say? Do you also know what to do when you are faced with, say, four forks and three knives? What if there are no forks or knives at all? Will you be surprised to find that Americans are the only people who eat American style? Do you know how people of other cultures view American table manners?

Chapter 10 is a summary of information arranged alphabetically by country. I recommend using this as a quick reference and not as a starting point.

There are certain ground rules we will observe in this book. The first one is that the masculine pronoun will be used in most cases. By a wide margin, it is still usually men who are involved in international business situations. This is not to say that this book will not benefit the American businesswoman; it is imperative that women be familiar with the usual business practices of other cultures to know when and how to make adjustments in their own behavior. Chapter 6 is devoted to the challenges faced by Western women doing business internationally. (The subject deserves an entire book of its own, which is forthcoming.)

The second ground rule is that it is assumed the reader of this book is American and has a general knowledge of U.S. business and social customs. If not, then the companion to this book, entitled *The American Game Plan: A Regional Approach to Business Protocol in the U.S.,* will be valuable.

Ground rule number three is the acknowledgment that the subject of ethics in business is an important one that cannot be adequately covered in this text. The approach to that subject in Chapter 7 serves to alert readers to possible areas of conflict, but not to solve such problems for them, for such might constitute legal advice and is beyond the scope of this book.

Not all nations of the world are included directly in this book, yet all are represented by culture type. The nations most likely to be visited by U.S. business people are highlighted with supplemental notes that contain specific information. This book will give readers a method for deducing the appropriate protocol in remote areas of the world to where they may be traveling.

As a trainer who specializes in the field of business protocol and etiquette, I have seen tremendous growth in corporate awareness of the importance of interpersonal behavior in business. Companies are willing to spend money to train their personnel to work together more effectively, to communicate more clearly, and generally to behave more professionally. This indicates that the purpose for these companies is to get the most out of their employees by enhancing employees' ability to perform in any business situation and achieve full potential. To accomplish that, all you need to know are the rules of the game.

Nan Leaptrott
Pinehurst, N.C.

CONTENTS

CHAPTER 9
THE EXCITING GAME OF INTERNATIONAL DINING   239

CHAPTER 10
CUT TO THE CHASE   253

1

The Game of Global Business

The game is global business and the rules of the game are called protocol. Protocol is a set of rules for interaction that must be observed in order to accomplish any business objective. Knowledge of protocol makes global business a game of strategy. Ignorance of the rules of behavior makes it a game of chance. Which type of game would you rather play?

Culture gives birth to protocol the way a game gives birth to rules. The rules of interaction—protocol—tell us what to do in order to achieve a certain result. The people of any nation are a group of players bound by a unique culture. Their society's protocol promotes the perpetuation of the society, its beliefs, and its objectives. By the method proposed in this book, you will understand any culture in the world by studying just three unique cultural models.

Mastering the game of global business requires two skills: understanding the rules of interaction and using the rules strategically. Note that the first skill says *understanding* the rules of interaction—not just *knowing* the rules. Understanding means to know where the rules come from and what purpose they serve, as well as knowledge of specific customs. No book can mention all of the potential situations an American businessperson might encounter. If one has an understanding of the governing principles that the rules of protocol grew out of—that is, the culture's underlying values—then in most instances the correct protocol can be deduced.

If your plane is about to land, I suggest you finish this chapter, then turn to Chapter 10, "Cut to the Chase." Chapter 10 offers in summary form detailed information about most countries. It is designed as a quick reference guide for those who have read Chapters 1 through 9. If you haven't, it contains important information that will at least keep you out of trouble if that is all you want to accomplish. What Chapter 10 will not give you is a true understanding of the culture you are about to enter. You will not be able to use the information strategically. Instead, you will be playing a game of chance.

Cross-cultural business heightens one's focus on personal interaction. At home we do business without thinking very much about how we behave and how we accomplish our objectives. We interact with businesspeople in our own culture very naturally. Going global causes one to focus more on the process of business. Effective personal interaction becomes a major factor in accomplishing objectives. The rules of protocol give structure to that business process.

ORIGINS OF THE GAME

Culture-based rules of interaction can seem baffling without an understanding of their origin or purpose. Quite simply, the rules reflect the ways in which people behave. Why people behave the way they do is a complex subject that can be simplified by the understanding that *people behave in a manner consistent with their perception of reality.*

Generally speaking, with emphasis on the word *generally*, the world's cultures can be divided into three fundamental classifications. They will be referred to as *tribal*, *collective*, and *pluralist*. Most cultures fall into one of these categories; some are combinations. In our simplified methodology, the world can be mapped by culture, as in Figure 1.1. Each is briefly explained here; a detailed discussion follows in Chapter 2.

Tribalism. The word *tribal* suggests primitive social structure, and yet you will notice that a large part of Western society may be termed tribal. What this means is that the primary focal point of the individual—the structure through which one derives one's identity—is the family unit. The family unit can be more accurately defined as a clan, or extended family. It is a close-knit group whose members are associated through heredity and who have a shared historical perspective. Members feel a sense of connection to the past through ancestors and to the future through children. In tribalist cultures, the family must survive at all costs, the family name must be protected, and the honor of the family must be defended.

Collectivism. Collectivism shares one similarity with tribalism: that of group association. However, collectivism engages a much broader concept of *group*. The group affiliation can be a town, a principality, a nation, or a race. The individual finds identity through affiliation with a large group. In order to maintain this group identity, it is important that the group foster homogeneity. All members are equal within the group. All participate, and all share. The individual is not singled out. It is important to an individual's identity that he or she be just like everyone else. It becomes fright-

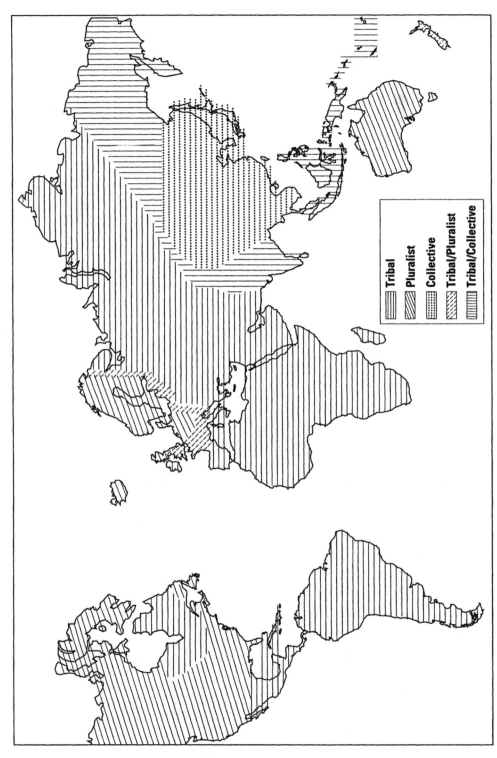

Figure 1.1
World Culture Map

Tribal
Pluralist
Collective
Tribal/Pluralist
Tribal/Collective

ening for those who exceed the group, go beyond, or reject the group and look for
something different, something personal. They are nothing without the group.

Pluralism. The pluralist society contains a variety of institutions or groups that provide social structure. One can choose to find personal identity through family, religious affiliation, social group, business, or political organization, most likely choosing
a combination of these. In a pluralist society, all are free to construct their own personal identity. They are not only free to, but must. Individuals are responsible for
themselves, the group will not care for them. It is through individual consent that any
group is maintained as a unit. Conformity is neither demanded nor assumed; it is accepted within a group as a means for maintaining the group's identity. Reliance on any
form of organization or institution is seen as a confession of weakness and dependence. Independence is the ultimate value; dependence, a form of failure. What ultimately binds a pluralist culture into an associative cultural unit is mutual consent. Its
members choose to remain in the culture and maintain basic civil laws to which all,
by logic, can consent.

THE PLAYERS

In international business it is important to know something about the people you will
meet. Do they think like you? Do they have the same priorities? How are you likely
to be received? To understand a culture means to understand the way its people act.

The cultural governing principles give you basic information about a player's tendencies. Such player characteristics will be summarized as **player portraits**. The portraits include information about a person's perceptions of time and physical space and
about how the player communicates most information, whether it is by language or
by gesture. The player portrait also will give you an idea of the player's power concept: Is he used to group power or to personal power? Is power distributed laterally
or hierarchically? A player's ability to deal with uncertainty, his degree of materialism,
and his self-awareness all are important factors in how an opponent or team member
will react to you and how he will attempt to achieve his own objectives.

TRIBAL PLAYER PORTRAIT

What does he believe is a person's responsibility?
To support his family. To be obedient to the rules of society.

What does he expect of others?
Mutual support, absolute loyalty.

How does he interact with others?
With strangers he is formal and aloof. With those he knows and trusts, he is warm and
   welcoming.

What impresses him? What does he respect in another?
Status, strength, cunning.

What is his attitude toward foreigners?
Cautious, defensive, formal, distrustful.

Why is he in the game?
He works to live.

What is his main objective?
To have the respect of his group, to do his job, to contribute to his family unit.

How does he define winning?
Getting what he asked for.

What is his business environment (physical and hierarchical)?
Strong vertical hierarchy with many levels. Top leaders are inaccessible. Offices are
   open plan for the lowest on the ladder, and managers have best offices.

How does he conduct business?
He must feel in control. Time and meeting content may be used for manipulation.
   Correspondence is controlled, limited, and personal.

How does he learn?
Content must be more visual than detailed text. Generalization of data, coaching, and
   repetition are helpful.

How does he give feedback?
He avoids detail and does not want to be held accountable. Feedback is usually
   subjective and not necessarily rational.

How does he make decisions?
Decisions are made at the top. Personal decisions are usually based on pride and
   emotion before objective benefits are considered.

What is his attitude toward time, schedules, plans, and change?
Time is linear, but he is process oriented, rather than goal oriented. Plans can grow,
   and project definitions tend to be fluid. He does not use detailed plans.

How does he approach problem solving?
More emphasis is put on assessment of blame than on solving problems. Where the
   blame falls, there are severe consequences.

COLLECTIVE PLAYER PORTRAIT

What does he believe is a person's responsibility?
Contribution to the group, maintaining the honor of the group, conformity.

What does he expect of others?
Humility, respect, mutual support.

How does he interact with others?

His actions do not stand out. He is friendly but noncommittal to strangers. He is loyal and forms strong relationships with friends.

What impresses him? What does he respect in another?

Strength and humility combined. Cleverness, knowledge.

What is his attitude toward foreigners?

Caution, distrust, aggressive but subtly defensive.

Why is he in the game?

He works to live.

What is his main objective?

He must succeed at the job he was given. He must get something from the opponent to improve the position of his group.

How does he define winning?

Zero-sum, total victory.

What is his business environment (physical and hierarchical)?

Power is shared, so there is more of a horizontally layered hierarchy. Managers do not stand out. The physical plan is very open, but location is important and symbolic.

How does he conduct business?

Everyone has his own job responsibility. Strategy is important in business dealings. Ritual is important. Correspondence is open and widely shared.

How does he learn?

He prefers to be shown rather than to read detailed text. He learns best with others (i.e., via group instruction).

How does he give feedback?

Feedback starts within the group. A consensus must be reached. If feedback is negative, it will be avoided.

How does he make decisions?

By consensus. Final decisions come from the top.

What is his attitude toward time, schedules, plans, and change?

He is more process than goal oriented. Things take as long as they take. Things happen when the time is right. Change may be construed as error in original thinking—and therefore resisted.

How does he approach problem solving?

Problems are evaded. Someone will lose face, and there will be conflict. Problems are passed off or handled very privately, ultimately not admitting to any problem.

PLURALIST PLAYER PORTRAIT

What does he believe is a person's responsibility?

Personal achievement, personal growth, independence.

What does he expect of others?

Integrity, performance, competence.

How does he interact with others?

Informally, with straightforward communication and fairness.

What impresses him? What does he respect in another?

Creativity, status gained through achievement.

What is his attitude toward foreigners?

Open, nonhostile, curious.

Why is he in the game?

He lives to work.

What is his main objective?

Success, achieving or exceeding his goals.

How does he define winning?

Zero-sum or win-win. On time and under budget.

What is his business environment (physical and hierarchical)?

Multilayered hierarchy of management, allowing movement within the company on
many levels. Physical space is private, with best spaces reserved for upper
management.

How does he conduct business?

Direct, gets down to business. More formal with strangers than coworkers. Correspondence is distributed along chain of command and to others who need to know.

How does he learn?

By detailed information, independent verification, and verbal text.

How does he give feedback?

Direct, specific, objective, impersonal.

How does he make decisions?

Independent, rational process. Approval of decisions by middle management.

What is his attitude toward time, schedules, plans, and change?

Time is linear; punctuality is important. He likes detailed plans and observes schedules.
Change is taken in stride.

How does he approach problem solving?

Problems are addressed quickly and rationally. What went wrong is analyzed after the
problem is solved.

THE GAME PLAN

Protocol consists not merely of knowing how to shake hands. It consists of knowing how to shake hands with the right person at the right time in the right way so that you communicate respect, knowledge, and self-confidence. You have the choice of either going through the motions or using your knowledge of protocol strategically, to your advantage. This could be compared to giving a presentation by simply listing facts, as opposed to preparing a presentation that focuses on the needs of your customer in order to solve that customer's business problems.

Your overall game plan should include the strategic use of protocol. Strategy is what gives us the opportunity to succeed or to fail. Strategy is necessary to any challenge if the player wants to be able to influence the results. The Chinese are famous for their use of elaborate military strategy and its application to business. *Bing Fa*, or the art of war, is studied by all Chinese. Similar to the rules of *Bing Fa*, we can devise a successful game plan for use anywhere around the globe.

To develop a game plan, we should look to the end result: What is the objective? Every player must know what he is trying to accomplish. How a player chooses to behave will depend on the goals and on whether or not the business objective requires a competitive or a noncompetitive approach. If we view business as a game for the moment, we can say that noncompetitive games involve any number of players working toward a common goal. The challenge lies in overcoming internal and external obstacles to success. In business, one of the noncompetitive games might be total quality management, in which each division of a company focuses on the improvement of its own process. Once each division has accomplished its goal, the entire company wins.

Competitive games are characterized by one player's or a group of players' presenting a challenge to another player or group of players. The goal is to enhance one player's position at the expense of another. In other words, someone wins and someone loses. This is survival of the fittest. In business, these games might be undertaken to increase market share or to monopolize a certain market sector. There is an aspect of competitive games that combines cooperation with competition. There can be a mutual quest for excellence through competition. Each side presents obstacles and challenges. Opposing sides must meet the challenge and improve their position. Both challengers can be winners.

A game plan for global business must consider the objective, the type of challenge being presented, and guidelines for interaction. Before looking at the culture-specific guidelines, consider the following three prime directives that should be part of any cross-cultural preparation.

1. *Never play the game by trying to become like your opponent, and never expect your opponent to become like you.* Each player must retain his own identity.

The purpose of learning about another culture is to give you information to use in planning strategy. If you were approached by someone whose purpose was to make you become like those in that person's group and play only by their rules, you would naturally resist them. Your identity would be threatened by their actions. You could not possibly trust them in any matter if you thought that the underlying objective was to make you become like them. Therefore, the objective of gaining trust will never be accomplished if you try to absorb another person's culture. No matter how hard you try, if you were raised an American, you will never become a Frenchman. And if you try, you will look something like a wolf in sheep's clothing. So, in order to obey the first rule of the game, you need to learn how to interact with those of another culture without losing your own cultural identity.

2. *Never judge another culture as being good or bad relative to your own.* You will find as you work through the games that some of the rules of protocol and some of the basic values look completely different from your own. In fact, there may be some cultures whose modes of operation are so completely opposed to yours that they may seem evil. But there is no such thing as good and bad in cultural values. Values are relative to a society. If you take the rules of, say, Saudi Arabia and apply them in Germany, you will have chaos. Your values and another player's values may be as opposite as two sides of a coin, but both sides are part of the same coin. Both sides are of equal value. You cannot truly respect another individual if you judge the person to be less than you. Respect is the consideration you give someone whom you deem to have inherent value. If this second fundamental rule is ignored, you might as well not play the game of global business, because you won't enjoy the game and you won't be very good at it either.

3. *Remember that the global business game is about people.* Generally speaking, business in the United States is conducted something like this: The goal is set, a plan is devised, the plan is executed, the results are evaluated. Or, as one American business executive put it, "Here's the product, where's my money?" To most Americans, business is a set of goals, plans, schedules, budgets, reviews, accounting, paychecks, and dividends. It is product, service, and payment for same. A company is defined by its stock value or net worth. And business is not seen as interaction among people; rather, we focus on numbers and products over people and the act of communication.

In fact, however, business is *senior executives* setting goals by consensus or decree and *communicating* those goals to their *management staff*, who then develop plans through information gathering and consultation *with others* in the company. *They* then meet with *subordinates* who are given a course of action with specific intermediate goals. Those actions require the *business-people* to *exchange* information, *negotiate* contracts, establish *partnerships*, work cooperatively *with others*, and provide feedback for their *managers*. While we remain so focused on the bottom line, we actually achieve our business goals through *people* who interact cooperatively and communicate effectively. Therefore, the importance of communication in the game is obvious:

> *"Business is the act of achieving a desired result through interaction between people."*

American players must remember: the game of global business is all about people. Before you begin a game, get that clearly in mind.

With these prime directives in mind, we can continue to develop general game plans for the three fundamental cultures. Chapters 4 and 5 contain more detailed game plans for specific countries and regions.

Tribal Game Plan

Approaching a tribal player on his own turf is very important. He is not by nature a risk taker and feels much more in control in his own territory. The need for a sense of control is great. He is distrustful of foreigners—or anyone outside the group—and will not extend an invitation unless there are clear benefits and low risk and unless introduction is by a mutual friend. Once a personal reference has been used, it is important in initial contact to appeal to the tribal player's ego and stature. Present your proposal in such a way as to minimize risk for him and to stress the gains that are possible.

Once an invitation has been extended, you should try to accommodate his schedule. You have a great opportunity to develop a strong business ally by accepting his hospitality. Your presence as a guest puts the tribal businessperson in a position of honor. It is a host's great honor to provide hospitality for a guest. By putting yourself in a position to accept his hospitality, you also put yourself in a position to establish a personal relationship, which in some tribal cultures is paramount to any business success.

The most obvious form of humility is to defer to another culture's customs or to play by its rules. This means the use or acknowledgment of local protocol, which we will explore in greater detail in later sections. In a tribal society, the protocol that guides business in the initial stages is aimed at establishing a relationship. Business moves forward only after a relationship has been established. During subsequent business meetings, protocol will focus on maintaining personal ties and perpetuating a sense of mutual respect. Such societies are strongly male dominant; male bonding, relative strength, and position are demonstrated and encouraged through the use of protocol. Image is important, and self-image is enhanced by the reflection of others. The image you present, which should be one of impeccable formality and conservatism, is an indication of respect. The better you look, the better it reflects on a tribal player's sense of self-esteem.

Consider it a necessary act of generosity and friendship to make concessions. Always approach tribal cultures with gifts—in the sense of something to concede. When making concessions, do so in the spirit of friendship, and make this offer clear by using flattering language. The poetic and emotional use of language is appreciated by tribal players. Any act will carry more meaning if enhanced by an appropriate speech.

Although tribal players work for the welfare of their tribal group, do not take this to mean that the player you are dealing with has no self-interest. He does, but it is different from the way you might perceive self-interest. Stature and being well-thought-of and respected by others are strong motivators, because self-image comes from outside the tribal player. It is not generated from within himself. He is worthy of respect if the group gives him respect. It is important in your business dealings to show him how he will benefit personally and how his position at work will be enhanced. This can be done subtly by clearly pointing out the less material merits of a deal. He will catch on. Highlighting the bottom line does not necessarily make a compelling argument.

Collective Game Plan

When you approach those in a collective culture on their turf, you have the special opportunity of being symbolically included within their group. As hosts, their hospitality will take you into some part of their group function. If they were to meet you first at your office, their group association would not include you. When you are in their office, you are physically a part of their group. Don't expect this to mean that they accept you as one of the family. You are still odd and do not conform to standards. But symbolically, you are one of them, interacting on common footing.

Travel to a collective culture only when invited. Collectivists, too, are wary of foreigners. They must feel ready and in control. They must have their group strategy in place. Everything they do in business is thought out in advance. Make the parties you contact the focus of your trip. Do not tell them that you are seeing several other groups while in their city or that you will be visiting so-and-so and will have some free time to drop by and meet them. All contacts have an undercurrent of symbolism and ritual. Expect formality. Everything is done for a reason.

The best initial contact is through a reference by a trade council or union, an international bank, or a government embassy. Note that these are references by respected *groups*, not necessarily individuals. In tribal cultures, personal references are more important. In a collective culture, your—or rather your company's—validation by a respected *organization* carries weight.

Humble yourself means, literally, to humble yourself. Once again, this requires that you must play by *their* rules; you must blend in, act conservatively, and not cause anyone to stand out. All are equal by conformity. Deference is to age and seniority. Look for symbolic behavior, and try to respond similarly. Always return a kindness or hospitality. This culture emphasizes sharing. You will never be totally accepted into the group, but sharing is symbolic of mutual respect.

Because you will never actually be part of the group, collectivists' view of group welfare may be at odds with your business purpose, no matter how schooled you are in their culture. The good of the group always comes first. For this reason, they will always require concessions. Don't deprive them of their way of doing business by throwing them a meaningless concession without making them work for it. They expect and enjoy the military strategy of business. It is what has kept their societal groups intact throughout history.

Showing respect and acknowledging a collectivist player's importance is a bit tricky. Collectivists are uncomfortable when singled out. Their accomplishments and talents belong to the group. They are proud of the honor their success bestows on the group. Be indirect and impersonal when you discuss people. Show respect for all groups that the person might be related to: his family, his company, his nation.

When pointing out the merits of any business offer or point of discussion, focus on how the outcome will benefit the group. Know the expertise and the relative authority of the opposing players in order to know how to best structure your remarks.

Pluralist Game Plan

In pluralist business cultures there may be no face-to-face meeting necessary until well into the discussion phase. Pluralists are generally more focused on the merits of a deal rather than who the people involved might be. But at some point the two parties will have to meet. Once discussions are in an advanced stage, it often makes more sense for the buyer to visit the seller, the major contractor to visit the subcontractor, or the client to visit the provider, because the person spending the money often wants to know what is behind the organization to which he is giving money. He is the power player whether he is on his own turf or not. That is a unique aspect of pluralist behavior.

Pluralists tend to take their power with them. Because one's rank or position in society is a function of one's accomplishments, rank and power are contained within the person, wherever he might go. That is why so many cultures view Americans as being inappropriately aggressive or arrogant. Americans do not naturally defer to those in power in other cultures because their personal power is part of their identity. Home field advantage is really only an advantage among pluralists if it is to one's advantage to have the entire organization on display to the opposing player. Alternatively, going to another pluralist's camp can have the effect of making you seem familiar to the players in their own environment, and they are therefore more comfortable doing business with you.

Initial contacts in pluralist societies are also best made by third-party referral. The most effective referral is often between professionals. Someone who knows you in your professional capacity can validate you as a professional. Sometimes a list of clients is all that is necessary to get in the door, without a personal letter from any of them.

Humility is shown merely by deferring to your host's hospitality and his schedule. All players are equal, but rank and position are maintained as a consequence of merit. The protocol of rank promotes the value of personal achievement. Bosses and subordinates may socialize together and are informal in their work environment, but hierarchy is maintained.

Unless one's objective is to survive by eliminating the competition, many pluralist transactions are win-win. That is why the United States has laws against monopolies. It is contrary to the inherent cultural value of fair play. In societies that foster the idea of equal opportunity, the focus of business is on the negotiation of terms that benefit both parties. Giant corporations are not in the business of putting smaller companies out of business by demanding terms that are detrimental to their subcontractors. Long-term business relationships are formed by mutual progress. It is recognized that all businesses have the profit motive and that if no room is left for profit, there is no basis for agreement. Allow a player some room to bargain in order to get the concessions that are most important to you. Think "give and take."

Personal achievement is important to the pluralist, but so is privacy. Some flaunt their financial achievements by way of the car they drive, the neighborhood in which they live, or the toys they have, but you will rarely see evidence of this at work. One's bank account or stock portfolio might be huge, but it is not talked about. It is a matter of personal pride and sense of accomplishment. What you *will* see in an office as evidence of achievement are college diplomas, trophies, letters of commendation, and location of one's office and its decoration. These may all be points of conversation in making your relationship more personal. Remember above all to respect a person's privacy and not bring up subjects that seem too personal.

Businesspeople in pluralist societies want to do their jobs well by improving their performance. They are usually open to ideas that will give them better information, more time, or a better bottom line. Any business offer should get right to the point and address one or all of these subjects. It is through improvement in these areas that the pluralist will find personal achievement that usually translates into improvement in material terms.

The aforementioned three strategies are techniques to be applied not only on initial contact or first meeting. They should be kept in mind during all encounters with people of these three cultures. The strategies are frameworks within which one can play the game to best advantage.

HOW DO YOU KNOW WHEN YOU'VE WON THE GAME?

One interesting truth about the game of global business is that winning is relative. You can define victory only for yourself or your company—not for your opponent or co-competitor. How is winning defined? It is the accomplishment of all the goals you set out to achieve. Once you attain your game objectives, you have won. Each player has different goals, even in competitive play. Each player has a different level of expectation, and once his own expectations and requirements have been met, each declares that he has won. What is winning to me may be losing to you if your objectives were aimed much higher than what I was content to accomplish.

Winning can have basically two results. The consequences of winning a competitive game are that someone wins and someone else loses. This is known as a zero-sum game. Your negative result is equal to my positive result, or, when added together, the sum of the consequences is zero. The other result is a win-win situation. This is possible in a noncompetitive game when all sides are competing against internal and external challenges for mutual benefit. Both sides win equally if they achieve their own personal or corporate objectives. Remember: winning is relative to one's own goals.

Zero-sum games usually do not lead to long-term business relationships. They are usually confrontational relationships, such as buying and selling or negotiating the terms of a contract. To maintain a business association requires a special competitive relationship in which neither side is asked to give up too much. Winning at business should not threaten the opponent's survival if a relationship is to be maintained.

The curious truth about the game of global business is that competitors may be playing differing types of games during the same transaction. What an American businessperson sees as a win-win situation, a Chinese businessperson may perceive as a win-lose situation. One American businessman who set up a distributorship in China recently had this comment: "I know he's stealing me blind, but I'm still making a huge profit." He saw that they were both making money, which fulfilled his criteria to open a profitable distribution network. His Chinese distributor who conducts business as if it were warfare sees the outcome—his additional income—as his win, which his American "competitor" subsequently loses. They have both won on their own terms.

This story leads to the question, what are acceptable losses? It is proper protocol and good strategy to have something to give up. But in order to win, you must maintain your absolutes. Know what you are willing to compromise and what you will not concede at any time. It is the attainment of your absolute goals that defines winning. The small losses along the way do not detract from the main goal. It is acceptable to lose a few battles but win the war.

Generally speaking, the player who knows the rules of the game so well that he develops the perfect strategy in each case, and who clearly knows and is committed to his objective will win the game. He will win the game on his own terms. Using the rules of protocol and etiquette to develop trust and respect will result in a relationship with the other businessperson. One of the tactics used to overcome an opponent's need to play a zero-sum game is the development of a personal relationship.

There comes a point when you seem to have achieved your goal. You declare to yourself and to your boss that you have won. In determining that you have won, can you trust the information you are receiving? The most obvious case in point is the Japanese creative use of the word *yes*. Japanese protocol prohibits Japanese from public confrontation, which would cause loss of face for one of the players. Therefore, they never answer a question in the negative. An American just wants the facts and couldn't care less if someone is offended by the answer. He wants to hear no if the answer is no, and yes if it is yes. If he asks of a Japanese, "Will you hire our company to design the new Osaka shipyard?" and the Japanese answers yes, then the American expects the contract to be signed and the work to proceed. He has won the job and the game. But the Japanese, having no intention of hiring the company, has indicated his position through subtle forms of communication that the American has not been trained to recognize. The American thinks he has won, but he has not.

Knowledge of the rules of protocol, then, also help us to understand what is being communicated. It will also enable an American to request feedback in an appropriate way—one that will result in receiving the factual information needed to evaluate his position and accomplish his goal.

The process of interaction is the focus of the game of global business, and the rules of protocol guide the action. So, in a sense the rules make the game. They establish the way the game is played. The excitement of the game is in the use of the rules for advancing, retreating, and overcoming setbacks. This is the significant action. This is where all your skill is required. Goal setting is a fundamental action. By way of analogy, a marathon runner is aware of the finish line but does not see it during most of the race: The course is set, but each step is taken one at a time; and a football player makes a series of first downs on his way to the end zone; and a baseball player has to get on base before being able to score a run. Protocol is the means that results in an end. It is the cause that produces the effect.

KEY POINTS

- The world can be divided into three fundamental cultures: tribal, collective, and pluralist.
- Prime directives for the game of global business:
  — Never play the game by trying to become like your opponent, and never expect your opponent to become like you.
  — Never judge another culture as being good or bad relative to your own.
  — The global business game is about people.

  These rules promote trust, respect, and communication.

- Mastering the game of global business requires:
  — An understanding of the rules of interaction.
  — Strategic use of the rules of interaction.

2

Discovering the Rules

The best way to simplify the vast amount of information on culture-based behavior is to use a method that focuses on the basic motivating factors in the world's cultures. Be assured that this is a highly simplified methodology and not a critical study of culture. In an attempt to present a unified approach, it is necessary to oversimplify cultures and their beliefs. The simplicity results in a theory, or framework, that works in most cases.

WHO MADE THE RULES?

Group behavior is founded on the shared values of the people making up the group. If we know the essential character of a group, the members' values, and their motivating forces, then we can derive for ourselves the general rules of interaction that are appropriate to that group. Specific motivating factors produce predictable behavior. Protocol does not evolve randomly. There is logic and purpose behind it. There is cause and effect. If we strip away the variety of cultural adaptations resulting from historical events and concentrate on a "pure" form of culture, then we can more easily see those cause and effect relationships. This is the basic method being proposed in this book.

The governing principles are the values of the group that are a reflection of the group's perception of reality. Every individual makes certain assumptions about the world and his own ability to affect it and to be affected by it. That essential understanding derives from each person's consciousness of being and from the fundamental concept of his relationship to a prime mover, a life-giving force, a supreme being, the cosmos, God—whatever it is called or however it is perceived. How the individual perceives his basic existence relative to that power will define his most important motivating forces. A person acts and reacts throughout his life in a manner consistent with his ultimate beliefs.

Consider the following possibilities:

- A man views himself in relationship to a supreme power as being totally separate from that power. He personifies that power, calling it God. There is a distinct difference between the man and God. God is the man's infinite superior. The man's perception of reality is hierarchical, with the most powerful at the top and down to the lowliest below. All his group institutions will be set up to reflect and maintain that view of reality.

- Now consider this same man as having the additional belief that he can improve himself and become closer to God. Then the character of the power hierarchy is changed. The society becomes a meritocracy, with those who achieve success being able to rise in the power hierarchy. The group values include the importance of individuality and personal achievement. The protocol of this society fosters individuality, gain, personal success, and a class system based on achievement.

- If instead of the belief in perfectibility, the man sees himself as being eternally inferior and completely controlled by God, then his social institutions will reflect not only a strong power hierarchy but also a strong sense of fatalism. The man will always feel completely dependent on God and be distrustful of anyone who does not share his concept of God. The protocol of this society fosters a strong power hierarchy, with those in command having exceptional power over others. The rule of law will be profound, and protocol will stress obedience. Showing respect to those in power is paramount. Human life at the bottom of the ladder is not valued as highly as human life at the top.

- Another man senses his connection to the infinite as being continuous. His ultimate selfhood is oneness with the eternal. He does not personify the power by giving the force a name or even a pronoun. The power is simply the infinite, and the man perceives his true nature to be part of the infinite. There is no true separation. The man's finite earthly form is merely illusion. This results in a completely different form of reality that is reflected in his daily life and social institutions. The individual and his personal achievements are not highly valued. It is achievement by the whole that is valued. The social structure is arranged so that people work together. Group identity is important. The protocol of this culture promotes the submersion of individual personality through the requirement of humility. Protocol promotes cooperation and sharing.

These fundamental perceptions of oneself relative to the divine define the individual's source of identity. One of the very basic human needs is identity. Identity consists in a sense of self—relative to something. A man's spiritual identity is his relationship to God. His personal identity is derived from his relationship to a group—a sense of being rooted in something. And one's identity within a group is formed through sharing some kind of essential characteristic with other members of the group. The individual could not survive without some form of association; hence, Adam and Eve.

The reciprocal is also true: The survival of the group can be ensured only if the group identity is maintained. If the group were to change its fundamental nature or disappear entirely, the members of the group would no longer have this associative identity. The person would no longer have the same personal reference points. His identity and the identity of the group do not survive. The purpose of protocol as a set of social rules is to support the unity of the group and foster its identity.

The group with which a person identifies consists of other individuals who share a similar perception of existence. They reflect each other and strengthen each other's beliefs. The group gains power through unity of action. Where there is unity of belief there is unity of action.

A culture develops as a group expression of values and beliefs. Those values and beliefs are expressed through symbolic communication, language, social institutions and structure, self-expression in the arts, and ritual. Within each culture is the programming for how members should value the individual; how they choose to live; how they behave; what they expect from life, from themselves, and from others; and how they express themselves. Culture is passed on through social institutions, including family, religious groups, and business and social institutions. Culture is one's link with the past and serves to validate one's values and beliefs in the present.

Each culture develops a set of laws. Members who act outside the mores and customs of the society are ostracized and possibly banished. They are a threat to the continuity and survival of the group. Even though neglect of normal protocol is not as threatening as breaking the criminal laws of society, neglect of protocol will signal the presence of an outsider—one who is working outside the system or one who may be working at cross purposes to the group. It causes confusion and uncertainty in interaction and makes progress difficult if not impossible.

Game theory, as a mathematical discipline, supports the idea that rules of protocol ensure stability in a society. In game theory there is an equilibrium point at which no player can gain anything by disregarding the rules of the game. The equilibrium point is a rule of behavior such that if all the players except one abide by it, the remaining player cannot do better than abide by it too. Playing by other rules keeps the player outside the game. The player will not achieve his goal relative to the group.

A case in point is the experience of an American who gave a technical presentation before a group of Japanese. After the presentation, the American solicited feedback on the ideas he presented. He wanted to be critiqued. However, Japanese protocol requires its members not to criticize, especially in public. The American continued to demand feedback but got smiles and nods and platitudes—and no useful information. He could not achieve his purpose as long as he requested the Japanese to do what was not allowed by their rules of conduct. The only way he could get the information he needed was to request it in terms their rules allowed.

GOVERNING PRINCIPLES

Theologists, anthropologists, sociologists, and many others may take exception to the simplicity of our model, but the point to remember is that we are presenting a simplistic model of the world in order to get a grasp on the unifying principles. We are by no means saying that all Asian or Middle Eastern countries observe the same rules of behavior. The tribal, collectivist, and pluralistic classifications represent the three fundamental concepts of culture that underlie social behavior.

Let's look more closely at the three basic cultures.

Tribalism. The structure through which the individual derives his identity is the family unit. The family unit can be defined as a clan, or extended family. It is a close-knit group that is associated through heredity. In tribal cultures, the family must survive at all costs. The family is a social structure that reflects the hierarchical view of reality. The individual has a fundamental sense of being separate from God. God is personified, is given a name, and is an infinitely superior power. At the same time, the profound sense of man's being unworthy increases the separation that the man feels. He finds himself in a strong power hierarchy with "God the Father" at the top. His perception of purpose in life is to do God's will—because God is supremely powerful—and to hope that divine grace will rescue him at his death.

Tribal societies demand conformity of all members. They tend to aggressively defend their social structure because it is so closely linked to their family. As a means of controlling their own local identity, tribal cultures look at the world subjectively, with a great deal of personal bias. People of these cultures are strongly opinionated, because their opinions and beliefs define their tribal group and their position within that group. Tribal power hierarchies do not promote individual achievement. Movement within the hierarchy comes from seniority.

Collectivism. In collective cultures, the individual finds his identity through affiliation with a large group. In order to maintain the group identity, it is important that the group foster homogeneity. The individual is not singled out. The collective nature is a reflection of the belief in the oneness of the universe. All people and all things are connected. There is no separation between the soul and the divine. Physical life is an illusion, and the spiritual direction of man is to return to the "absolute." The essence of man is an emanation from the divine. The divine is not personalized or rationalized. It is the "infinite," the "absolute." It is an organized power. There are consistent laws of the universe. The universe is not random or chaotic. It is supervised by the absolute nature of all things. Collective social order emphasizes harmony of all things. The life of the individual is subordinate to the laws that rule the universe. In tribal society, conformity is demanded. In collectivist society, conformity is assumed.

Religion or spirituality is an inherent quality of collective societies. It does not require the tenets of dogma. It is nonevolutionary. One cannot change the laws of the universe. Religion is not revealed throughout history; it is inherent in the nature of the individual. Actually, a more accurate perspective is that the individual is an inherent part of spiritual reality. The individual is merely a concept of this world. The person's existential objective is to merge his consciousness with the divine, to be reabsorbed into the oneness of all things. Therefore, the collective society—as a structure of reality—pays very little attention to the individual and makes total commitment to the good of the whole.

Pluralism. In a pluralist society everyone is free to construct his own personal identity. The individual is responsible for himself. What ultimately binds a pluralist culture into an associative cultural unit is mutual consent. Its members choose to remain in the culture and maintain basic civil laws to which all, by logic, can consent. A man in this society receives his independence through God. His spiritual reality is one of separateness from God. God is personified. He is all-powerful, as in tribal culture. Yet God is viewed as being in a beneficent relationship with man. Man has fallen from divinity. He is, however, inherently perfectible, and God assists him throughout his life in perfecting himself. He works out his own salvation with God as his guide and partner. A man's actions are important. Not to take action to take control of one's life is to ignore the challenge and hope of perfectibility. "God helps those who help themselves."

In a pluralist society, religion is not a fundamental social structure as it is in tribal culture; nor is it an inherent quality as in a collective culture. Religion is a personal relationship. Each individual relates to God in his own way. Even religious institutions are plural, with numerous denominations from which to choose affiliation. Free will is a fundamental religious and social value.

Although all three cultural models are based on religious beliefs, they do not necessarily imply a uniform religion. Among the tribal cultures there are Moslem, Roman Catholic, Jewish, Anglican, and Eastern Orthodox countries. Collective cultures embrace Buddhism, Taoism, Confucianism, and Hinduism. Pluralist countries offer numerous denominations of predominantly Protestant religions.

Religion is the most direct expression of our spiritual realities. Whereas the shared perception of reality is what defines and unifies a culture, all cultures that are fundamentally alike do not necessarily share a common religion. Their particular religious expression may express local influences. The religion that comes to dominate a certain region reflects tribal, collective, or pluralist reality as it is understood in that environment.

The tribal religions previously mentioned—Judaism, Roman Catholicism, Eastern Orthodoxy, Anglicanism, and Islam—all grew out of one religion. They all believe in the same God. To all of them God is a separate, personified "being." He is the father, the ruler of heaven. He is at the top of the power hierarchy. Not many of these cultures would acknowledge that they have anything in common with one another, and yet they all have very strong power hierarchies and accompanying class structures. They have strong focus on the family, and their members' lives revolve around the family. They have similar views of time, and similar work ethics. Their differences are largely based on their environment.

The Arab Moslems live in areas that have been perpetually threatened by foreign invasion. Their culture tends to be more closed and withdrawn. It is defensive first, and suspicious of outsiders. The difference between Roman and Eastern Catholicism is one of anthropology versus cosmology. The Roman focus is more on the human being through its patristic tradition, whereas the Hellenic and eastern European countries' early spiritual roots were in nature and Mother Earth. This leads the Eastern church to find its religion revealed in physical form, such as artwork. Worship is heavily symbolic. For each region, the dominant religion reflects long-established cultural values and beliefs.

The first task in discovering the rules of protocol is to determine which of the three major cultural models is in force. The culture map in Figure 1.1 (see page 3) will help. In addition to the major cultural designation, you also will need information on religion and on any historical or current invasions by other cultures, that deeply influence a particular region or nation. These additional cultural variations will affect the social behavior of those in the region.

EACH NATION HAS ITS VARIATIONS ON THE RULES

Each nation belongs to one of the three governing cultures, but some, due to historical events and geographical proximity, have developed a culture that combines two of those major realities. Long occupations by foreign cultures always left their mark on native cultures. Spanish, Portuguese, English, and Dutch explorers, together with Moslem traders—all actively colonizing between the 15th and 20th centuries—altered the cultures they dominated. Yet the most basic perceptions of reality—imprinted and programmed into civilizations over thousands of years—can never be completely eradicated.

As an example, it is generally safe to say that Asia and Southeast Asia are fundamentally collective. Yet Malaysia and Indonesia are predominantly Moslem and therefore share cultural behavior with the Arab countries, which are based on a tribal society. The Moslem influence arrived through Arab traders in the 15th century who imposed the Islamic rule of law. The religion was embraced after centuries of influence, but the collective attitudes underlie its expression in Malaysia and Indonesia. The strong, aggressive power hierarchy is softened by the egalitarian mind-set of the underlying collectivist culture. Women are not severely restrained from participation in society as they are in Arab states. Reverence for ancestors is maintained as in all collective societies. The predominant influence of the imported religion is its sense of fatalism and surrender to God's will. There is a greater sense of individualism due to the belief in a personified God, yet the individual finds his identity in the family unit.

The same can be said of the Philippines. The underlying, ancient culture is collective. In the 16th century, Spain gained control of the country and held it for nearly 400 years. The Spanish culture brought Roman Catholicism to the Philippines, altering the latter's beliefs to include a separation from God. Again, this resulted in a culture with a power hierarchy that is not so aggressive as those under Moslem influence, yet one that brought the collective focal point down to the level of the family unit.

Culture and its rules are not static. What was appropriate behavior a thousand years ago may not be adequate to promote the goals of today's society. Japan had a culture that changed quickly from an isolated feudal society to a major industrialized nation after World War II. Ancient Japanese customs became overlaid with Western values. Therefore, the Japanese cannot be seen strictly as a collective society, but one that also displays strong forms of the pluralist achievement power hierarchies. The result is a power hierarchy that encourages achievement—but for the good of the group.

An American who looks at Figure 1.1 and sees that England has been branded a tribal culture, may have some doubt. Wasn't it mainly England that gave rise to the American colonies? Shouldn't the American and British cultures be similar? A brief review of history might remind us that most colonists came to America seeking the opportunity for self-expression—in both religion and society. Britain is a hybrid area resulting from its invasion by the Normans (of France) in the 11th century. The invasion brought to England a strong power hierarchy, a strong monarchy that has perpetuated the social power hierarchy to this day. Even before the Norman conquest, the Roman Empire included England. But from the north, England was also greatly influenced by the Saxons of northern Europe. The Norse Vikings also had an influence, with their strong emphasis on the individual and free will. The two influences have been blended quite well in the Anglican church, which replaced Roman Catholicism in the 17th century.

Not only do foreign cultures influence the regions their people invade, but the foreign culture can also be redefined as it is assimilated into the indigenous culture. At one time, all of western Europe was Roman Catholic. But eventually the fundamental perceptions of reality in northern Europe had to bubble up through the imposed religious culture, giving birth to the Reformation. It could only happen there. It was a result of the strong desire of the people of that pluralist culture to reflect their individualistic idea of reality through their social and religious institutions.

Similarly, Roman Catholicism was ultimately modified in Greece and spread to eastern Europe in the form of the Eastern Orthodox church. The Hellenic tradition stressed cosmology and the forces of nature in its perception of the world. A personified God and man were still separate, but man finds his relationship to God through his experience of the physical world. The Eastern Orthodox church expresses that reality through its extensive use of art and ritual. It uses iconography and paintings to portray the beliefs that Roman Catholics tend to portray more in language. Eastern Orthodoxy was a compatible religion that gained wide acceptance in eastern Europe, for it supported the strong relationship to the natural, physical world. The power hierarchy was retained, but the religion was adapted to fit the cultural expression of spiritual reality.

The primary factor that determines governing principles is the indigenous perception of reality. The secondary factor is the outside influence of any occupying cultures. Intrusions by other cultures affect specific details of the rules of behavior, but rarely change the most basic perceptions.

PROTOCOL VERSUS ETIQUETTE

The previous sections have discussed at some length the origin and purpose of protocol. Protocol is what to do in a given situation. Many people use the terms *etiquette* and *protocol* interchangeably, but in fact they are different. Protocol is *what* to do. Etiquette is *how* to do it—and how to do it gracefully. Take figure skating as an analogy. In competition, each skater is given a set of marks by the judges—one for technical merit and another for artistic impression. For our analogy, protocol would be the technical merit, and etiquette the artistic impression. They both are important in making the best possible impression on an audience.

Etiquette is learning to yawn with your mouth closed. Etiquette is actually quite practical and easy to accomplish. As long as you understand the correct protocol, etiquette can usually be adapted to doing gracefully and respectfully what needs to be done. With this background and distinction let's look at some examples of protocol and etiquette that will demonstrate the relationship between the two. Each example also discusses how protocol reinforces cultural belief. The strategies that are included give additional insight into how to make the most effective use of the point of protocol.

Example 1: Exchanging Business Cards in Japan

Protocol: In Japan, upon first meeting, all players exchange business cards.

Etiquette: Business cards are exchanged in a very ritualistic manner. The card is presented with both hands so that the recipient can read it. The Japanese person may bow. All that is required of you is to nod your head. This is done simultaneously. Upon receipt, the player examines the card thoroughly, making note of the person's title, name pronunciation, and generally regarding the card with reverence. Never take a card and stuff it into your pocket. Never put the card away in the presence of the giver. Never write on the card. Place the card in front of you during a meeting if seated.

Cultural reinforcement: Japan is a collectivist society—very uniform and nonindividual. To the Japanese there is a weak concept of self. The Japanese business card carries the identity of the person. It identifies his "group," or company; it points out his title; it carries his family name. To casually put it aside without due regard is to disregard the human being that gave it to you.

Strategy: Be sure your own cards are of high-quality paper and print. The card should be bilingual. Be prepared to hand out a large number.

Example 2: First Meeting in Mexico

Protocol: In Mexico you meet your prospective client. Before meetings begin, he takes you to lunch, which lasts four hours. No business is discussed. This is common business practice. You should not suggest getting down to business. The host will decide when and whether this is to happen.

Etiquette: Accept the invitation to lunch. Don't be surprised at how much Mexicans drink. Do not try to match your host glass for glass unless you are used to drinking alcohol. Answer questions about your place in the company you represent, your family, and your hobbies. Remain formal and respectful, though friendly. Latin Americans appreciate machismo. Find common ground whenever possible. Avoid comparing Mexico with the United States. Do not talk about crime, corruption, illegal aliens, or other sensitive issues. If pressed, be noncommittal.

Cultural reinforcement: Mexico is a tribal society. People will not do business with you unless you are trusted and are accepted into the group. The long social lunch gives the Mexican an opportunity to size you up. He is deciding if you are the type of person with whom he wants to have a relationship. Even if you are an expert in your field, he will not do business with you if he doesn't like you.

Strategy: In order to give your company a better chance of succeeding, it would be wise to send more than one person to this first meeting. This way, if the Mexican businessman doesn't like the lead player but wants to do business with your company, he can choose to do so through the representative with whom he feels most comfortable.

Example 3: A Business Proposal for Germany

Protocol: In Germany your business proposal should be detailed, precise, and completely unambiguous. Plans and schedules should be detailed and realistic.

Etiquette: Proposals should be translated into German, and presentation should be professional, well-organized, and neat.

Cultural reinforcement: German culture is highly ordered and places great value on the physical world. Germany has a materialistic culture. Concrete information, facts, and technical precision are reflections of the concreteness of the physical world in which Germans live. Plans are important. Order is perceived to be under human control. Germans are not fatalistic. They believe they can affect the world, so creating order is one of their main values, reflected in the way they conduct business.

Strategy: Reduce risks whenever possible. Include many milestones in your schedules. Provide backup systems and evaluation points. Build in feedback loops to provide information for decision making.

Example 4: Greeting the Chinese

Protocol: Until recently, when Western influence began to modify behavior, the proper greeting in China was to bow from the waist. Now, Westerners are greeted with a handshake along with a slight bow.

Etiquette: A younger person should bow lower to an older person: the deeper the bow, the greater the respect that is shown. Handshakes should be slightly soft and never aggressive.

Cultural reinforcement: The Asian collectivist cultures are not physically oriented. They do not display the need or desire for physical contact with people they meet. The head is the most sacred part of the body. Inclining it toward another is a sign of respect. Asian etiquette always enables the Chinese to show others respect.

Strategy: Do not try to greet a Chinese in the customary fashion. There are many nuances to the form of the bow. Unless you understand this ceremony completely, you may look awkward and be offensive. A slight bow of the head, however, is a gesture that is appreciated.

Example 5: Meeting Behavior in Northern Europe

Protocol: If you are at a meeting in northern Europe, give the speaker your full attention and strong eye contact.

Etiquette: Sit up and show interest in what is being said. Do not interrupt the speaker with questions unless he has asked the audience to do so. If people are taking turns in a group, try to take notes after the person is finished with his remarks.

Cultural reinforcement: In pluralist societies like those of northern Europe, the individual's thoughts and opinions are valued. Listeners should be present with the speaker and receive his ideas. This culture values a focus that is on the individual.

Strategy: It is useful—after long remarks have been made—to paraphrase the speaker's main ideas. That way he will know if he has been successful in communicating his meaning, and you will be sure that you understand.

Example 6: The Negative Statement in Taiwan

Protocol: In Taiwan and other Asian countries, never say no directly.

Etiquette: Instead of saying no, Taiwanese may say yes along with body language that truly indicates their meaning. They may also use such language as, "It is difficult."

Cultural reinforcement: No implies conflict and disagreement. Conflict destabilizes the group, so it is not permitted. It also causes a person to lose face when his ideas are not accepted. Causing someone to lose face is never allowed.

Strategy: Unless you live in Taiwanese culture or have studied it extensively, it will be very difficult for you to ever read the paralanguage that comes along with the word *yes.* It is wise to employ a local person as agent or assistant who can translate inner meaning and advise you on your next move.

Example 7: Showing Rank in Saudi Arabia

Protocol: On a visit to Saudi Arabia, the person of highest rank traveling with subordinates should show the distinction of his rank.

Etiquette: He should maintain formality with his subordinates, even though he may be on a first-name basis with them at home. He should dress better, have the best hotel room, and be deferred to by subordinates. He should always be the first person in the team to be introduced. At meetings he should be the one to speak, unless he designates an assistant and validates that person's qualifications.

Cultural reinforcement: Tribal cultures value hierarchy. A strong hierarchy supports their view of reality. They expect a distinction between top leadership and middle management. A strong leader is respected.

Strategy: To prove yourself to your Saudi client you must exude strong leadership qualities. You can do this when you make sure your client knows how respected you are in your company by the rank you hold. Make sure when negotiating with your Saudi clients you show respect to your subordinates while maintaining your level of distinction.

Example 8: Posture in Korea

Protocol: In Korea, when sitting or standing, always use good posture.

Etiquette: When sitting, keep knees together. The feet should always be on the floor, never on furniture or propped on a knee. Do not rest hands in pockets. Sit or stand attentively. The soles of the feet should never be shown.

Cultural reinforcement: Remember that in Asia physical action is symbolic. If your body is under control, then you are under control. Good posture is symbolic of good moral fiber.

Strategy: In all your actions and reactions, display control and discipline over your body movements with silence, and your time constraints.

Example 9: Punctuality in Switzerland

Protocol: In Switzerland, punctuality is of prime importance.

Etiquette: It is rude not to be on time for a meeting. If you must be late for some valid reason, call ahead and reschedule as soon as you know you might be late.

Cultural reinforcement: In a society of individuals, everyone has his own agenda, his own plans, and his own priorities. Such attitudes are respected and encouraged. When an appointment has been made, it fits into a person's daily schedule. If someone is late, every other plan is affected. The individual is hampered in fulfilling the goals he established for himself. Ultimately, this is extended to imply that the person's freedom to self-determination is restricted, which is unacceptable in Swiss society.

Strategy: Plan to arrive half an hour early near your destination. Do not sit in the office lobby and wait. If your host knows you are there so early, it will disrupt his schedule. Be nearby, but plan to arrive at the office exactly on time.

Example 10: Addressing a Meeting in China

Protocol: In China—and other collective societies, make your presentation or remarks to all present during a meeting. Do not address your remarks only to the person you think is highest in rank. It is ambiguous who actually makes the final decision. Most decisions are by consensus.

Etiquette: In a collective society it is not proper to single out any one person, and eye contact is best kept indirect. However, group leadership is acknowledged. Your highest-ranking team member should do the talking. The seating arrangement is important in establishing rank as well, with the most important person in the middle, flanked by subordinates. The eldest players should receive special deference as group leaders. Direct your comments to the eldest, even if he does not speak English and even though you know he is not in charge.

Cultural reinforcement: All members are equal and the group is homogeneous. No one is singled out as being more important. However, the focus of the group rests on its elders. The group should receive information and process information as a group. The people all are one. Age is respected. Those of advanced years have contributed most to the group solely by having been part of the group and promoting its survival for so long.

Strategy: Look around the room as you speak. Incline your head slightly when your remarks are addressed to the eldest. Do not rest your eyes on any one person for very long. Speak moderately and slowly.

Example 11: Refusing and Accepting Food in the Far East

Protocol: In many countries of the Far East, it is proper to refuse food the first two times it is offered. Accept on the third offering.

Etiquette: Before accepting, use such expressions as "I couldn't" or "I shouldn't." At each refusal you might note the server's kindness in offering. Avoid the word *no.*

Cultural reinforcement: The server is made equal to the guest. This behavior elevates the giver, making the gift more valuable. It also humbles the receiver. Giving is humbling. Receiving should be, also.

Strategy: Building the relationship is carried over into your dining situations. Learn to eat foods that aren't familiar to you. In Arab countries be prepared to eat without utensils. Learn to make your client/host feel important by taking the emphasis off yourself and placing it on them.

Example 12: Using First Names in the United States

Protocol: In most companies in the United States, employees are on a first-name basis with those they come in contact with regularly, including managers. Also, professionals of different companies meeting for managers who are infrequently met will be referred to by their surname.

Etiquette: When introducing yourself to new coworkers, use your full name. Some secretaries or other assistants choose to keep a formal relationship with the professionals they work with by using Mr. or Mrs. or Miss. Most peers should use first names when asked to do so. When others address you formally but you prefer to be informal, ask them to use your first name. Allow them to do this or to continue being formal, whichever is more comfortable for them.

Cultural reinforcement: Informality promotes equality. Among those working together, teamwork and cooperation are fostered by a more personal and direct form of interaction. Americans usually cut through formality to get things done. The individual must be able to reach his goals—even cooperative goals—with as few barriers as possible.

Strategy: When speaking to someone for the first time on the phone, as in a cold call, be formal at first. As the talk progresses and rapport seems to be building, you might feel comfortable ending the call by using the person's first name. Use his first name if he uses your first name.

Example 13: Serving Wine in Japan

Protocol: In Japan, when entertaining, the host pours wine for the guest; the guest reciprocates by pouring wine for the host.

Etiquette: Reciprocate for your host before drinking the wine poured for you. Wait for a toast. Always reciprocate a toast.

Cultural reinforcement: The act of reciprocating is very important. It indicates equality. Giving and receiving are equally important acts. They simultaneously indicate respect and humility. Reciprocation indicates that both people have the good of the other in mind. This promotes group harmony.

Strategy: If you don't drink, don't turn your glass upside down. Allow it to be filled. Pretend to sip the wine during toasts. If you finish a glass, it will be refilled by your host.

These examples of protocol and etiquette illustrate how protocol is used to promote or maintain the values of a culture. The etiquette used to achieve the purpose of the protocol may be different for many locales within a broad cultural region. For instance, some form of noncontact greeting is traditionally used in all parts of the collective Far East. However, Cambodia, Laos, and Thailand perform this greeting differently from the Chinese or Japanese. Their greeting includes using the hands at about chest level, palms together as if in prayer, and dipping the head toward the hands with a slight bow or curtsy from a woman. The higher the hands, the greater the show of respect. Hands may be placed anywhere between the solar plexus and the forehead. The Chinese and Japanese simply bow from the waist.

Local influences and history affect etiquette more than protocol. What should be done in the general sense will always be consistent with the values of the collective, tribal, or pluralist group. How it is done will depend on the climate of the area, the natural resources, the relative wealth and educational level of the society, and the level of technological development.

It's becoming more obvious how Western technology influences many traditional customs around the globe. Some cultures simply never invented the fork. They eat with their hands or chopsticks. This is good etiquette for their indigenous culture. A Westerner arrives with forks, spoons, and knives. Gradually the use of them is accepted into the local society, and dining customs change. Similarly, Western dress has become accepted in most parts of the world by those conducting business. Much of this influence came from the imperial presence of many European nations in all parts of the world during the past several centuries.

Traditional dress was modified over time. The collective cultures may have assumed Western dress as a unifying image of modern business. Dress is a form of personal expression. Those in collectivist cultures dress homogeneously and therefore express the same "personal" style. Tribal cultures tend to dress in a way that is unique to their group. Their group may even identify with a particular form of dress, as in Saudi Arabia. In pluralist societies, individuals use style to express themselves. In business this means the expression of concurrence and cooperation within the group. But only in a pluralist society can a person actually move up in the hierarchy as a partial result of the personal image he projects.

Following is a brief exercise that will test your ability to recognize the type of culture supported by certain forms of protocol. For each statement below, choose whether the protocol applies to tribal, collective, or pluralist culture, and why.

1. Do not discuss business during meals.
2. When speaking, pause now and then to allow quiet time.
3. During a meeting, distractions and interruptions are considered normal.
4. Discuss your company, not yourself.
5. Discuss your position within your company.
6. Discuss the deal, not yourself.
7. Never call someone without first sending a letter of introduction.
8. Use good eye contact.
9. Do not use direct eye contact.
10. Introduce the most senior person first.
11. When someone is giving a speech, sitting in the audience with eyes closed is a compliment.
12. It will be assumed that the oldest person of your team is the team leader.
13. Managers and subordinates should not appear different.
14. Do everything by the book.
15. When you are a guest for a meal in someone's home, always ask for seconds.
16. Never publicly or directly criticize others.
17. Never ask anyone to work after hours or on weekends.
18. A host gives gifts to his guests.
19. Gift giving is ritualistic and reciprocal.
20. Gift giving is a personal expression of one's feelings and need not be reciprocated.
21. Use gestures and emotion to get your point across.
22. Respond to questions directly with precise information.

Following are the answers with brief explanations.
1. Do not discuss business during meals.
   Culture: Tribal, Collective

This is important to both cultures for slightly different reasons. Collective societies believe that everything happens in its own time. The time for eating is for eating. Tribal cultures consider this a social opportunity, and because relationship building is their focus, they want to talk to you—and not about your business.

2. When speaking, pause now and then to allow quiet time.
    Culture: Collective
    > Collective societies value silence for reflection on ideas. Taking time to reflect is a sign of respect.

3. During a meeting, distractions and interruptions are considered normal.
    Culture: Tribal
    > Neither time nor process is linear. Many things happen at once. This reflects tribal cultures' perception of time.

4. Discuss your company, not yourself.
    Culture: Collective
    > To them, you are defined by your company. The individual is not important except in how he relates to his group.

5. Discuss your position within your company.
    Culture: Tribal
    > The family unit is the most important focus group, not the company. Your position and title elevate you and your family in others' eyes. They know something about you by how others have honored you (i.e., with position and rank).

6. Discuss the deal, not yourself.
    Culture: Pluralist
    > Every person has his own agenda and his own need to serve. Business is done to serve that need. Your counterpart wants to get down to business first and maybe get to know you later.

7. Never call someone without first sending a letter of introduction.
    Culture: Tribal, Collective, Pluralist
    > For different reasons, this holds true everywhere. In tribal cultures, society is closed. Strangers must earn trust before dealing with the group. Collective cultures work with people who are perceived to be of benefit to the group and not threatening. Introduction assures them of your good intentions. Pluralist societies keep to schedules and priorities. It is disruptive and rude to call others without their anticipating the call by prior introduction or advance correspondence.

8. Use good eye contact.

Culture: Pluralist, Tribal

> Pluralist cultures focus on the individual. Eye contact shows respect and interest in the person. Those in tribal cultures do not trust someone who will not look them in the eye.

9. Do not use direct eye contact.

Culture: Collective

> Direct eye contact singles out the person and is considered to be intimate.

10. Introduce the most senior person first.

Culture: Tribal, Collective, Pluralist

> This is done to maintain and recognize the power hierarchy and to show respect for age and accomplishment, depending on the culture.

11. When someone is giving a speech, sitting in the audience with eyes closed is a compliment.

Culture: Collective

> Focus is not on the speaker but what is being said. Closing the eyes allows a person to concentrate and understand the full meaning of an idea.

12. It will be assumed that the oldest person of your group is the team leader.

Culture: Collective, Tribal

> In tribal and collective societies, advancement is largely through seniority—not necessarily merit: the older the person, the longer he has been with the company and the higher his position. People tend not to move around much; they usually stay with one company nearly all their working life.

13. Managers and subordinates should not appear different.

Culture: Collective

> Appearance is uniform, and managers can socialize with employees. The purpose is to perpetuate equality. Everyone in the group appears to be the same.

14. Do everything by the book.

Culture: Pluralist, Collective

> Life has order, whether that order is caused by man or by the divine laws of the universe. Rules and protocol are to be followed.

15. When you are a guest for a meal in someone's home, always ask for seconds.

Culture: Pluralist

> It is a compliment to the cook, and it is expected that each person will ask for what is wanted.

16. Never publicly or directly criticize others.
    Culture: Collective

    > Criticism automatically makes the person being criticized lose face. Criticism is never direct. There are other ways to improve performance, and focusing on the group performance is how this is done.

17. Never ask anyone to work after hours or on weekends.
    Culture: Tribal, Collective

    > These people work to live; they do not live to work. Their leisure time with their families is very important. Some pluralist societies also feel this way. The individual's personal time is to be respected. An employer should not expect an employee to work after hours if the employee chooses not to.

18. A host gives gifts to his guests.
    Culture: Tribal, Collective

    > A guest is a gift from God. A guest honors the host. The host takes care of the guest and expresses appreciation for the guest's visit. The guest returns that appreciation, as give-and-take and sharing in general are cultural values.

19. Gift giving is ritualistic and reciprocal.
    Culture: Collective

    > Physical things are symbolic. A gift is symbolic of honor, respect, and sharing. Ritual is important in collective cultures.

20. Gift giving is a personal expression of one's feelings and need not be reciprocated.
    Culture: Pluralist

    > Giving and sharing are not expected of an individual, as free will is paramount. But giving someone a gift enhances the recipient's self-esteem, and so it is greatly appreciated.

21. Use gestures and emotion to get your point across.
    Culture: Tribal

    > Subjective opinions are backed by emotion. Emotional content reinforces one's opinion with one's own signature. Emotion is also used to convince and persuade. The exception to this rule would be England.

22. Respond to questions directly with precise information.
    Culture: Pluralist

    > Pluralist cultures are comfortable with concrete ideas. They want no ambiguity, because it conflicts with their ability to achieve their goals.

UNIVERSAL ETIQUETTE

Although etiquette is strongly influenced by local factors, a study of global customs does reveal some recurring themes. Following is a general list of dos and don'ts that applies worldwide.

Keep your hands to yourself, off yourself, and out of your pockets.

Gesture only with your full hand, not with fingers.

Keep your mouth closed when not speaking.

Keep your feet on the ground.

Shake hands moderately. Return the grip you are given.

Respect age.

Avoid the colors yellow, purple, black, white, and red. Although fine in some countries, these are the colors that most often cause problems. Do not give chrysanthemums, roses, or lilies. Never give an even number of flowers (but not 13).

Err on the side of formality.

Dress conservatively. Be clean and neat.

Don't use given names unless invited to.

Reciprocate hospitality when it is possible.

Don't tell jokes or attempt humor.

Be punctual in business, even if others are not. Don't show annoyance at being kept waiting. If you are invited to someone's home, find out the local custom. Punctuality varies widely. You may catch your host in the shower.

At a meal, wait for your host to start. If nothing happens for a long time and people are staring at you, it may be their custom for the guest to begin first. Be observant and do as others do.

Don't discuss politics, crime, religion, or personal topics.

KEY POINTS

- An individual's spiritual identity leads to a perception of reality, shared by a group, which leads to culture that reflects that reality through its group behavior.
- The rules that secure and perpetuate that behavior are called protocol.
- The world's cultures can be classified into three groups for understanding culture-based protocol. These are called:
  — Tribal
  — Collective
  — Pluralist

- Player portraits can be derived from the governing principles of their distinct culture.
- Protocol is *what* to do in a certain situation. Etiquette is *how* to do something gracefully and respectfully.
- Protocol and etiquette can be used strategically.
- It is sometimes helpful to consult the section Universal Etiquette if you have doubts that you may be doing something wrong. But it is preferable to deduce or study local manners.

3

How to Play the Game Anywhere
in the World

The steps you take to prepare for a cross-cultural business encounter are the same in every case. The game analogy is useful here. Consider what you do spontaneously when you prepare to play a game. If you are competitive, the first thing you do is size up your competition. Then you prepare yourself mentally by thinking of the game as a whole: the objective and the rules. Next, you decide what your first move will be and what you expect your opponent's response to be. The same activities must be discharged when preparing to do business.

With your business objective in mind, you determine who must be contacted. You define the decisions or agreements to be reached and any obstacles you expect to encounter. Before you take action, you consider the best avenue of introduction and where that first meeting should take place. Before you make contact, you consider your schedule and time frame for completing your objectives.

Businesspeople of other cultures might appear to do business differently from American businesspeople, but they do not. They must take all the same steps in order to conduct business. Business in a foreign culture appears different because the people's perceptions of basic concepts differ from our own. The concepts that vary by culture include time, space, power, material gain, self-awareness, work ethic, and communication. The game of business is the same anywhere in the world. It only looks different to each of us because we see it through our cultural lenses.

There are two essential components to every game: the game's structure as defined by its rules and the game's players. Protocol—the rules of the game—is defined by each culture. So too are the players. The people with whom you do business reflect their various cultures. The better you understand the other player, whether he be opponent or team member, the better you can plan your course of action.

The three fundamental cultures lead to three sets of fundamental player characteristics, presented as player portraits in Chapter 1. When applying that player information to any particular country, keep in mind that the population of many nations is a composite of regional nationalities. For example, Malaysia and Thailand have very large Chinese populations. Indonesia has a large Malaysian population. Sri Lanka has a significant Indian population. In many countries you may encounter members of the business class whose cultural background is different from the national majority. Therefore, knowledge of the governing principles of an entire region, and not just the customs of one country, is essential for success. Each playing field's governing principles are known before the game begins, so that the philosophical and historical background affecting an entire region is known, and not just that of one country. This broader approach to international culture and protocol gives the businessperson a greater opportunity for success.

DEVELOPING A PLAYER PORTRAIT

Given the overall governing principles for a region, one can draw conclusions about the people of that specific culture. Cultural psyche is passed down among generations and creates within each individual a consistent culture-specific character.

Before we play the game of business with a new opponent or team member of another culture, we would like to know something about him. How well does he know the game? What are his objectives and motivations? What are his expectations and attitudes toward both his opponents and his teammates? In business, we want to know whom the person is that we will be dealing. But we need to know more than his name, rank, and expertise. In order to strategize properly, we must know what he hopes to gain for himself and for his company. What is his attitude toward doing business with Americans? How are his assumptions and perceptions different from ours such that they might cause obstacles to success? How do we best communicate with this person?

In the game of global business we must identify the other player before we can attempt to strategize and take action. We develop a player portrait by considering perceptions of time, space, communication style, materialism, power, self-awareness, and work ethic.

Time

It is hard for us as well as for people in any culture to conceive that there might be a differing interpretation of something so basic, so absolute as time. But there is. Time is one of those qualities of reality that reflects the nature of the divine, as we know it. In our pluralistic society—where the individual is separate and motivated by continuous improvement—time is linear and measurable. We are goal oriented. We do one thing at a time. We make plans and follow them until the goal is achieved. We take time commitments seriously and emphasize promptness.

In tribal societies time is relative. God controls everything, and time is regarded as fate. What happens will happen. One has no control over time or God or fate. Time is linear, but inconsequential. The process is far more important than the goal. Plans are made but rarely followed, and often changed without notice. Time commitments are taken lightly, and tribal people are almost never on time. They tend to do many things at once and are highly distractible. They could be thought of as "flowing" with time.

Collective cultures gain their understanding of time from the belief in the infinite, the eternal, and the laws of the universe. Time is not necessarily linear; neither is life or death. History and perceptions give collective cultures a very long-term approach to time. Plans are allowed to form, goals to manifest. Everything happens in its own time according to the laws of the universe. Collectivists take the time necessary for all the pieces of a puzzle to fall together; then they act. They are very patient people. People of this culture do what has to be done when it is necessary, and they are not often punctual unless it is the right time. Plans change easily as the process flows. Time has a very fluid quality.

Space

Space perception is another relative quality of culture. Generally, cultures that stress the importance of the individual respect a person's privacy and physical autonomy. During personal interaction, they are most comfortable maintaining a distance of about one and a half to four feet. Distance for social interaction is comfortable beyond four feet. Pluralist cultures like to define their space and to control their personal territory. Not so with a tribal culture. Tribal people perceive all personal interaction to be intimate—as between friends or family. They must trust you as they would a close friend if they are to do business with you, and so their comfort zone is much closer: six inches to two feet. In Arab countries, distances between the sexes are much greater. The sexes are not permitted to show intimacy in public. Standing in very close proximity is a sign of intimacy.

Collective cultures are comfortable with proximity because of their sense of oneness and strong group identity. Japan is an exception, but it is also not purely collective, as we will see in the Pacific Rim game. It is also awkward to bow when standing closer than two feet together.

Communication Style

Communication can be achieved both verbally and nonverbally. *Body language* is the colloquial term given to the use of gestures in communicating meaning. Body language can range from gesturing with the hands to rolling the eyes and making other facial expressions. A person's stance can indicate attitude as well. Various cultures mix verbal and nonverbal communication to differing degrees. Language itself is developed with the use of such paralanguage implied. Such languages often have words with ambiguous meanings, and exact content needs to be determined by paralanguage at each instance of use. Words and phrases often depend on their context. Other languages allow the speaker to be very precise, with a variety of words with nearly identical meanings to choose from.

Pluralist cultures tend to expect verbal language to be precise. They do not rely on paralanguage to transmit meaning. Because of their own cultural perspective, they are often inept at recognizing paralanguage when used by those of another culture. They don't expect it, so they don't look for it. They may thus lose part of the communication, which results in misunderstanding. Their communication style also prompts them to ask detailed questions and expect specific instructions. No meaning is left ambiguous. Communication and information are given and received along formal hierarchical lines.

Tribal cultures generally use verbal language in a nonspecific sense. They reserve the right to add meaning to their communications by personal physical expression (i.e., body language). When speaking with a Westerner, they may be confused by the lack of emphasis or emotion in the Westerner's speech. Beyond body language, they use inflection to add emotional content to their communication. They tend to acquire information through informal means, such as networks and casual conversations. They are wary of information they have not gathered themselves, and they prefer to learn on their own how things are done.

Collective cultures usually develop languages that are more diffuse in their meaning. Their language is highly symbolic, with analogies from nature used to express meaning. The added dimension of their verbal communication is not so much with body language as it is with symbolic content. Facts are not expressed directly. Meanings are implied. It takes great skill for a foreigner who is used to precise, direct communication to understand the complete meaning of such a communication style. This tendency toward symbolic communication extends to factual content as well. Instructions must be shown as well as verbalized. Collectivists are not accustomed to receiving specific guidelines or rules.

Materialism

Materialism is commonly defined as a strong focus on achievement and the acquisition of possessions. Pluralist cultures that promote individualism naturally tend toward personal ownership and therefore focus on acquiring possessions. Tribal cultures tend to hold possessions in the tribal group. Possessions belong to the family, and not to one person. More recently, Western nations, with their pride in possessions, have impressed upon many tribal cultures that ownership implies respect and honor. Tribal people have thereby learned to express their cultural values in a formerly unsought way. Similarly, in collective societies, possessions are communal. Collective cultures find *things* to be of a symbolic nature. Among such cultures that were once not much concerned with owning things, however, the influence of the West has caused physical possessions to take on the symbolic meaning of power.

Power

The word *power* usually evokes a strong emotional response from people. To some it is threatening; to others it is what they strive for. For many it is accepted that power resides with the elite and always will. Attitudes toward the acceptance of power, the gaining of power, and the use of power are often culturally based. The perception of the degree of inequality that should exist in a society is a related issue. Should power be distributed vertically or horizontally? That is to say, should one supreme ruler be in charge, with descending authority levels? Or should power be shared?

All cultures exhibit a sense of a power greater than they on the physical plane. Even collective societies consider the laws of nature to be greater than the laws of man. It is natural to assume that they all will have some sort of vertical, or semivertical, power structure in their society.

Pluralist societies are founded on concepts of equality. Anyone may be in a position to lead. Those in power are accessible and accountable; they are not considered to be a different type of person or to be ones who deserve or have the right to power. The power structure is based on merit, and the use of power is by consent. Authority is respected, but not venerated.

Tribal societies have the strongest power structures, which are a direct representation of their concept of their relationship with God. To them that hierarchy implies natural inequality. There is an order of inequality in which everyone has his rightful place. Power is a basic fact of life. Those in power are not questioned. They enjoy special privileges. In strong power hierarchies, those in power—those who are superior— are viewed as different kinds of persons, thus amplifying the notion of inequality. Superiors in any social institution are generally inaccessible. Tribal societies have a large number of written rules and expect obedience and conformity.

The collective cultures fall somewhere in between. All members of society are spiritually equal, and authority tends to be shared at most levels, but in large collective groups, strong leaders are present. Those leaders are atypical of the normal citizen and are often perceived as having some divine blessing. Authority and power are absolute, as is the structure of a collective society. There is not a strong vertical power structure, but the power at the top dictates the conformity of the masses below. Power is generally in the hands of the elders, for age is venerated.

Self-Awareness

The three distinct cultures of our global model exhibit self-awareness to different degrees. Self-awareness means the awareness of oneself as an individual. At one end of the scale is the pluralist society, with its profound emphasis on the individual. Personal achievement is placed above all else. As it is succinctly stated in the U.S. Declaration of Independence, "life, liberty and the pursuit of happiness" are the inalienable rights of mankind—at least to the American way of thinking.

The collectivist, at the other extreme, believes that ego is merely a worldly manifestation and not our true nature. We are all part of "Big Mind," we are all one, and therefore there should be no distinction between us. The collective notion of equality is quite different from the pluralist notion of equality. The former holds an enforced equality for the good of all in the group. It is an equality of conformity. The pluralist equality is for the good of the individual, implying that we all are equal in our opportunities but not necessarily in our achievements. Those in collective societies are conscious of themselves as separate human beings, but their motivations, their judgments, and their sense of honor and worth are derived from their group. The individual's achievements bring honor to the group, not to the individual.

Tribal cultures lie in between. They are not unconscious of the individual, but the needs of the individual are secondary to the needs of the tribal group. Tribal people achieve through interpersonal relationships. It is the relationship itself that is important, not what is achieved. Their sense of personal identity is strong as it relates to their family group. The motivations of the individual are largely for the protection and advancement of one's own family group.

It is important and interesting to note that in both tribal and collective cultures, honor and pride are strong motivating forces. At first look, these two values would seem to indicate strong self-awareness. In fact, they are the natural result of human beings having their focus outside themselves, having a very weak individual identity. Pride and honor are qualities that exist only relative to someone else or some group. Pride and honor are name tags worn on the psyche. They tell the observer, "This is a great or honorable man." It is because this quality is not born on the inside that it must be shown on the outside. It is part of a man identifying through the group.

Work Ethic

Cultural attitudes toward work are strongly influenced by our concept of personal responsibility. Personal responsibility may be directed inward or outward. In pluralist societies, the individual's responsibility is to himself; personal achievement is an inner motivation. This culture takes work very seriously. Those who do not excel or cannot excel are valued less highly than those who do. Pluralists tend to give greatest respect to those who have improved their rank and their wealth through personal effort.

When achievement is for the individual, his work is an expression of himself. He lives to work instead of works to live.

In tribal cultures, the person's responsibility is outward—toward the good of the group. Each person's responsibility is to work to support the family group. The decisions a person makes about which job to take and where and for how much are highly dependent on the needs of the tribal group. People in these cultures tend not to move far from the core group or to change jobs, and they are insistent on receiving a set salary. They need more security in their employment. The culture recognizes this, and so social and business institutions are set up to provide for these cultural needs and perpetuate them. People in this society tend to work so that they can live and enjoy life with their families.

Similarly, collective societies view the responsibility of all members to be the continuous contribution of efforts to the good of the group so that the group can take care of those who cannot contribute. Again, the focus is outward. The person's responsibility is to achieve something outside himself. Steady employment is a need of the members of this culture. Often the society and its institutions dictate what job a person will hold. There is not much change in jobs except through seniority. The workers tend to work to live instead of live to work. They fulfill their obligation to society and in return are protected and validated by their society.

When these concepts are understood with respect to their cultural interpretations, we gain insight that will help us to interact effectively with others. Now it is time to apply these concepts to develop a player portrait for use in a sample game. Together with governing principles and protocol, the player portrait allows us to devise a game plan that will guide us toward achieving our goal.

HOW THE GAME WORKS: A CHALLENGE

For the remainder of this chapter, we will apply the fundamentals of cultural perception to a hypothetical scenario in order to demonstrate how to approach an unfamiliar culture. The playing field we will consider in this example is an actual country. The information will be useful when we tour the world's playing fields in the next chapter. In this test case, one critical historical factor has been removed as an influence in the region. In Chapter 4 it will be interesting to compare the game plan for our test case with the game plan for the actual country to see how a historical event can change behavior.

Enter the playing field, and you will immediately see the country's distinguishing geographical features: its terrain, forests, coastal access, rivers, agricultural land, and mountains. Its physical characteristics are your initial clues as to what factors might have shaped its ancient resident culture. If the land were barren desert as opposed to snowcapped mountains or dense rain forest or if the climate were warm and sunny instead of having extremes of cold and heat, then the residents' relationship to nature and God's manifest reality as a natural occurrence, would vary. Those in countries that are deeply affected by the rhythms and bounty of the ocean perceive of reality differently from those who earn a living farming the inland plains. Herdsmen, farmers, and fishermen will all have different perspectives. Your first move is to guess how the physical world has influenced the native people.

On our hypothetical playing field, we see plains, rivers, and forests, which suggest good, fertile lands. The assumption of an agricultural society can be made. What does this tell us? It is probably not a mobile society. Affairs were probably localized. This could be a tribal culture, because agriculture requires cooperation in production and distribution. It also allows self-sufficiency to an extended family. Or this could be a collective culture. Because the territory is large, the perspective of this culture might be broader than just a family tribe. It could include a larger group spanning a larger natural area. A specific local culture can be a combination of the three dominant cultures. The proximity of variant cultures and the flow of populations across regional boundaries can cause cultural influences to blend, forming a unique cultural mix.

Governing Principles

In our test case, the culture has grown up with a deep connection to the land. It supports them with its yield. It provides food, shelter, and clothing. It is the most important organizing principle in society. The physical extremes of climate, the cycles of sunlight, and the seasons shape the inhabitants' sense of physical reality and physical security. Mother Nature takes care of them.

Mother Nature is a personification. The power that molds reality in this culture is made out to be a separate entity that benevolently provides for the inhabitants. Thus God's presence is revealed to them through the physical world. Nature is a powerful force. Nature, with its cycles and extremes of climate, defines their lives. They are reactive to a superior proactive force.

The act of personification indicates a separation from God, which is indicative of the tribal mind-set. But the pure tribal culture is modified by the strong influence of God in nature. The focus is turned more outward. This results in a lessened power hierarchy. Power comes from outside the group. All of the members of the group must react to this power—even the leaders of the group. The vertical strength of the tribal hierarchy is muted somewhat, and social ties beyond the group become more important. The family is an extended family—more of a clan. There is more of a sense of equality than there is in a purely tribal culture. There is a sense of equality of contributions, but not exactly the equality of uniformity that defines the collective frame of mind. All members must contribute to society. All members know they have to work for what they get.

Construct a Player Portrait

With this understanding of the culture's governing principles, we move on to look at the character of the individual. The spiritual and physical reality of the culture causes definite culture-based perceptions. Regarding time, this culture will likely have a relaxed concept of time. It is not strongly linear, but more cyclic. The rhythms of nature are cyclic. Events are controlled by natural forces. People do not control time or events. Something happens, and they react. This culture is probably not capable of extrapolating cause and effect far into the future.

Additionally, the notion of events being out of the inhabitants' control translates to the individual in the group to mean that events are controlled by others. There is not a strong take-charge mentality. It is more of a do-what-is-asked mentality. To completely take control of a project and define each step in great detail with lines of communication clarified and a precise schedule to follow would not be expected.

The perception of events being beyond one's control would also lead to an aversion toward taking risks. If a person does not feel he has the personal power to shape events, to initiate action, or to change the course of troubled projects, he will not put himself in a position to fail. This person's sense of physical and professional security must be maintained to reduce stress.

The cultural concept of space is twofold. The sense of physical space borders on infinite, but they are a communal society, so their social distance is more communal. In effect, their comfort distance for personal interaction should be greater than tribal, but closer than pluralist. They have more of a sense of the physical than collective societies, and so touching, as in handshakes, is to be expected. Closeness affords a greater sense of physical security.

The tribal approach to communication would seem a good place to start in getting a handle on their communication style. Expect vague language compared with English, which allows more precision. Since they experience reality through nature, expect them to use visual symbolism in their communication. This might mean translating abstract or theoretical notions into concrete, physical examples. In fact, their thinking is likely to be more concrete than theoretical.

For a society that has its spiritual foundations in nature and the physical world, this culture is in a sense materialistic. Members respond to physical symbols. But their tribal/collective culture does not encourage personal ownership, and so our notion of materialism does not translate. Things count, but not necessarily personal things. The members are material in the sense that they express themselves, their spirituality, and their reality through physical forms (e.g., the visual and performing arts). This is what is meant when we say that their personal expression is materialistic.

Their concept of power is abstract, lying in a loosely personified force. On a human level, power is not so much power in the sense of supremacy as it is authority. Those in the clan who have the authority to lead the group do not necessarily have power as they perceive natural power. In the tribal group it would seem natural that those in authority would be one's parents—or the group elders. We should expect the people of this culture to take direction from their parents at home and from older figures of authority in business. They most likely will defer to age.

As there is a void in leadership, it should also be expected that there should be a void in accountability. There should be harmony. No one should be singled out and humiliated, so failure is not a subject for discussion. Expect there to be an extensive avoidance tendency and secretiveness.

The people in this culture exhibit self-awareness as an extension of their family or clan. All members of the group are transient, as is all life on earth. However, the group survives. People pass away. When someone dies there is a void in the group. A form of self-awareness in collective and tribal cultures is the veneration of ancestors. The ancestor is retained as a permanent part of the group even after physical death. No one person may be singled out and held in high esteem during their lifetime; one must maintain equality of conformity. But after someone dies, leaving the group, a method of retaining individuals in the group is to continue to recognize them after their death.

Pride and honor should be motivating factors for a person of this culture because the focus of the individual is turned outward. The person's self-esteem is rooted in the respect given him by others and not by his internal sense of self-satisfaction. Achievements are made relative to other individuals in the group. We should expect relationship building to be an important factor in business, as well as the values of sharing and cooperation.

One aspect of personal achievement is highly valued, and that is achievement in the arts. This is because the physical expression of humanity through visual, performing, and practical arts is sacred to all in the society. It represents the fundamental spirit of all members of the culture. Artists are greatly honored.

Because cultural attitudes toward work are strongly influenced by the concept of personal responsibility, one can expect the businesspeople to be good at teamwork. Their cultural background supports a tendency toward reaction versus action, but it also requires them to work for what they need. Expect that these people will work well and productively in groups when guided by unambiguous management.

With the cultural profiles we have derived from the region's governing principles, we can now construct a player portrait.

TEST CASE PLAYER PORTRAIT

What does he believe is a person's responsibility?

To take care of and/or contribute to his family group. To share the work of the group with others.

What does he expect of others?

Mutual support, family loyalty, honesty.

How does he interact with others?

He assumes equality of all players. He does not show deference, but is modest in his interactions at first. He must build a relationship before he trusts enough to interact openly.

What impresses him? What does he respect in another?

Competence, loyalty, honesty

What is his attitude toward foreigners?

His first responsibility is to the family clan, so he is reserved with strangers. When it is perceived that there is no threat to the group and that the foreigner will benefit the group, the foreigner is welcomed, and treated with warm hospitality.

Why is he in the game?

This player works to live.

What is his main objective?

His main objective in completing his business is achieving a minimum of disruption to life. His work should not cause stress in his family life. Harmony should be maintained.

How does he define winning?

Win-win.

What is his business environment (physical and hierarchical)?

There is a loose hierarchical structure, with authority accepted at the top. Requests for decisions flow up the ladder, and causal goal setting flows down. The physical arrangement should be open, but close-knit. People are not likely to be singled out for prime office space. Functionality should direct the physical plant. Aesthetics might be important, as are light and windows.

How does he conduct business?

He prefers to conduct business by partnerships and teamwork. Communication is restricted and indirect. Only those who need to know will get the information so as to limit the possibility of negative feedback. Criticism is not given, in general. There are no performance reviews.

How does he learn?

He tends to work from the general to the specific, and he relates abstract concepts to concrete knowledge. Use of physical analogies and visual description is recommended.

How does he give feedback?

So as not to be disruptive or held accountable, he gives only feedback that is sparse and vague. He tells you what you want to hear.

How does he make decisions?

He is not accustomed to being responsible. Action items are bumped upstairs to the person accepting ultimate authority for the business unit's work. Decisions are difficult because issues are not well-defined.

What is his attitude toward time, schedules, plans, and change?

Time is not linear. There is not much regard for keeping to schedules. There is no association between time and money. He is process oriented and may become absorbed in the process at the expense of the schedule. Change is accepted if it is not disruptive. New information can be absorbed into the process.

What is his approach to problem solving?

There are no problems. Whatever happens is absorbed into the process. The entire project may become redefined because a problem must be assimilated into it. Problems are simply thought of as change orders. All this is because no one wants to give bad news, so bad news is changed to neutral news. He is reactive by nature. He does what he can do. Those in authority may never even be informed of the change.

Develop a Game Plan

Now that we know the likely behavior of opposing players, we can use this information to develop a strategic game plan.

Test Case Strategic Game Plan

This culture forms closed groups for mutual support and security. The members will definitely feel more comfortable remaining on their own turf. They are wary of strangers—especially foreigners who appear more powerful than they. If the opposing player discerns clear benefits to working with you, he will welcome you, but keep dealings strictly business. Your goal is to communicate that you seek mutual benefits in approaching this culture to do business.

Relationships are exceedingly important in business. In order to minimize any perceived threat from you and to open the way for relationship building, you must approach with an introduction. A professional, yet impersonal introduction will be accepted because the members highly regard competence, which is attested to by a professional reference. A personal introduction is especially useful, as it will break down barriers and open doors more quickly. These businesspeople are not so suspicious of strangers that they will let their fears get in the way of a clear benefit, yet the form of a congenial business relationship is necessary before substantive talks can begin.

Humility is the recognition of and respect for a culture's brand of conformity and modesty. You should not exceed the culture's ability to provide material goods. This means you should not dress in an ostentatious or expensive manner. Do not entertain lavishly. Do not assert the American values of personal gain in order to motivate them. Accept their modest and moderate ways. Accept their way of doing things and their group accomplishments. Don't try to fix them. Show that you respectfully propose business that will benefit the group on its terms. This means for the good of the group. Because this culture is a combination tribal/collective, it is both family and state.

All tribal players feel an obligation to better the position of their group. All need to demonstrate their competence by receiving value from the outsider. However, this culture believes in the value of mutual support and sharing. The members are win-win players, as are most Americans, and they will negotiate for the good of both parties once their group is taken care of. Be prepared to give them a guaranteed gain in exchange for equal value. Minimize risk to them in what they are to receive and in what they are to give.

Valuing the person is valuing the relationship. Focus on the shared respect you have for each other and on your enthusiasm for the new relationship that is being forged. The person's prime identity is through his family group. Ultimately, showing respect and concern for his family is a great compliment to the man. Always be sincere, for honesty is highly valued.

Don't entice a person with personal material wealth unless it will benefit his entire clan. Great wealth is not sought, because it would cause one's immediate family to stand out far beyond the moderate means of the larger collective group. Wealth is shared. Those less fortunate are cared for first. This player's welfare in business is most commonly defined as the path of least resistance. Show these businesspeople how to do their job more easily, more harmoniously, and with less risk of failure. This is their objective.

With your own objective clearly in mind, you will know from your personal perspective whether the game you have chosen is competitive or cooperative (i.e., win-win or zero-sum). Once you have determined this for yourself, consider the culture you are dealing with and determine the same issue for your opponent. You may have different objectives and different motivations, which influence the strategy each player will use. It is always wise to anticipate your opponent's level of motivation and his definition of winning.

For our test case let's assume that your objective is to hire a subcontractor to provide computer programming services for your company in the United States. The targeted country has a large pool of proficient programmers who work at lower wages than programmers in the United States. Your objective is to make contact with a group of programmers that was recommended to you by that country's embassy trade mission to the United States.

You know by your objective that you will be dealing with educated professionals, who may or may not have experience interacting with foreigners. Assume they do not. They might speak English, but it is probably technical English. An interpreter may still be a good idea to communicate business concepts that may not be directly translatable.

Advancing Play

The steps that will be required to advance you through the game toward your goal are the following.

Step 1. Make initial contact.
Step 2. Meet the potential subcontractor at the latter's site.
Step 3. Evaluate the subcontractor's ability to do the job.
Step 4. Negotiate a service agreement and pay scale.
Step 5. Establish procedures for project management.

Your opponent's list will differ. It may look something like this.

Step 1. Consider a request from an American company.
Step 2. Meet with American businesspeople.
Step 3. Listen to their proposal.
Step 4. Decide if the job is of interest.
Step 5. Agree on contract terms.

Your perspective may be that they should be eager to do business with you and will do everything they can to impress you to get the job. But to them, they are the most important participant, and they do what is in their best interest. They are interviewing you every bit as much as you are interviewing them.

What will probably be your greatest obstacles to achieving your intermediate goals?

- Difficulties in communication
- Perception of you as powerful foreigner
- Their need for respect
- Differences in motivation
- Their inability to link time and money
- Difficulties in obtaining critical feedback and realistic information
- Their lack of a strong, achievement-based power hierarchy

To overcome these obstacles, we use protocol that establishes trust and respect and maximizes efficient communication.

LET THE GAMES BEGIN!

You have entered the hypothetical playing field with a referral from the country's embassy trade mission to the United States. That's a good start. Now, how do you initiate contact with the company to which you were referred?

Protocol Challenge

An appropriate company has been identified through the foreign trade mission. Your next move is to
a. telephone the company and make an appointment to discuss your proposal.
b. ask the trade mission officer to write a letter of introduction on your behalf.

If you chose (a), you probably have to start over with a new company referral. In this case, you did not approach as a friend, having been introduced by a third party. You called the company out of the blue, and it, not being predisposed to trust strangers, refused your call. Perhaps if you are IBM you can get away with it, but it is still arrogant and presumptuous and will cause future problems in negotiations.

Protocol Challenge

You follow up the letter of introduction with
a. an invitation to the top manager for dinner at the city's most exclusive restaurant.
b. a letter proposal stating your hopes of doing business with them, your ideas for a cooperative effort, and a request for a meeting.

The correct move is (b) because not only would the manager feel uncomfortable being singled out and shown hospitality far beyond his means, but you have not yet established credibility and a foundation of mutual trust.

STRATEGY

Courier the letter to be sure it arrives safely. Be sure to have the document translated into the foreign culture's language to speed up the process. Be direct, clear, and brief as to your proposition. Make clear what they will gain and what you would like to receive in return. Clearly state the purpose for an introductory meeting. Demonstrate your company's competence and high standing. Make reference to the letter of introduction from their embassy. Request that they consider the benefits of the business proposal. Ask for what you want: a meeting to explore opportunities. Don't assume they understand anything you have not explicitly stated. Give them an estimate of the time line you envision but without stating a detailed schedule. Tell them you are very willing to travel to their offices. Formally request a meeting, and let them know the most appropriate medium for response: fax, e-mail, courier. Your tone should be friendly but professional. Do not use first names; use titles and family names. Do not send a massive brochure about your company.

Be patient in waiting for a response. Let's assume you receive an invitation.

Protocol Challenge

You have received an invitation to talk. How do you respond?
a. You phone them immediately to say when you will be in their country, give them your flight schedule, and ask them to meet you at the airport.
b. You respond in writing that you accept their invitation. Suggest several possible dates, and ask them to select the date that is best for them. State how many people you will be bringing, who they are, and what their function is.

If you chose (a) go back to the trade mission and begin again. If you chose (b), congratulations. You wisely knew to allow them flexibility with time and to prepare them for whom they will be meeting in order to lessen uncertainty.

Protocol Challenge

You respond to the invitation in writing and send it by
a. fax.
b. e-mail.
c. courier.

Unless you had been requested by them to do otherwise, you should choose (c). Their response finally comes, with a date set for your meeting.

Protocol Challenge

You confirm the meeting by
a. calling the party you will be meeting and asking him to make local hotel reservations for you.
b. writing to confirm time, date, and place and to request any necessary help in obtaining a visa.

If you choose (a) it's back to the beginning. Selection (b) allows you to move forward.

STRATEGY

Contact the trade mission for assistance with travel plans. Get information about local restaurants, hotels, shops, airport transfers, and currency. Obtain a city map. Do these things to prepare to fend for yourself if necessary, return or initiate hospitality, and locate yourself strategically near their site. Also get information on their commercial laws for drafting a preliminary contract.

You have now completed the first step in reaching your objective. This was first contact. You are now ready to move on to the first meeting. Your strategic objective in the first meeting is to establish trust and mutual respect and to open communications.

Protocol Challenge

You choose to wear to your first meeting
a. an expensive designer suit with a tie (or scarf) that suits your personality.
b. a conservative business suit, formal yet not too severe; colors of accessories are muted; clothing is clean and neatly pressed.

You realize that people in this culture feel more comfortable blending in and conforming to the group, so (a) is out. That leaves (b). Move on to the next challenge.

Protocol Challenge

The meeting is scheduled for 10 o'clock. You arrive at the building at
a. 10 o'clock—give or take 10 minutes.
b. 9:50.

Because arrival at the building even at 10 o'clock will not put you in the correct office until sometime after 10, you know to choose (b). Even though these people have a nonlinear concept of time, that perception may apply more to their process thinking than their start times. In collective societies where harmony is important, gathering at a prescribed time promotes harmony and shows respect for others. You would be wise not to gamble. Be on time, and let time flow from there as it will.

Protocol Challenge

You and your two associates have been announced and led into a large conference room. Four people walk in the door—three men and one woman. You are the leader of your team. When the others enter the room, you

a. walk toward the first person in the door, shake hands, and introduce yourself; the others on your team do likewise.
b. stand and wait for the leader among them to emerge; the leader will introduce himself to you, the team leader; you then introduce your associates to the leader; then he will introduce his people to you.

In pluralistic business societies, all meeting participants are equal until they get down to business. An American would naturally introduce himself to anyone at the meeting. But in a tribal/collective society, position is recognized. In purely tribal cultures, the leader would be recognized because of the strong power hierarchy and the need to maintain distinctions within the hierarchy. In collective cultures, the leader is the representative of the group. He is equal to every member of the group, so if you have met the leader, you have met the group. In our test case, the culture is a mixed tribal/collective society. The hierarchy is not strong, but leaders are the focal point of the group. Selection (b) is the correct answer.

Protocol Challenge

Both sides have been introduced. You and your team
a. take seats at the meeting table, lining up on one side.
b. stand and talk for a few minutes.

Nonpluralist societies need to form relationships before getting down to business. They aren't sure they even want to do business until they find out what sort of person you are. Although (a) is the right answer for a pluralist culture, in this culture (b) is correct.

Etiquette Technique

Introductory conversation should be limited to your appreciation for the invitation, your interest in the country and culture, and your mutual interest in the industry in which you are both employed. Depending on their experience with Westerners, your hosts may choose to get down to business by directing you to the meeting table. Don't prolong or monopolize the preliminary conversations just to have them learn something about you. They may prefer to do this over a longer period of time. Let your host set the pace and decide when it is time to talk business.

Protocol Challenge

Your host indicates that you should sit facing them at a long table. The next thing you do is
a. pull out your business cards and hand one to each person; your team members do likewise.

b. wait for your host to present a gift of welcome; then reciprocate with a token gift from your company.

You probably chose (b), but (a) is correct also. Either may happen first. Business cards may be exchanged, with no formality attached other than being sure to read each one and not write notes on it. After all have sorted out their cards and their seats, the host will usually offer some small gift, like lapel pins, to each of your team. You should be prepared to return the gesture with a small token that represents your company or something symbolizing your country or local community. Gifts symbolize acceptance and sharing. It is important to reciprocate. You came prepared to offer gifts.

Protocol Challenge

You expect to get down to business now. Your host presents you with what looks like a contract and is called an agreement of cooperation. You respond by
a. hesitating and then suggesting that you will take it home to your legal department for its approval; you open your presentation material and begin your presentation.
b. take the contract and pleasantly, matter-of-factly, look it over (along with an interpreter, if it is not translated), heartily agree to such friendly cooperation, and sign it.

If you chose (a), return to square one and get a new prospect from the trade mission. But, of course you chose (b) because your pretrip study of national commercial law indicated that contracts are vague and largely unenforceable. Contracts primarily set forth an intent to begin a business relationship. Any contract your hosts propose should not be assumed to have much detailed substance. It is the spoken agreement that carries more weight. Often, businesspeople from cultures such as this will in turn sign any contract you give them in an effort to engage you to their benefit. The specific terms of a truly substantive contract should be discussed at great length and accepted by both sides as mutually beneficial.

You have now successfully established mutual intent to do business. Your next step is to exchange information.

Protocol Challenge

You have been asked to proceed with your remarks. You open your presentation with
a. an overview of your company and its market share, sales volume, physical plant, and workforce.
b. a discussion of your hosts' capabilities as you perceive them, your need for their capabilities, and the potential for business should the two of you agree to work together.

Selection (b) is the correct answer. But (a) is good information, too. You just don't want to start off with it. You risk being perceived as arrogant and selfish if you talk only about yourself. They will be looking for the benefit to their group. Get their attention up front by giving them the information that is most important to them. This will open barriers faster and relax any tension or fear of you as a superior power.

STRATEGY

When presenting the benefits of a possible cooperative arrangement, be conservative. Do not exaggerate. There is a risk that they may see you as their savior, and you may not be able to, or may not want to, live up to their expectations. Be very precise, not vague, moving from point to point in an organized way. An outline or agenda would be helpful to keep them focused. Even handing out a summary sheet of each subject would be useful. Visual reinforcement via simple charts or flow diagrams can also help your message be understood. Don't cover too many topics at once. Your opponents are distractible and may go off on tangents. Summarize your statements often. Always make an effort to show cause and effect, especially between time and money and performance. The use of physical analogies is effective.

Etiquette Technique

When you make a presentation, your voice should be moderate and relaxed. Some emotion may be effective. Never allow your voice to become stern or commanding; you are talking to friends. However, maintain formality in your speech. Keep good eye contact with all members of the group. Address the most important remarks or emphasis to the leader.

Now you are ready to move on to their part of the information exchange.

Protocol Challenge

You now want to talk about their qualifications to do the work. You ask them
a. to discuss their company's capabilities.
b. to discuss their key personnel's experience.

This is a trick question. You would think that because theirs is a tribal/collective society, they would be focused on the group identity: the company. And they are. But because the group and its survival are so much more important than the individual, the group members are reluctant to give away to a relative stranger too much information about their operation for fear that it will weaken their defenses and render the group susceptible to attack. The individual, however, feels no personal threat and will most willingly tell you his abilities and areas of knowledge. It is not wrong to proceed as in (a), but you won't get the information you need.

STRATEGY

When soliciting information, do not ask yes- or no-type questions. You will receive a yes or no. Your hosts will not elaborate or volunteer information. They will not anticipate your need for the information for which you are looking. Ask precise questions that are process-oriented. Use hypothetical questions to learn their thought process and problem-solving approach. Steer them toward the subjects you want to discuss. Encourage input from the entire group.

You've made huge advances toward your goal. (Always keep your goal in mind.) You have gathered the information you need and feel confident that they have been truthful.

Protocol Challenge

You and your associates are in agreement that you would like to work with this company. Your next move is to

a. tell them you are impressed with their capabilities, you are confident they can do the work, and the two companies will both benefit; you pull out of your briefcase a contract that you propose for the venture and suggest both parties begin the detailed work of negotiating payment and work descriptions.

b. delay informing them that you have made a decision; you thank them for the information, being positive in assessing the possibility of working together; then you invite them all to lunch.

Remember, they treat contracts lightly. Until you have established some sort of personal bond, your welfare is of no concern to them. It is hard for them to let a friend down. They must have some basis on which to give you loyalty and commitment. It is the personal commitment of the people involved that makes the deal work—not signatures on a piece of paper. This is true in most cultures that do not have a strong power hierarchy. The stronger the organization, the stronger is the coercive rule of law. It is because of the loose organization that each group or individual must have motivation for cooperation.

You have now entered the most treacherous part of the game: socializing. The world is full of local customs and rituals, and many can be specific to particular families. Think of your own family or social group. Your behavior in social settings is very different depending on who makes up the group. There is etiquette for intimate gatherings. There is etiquette for large family gatherings. There are etiquettes for formal social functions and for business social functions. Social protocol, business protocol, diplomatic protocol, and military protocol all have different objectives. We will be concerned here with social business protocol.

Protocol Challenge

You have chosen a restaurant nearby. You arrive at the restaurant together, and as your first act as host you
a. sit at the head of the table and expect your counterpart to sit opposite you.
b. take a central location and ask your guest of honor—the head person—to sit to your right.

You know that the answer will be (b). Why? You want the seating to be less confrontational. You are trying to break down barriers at this point. If the local etiquette is uncertain, do what is graceful and practical, and by all means use it to accomplish what you want—in this case, getting the person of most importance next to you.

Protocol Challenge

It is time to order the food. You as host
a. order the most Western-looking item and look to the next person to order theirs.
b. ask your new associates to explain several of the local dishes and recommend their favorites; then you order something they recommend.

Etiquette Techniques

When it is you who are the host, it is polite to either order or indicate that you are considering ordering one of the more expensive items. This gives your guests permission to choose something in that price range. If you are a guest, never order something that is significantly more expensive than what your host has ordered. Don't be extravagant, but be generous. Extravagance in a culture whose standard of living is considerably lower than your own may be taken as an affront. Using money recklessly or passing it all off because of the availability of a company expense account is inappropriate behavior and can polarize the two parties. In a purely tribal society, lavish entertaining may be appropriate to show respect for another, but under the collective influence, ostentatious behavior of any kind is not appropriate.

Protocol Challenge

What is the appropriate method of eating?

This throws you for a moment, because you have to come up with your own answers. And in many cases you will find that you must do just that. Eating behavior is highly localized in less developed parts of the world. Western countries have more or less standardized formal dining protocol and etiquette, but even within the United States protocol varies remarkably. Here are a few clues.

- Observe the place setting. Are there knives, forks, and spoons in the normal places? If so, you can assume the Continental method, which is summarized in Chapter 9. If there are no utensils—or only, say, a spoon—the proper etiquette may be to eat with your hands. If there are chopsticks, use them as your utensils, except as common sense dictates (e.g., soup).
- Observe the natives. As hosts, they may expect you to begin first. You might pick up a utensil and approach the food, which is usually signal enough to begin. Then pause to observe what others are doing. If they all slurp their soup, slurp your soup.
- Note that cultures with less intense power hierarchies have less interest in formalized etiquette. Do what seems proper, and study the Universal Etiquette section before you go.

You know that you are dealing here with a loosely tribal, and originally agrarian, culture. You reason that your hosts' approach to eating might be more communal and include common serving bowls, passing bread and condiments, and serving each other. You might even use dining etiquette symbolically—pouring wine for your guest of honor and having your other team members pour wine for the others. This may not be the local custom, but in this culture it might be a nice touch, indicative of your willingness to share.

STRATEGY

Keep the conversation social. Your objective at this meal is bonding. If you want them to be dependable subcontractors, you need their personal commitment. Find out about their families. They are probably a lot like yours. Just to be safe, do not ask about their wives or daughters unless information is volunteered. Your objective is to find common ground. Note similarities whenever you can. Another good subject is education—especially their university experiences. Professional people love to talk about their universities. Use this time to assess their attitude toward you. Do they seem interested in forming a relationship—business or otherwise? You may have decided to do business with them, but they may not want to do business with you.

Protocol Challenge

At the end of the meal you, as host,
a. wave your arms to get the attention of the waiter and ask for the check.
b. say to your counterpart, "I would like to ask for the check," as you look for the waiter.

There are many different customs for flagging down a waiter for the bill. Most of them will be offensive to someone else. The most inconspicuous method is always the best. You chose (b) because, not knowing the custom, your comment might elicit help from your guest. Do not use hand gestures if at all possible. Wait until the waiter is nearby, and look him down if you don't get any other help.

Protocol Challenge

Walking back to the office, where, by the way, you have left your briefcase (but taken valuables with you), you say to the person in charge,
a. "I think we might be able to get a contract hammered out this afternoon."
b. "I feel that our meeting this morning was very valuable; I recommend we both consider the comments made this morning and reconvene tomorrow to discuss our next step. I would like to take a minute to write down a few summary notes for both of us if I may."

Answer (b) gets you all the cooperation you ask for. You return to the meeting room and make a brief list of key points. You follow this with a brief list of action items. Be simple and specific. Take nothing for granted. Guide them through the thought process. They tend to be nonlinear and respond best to concrete communication. Upon leaving, you shake hands again.

Even though business could have been concluded that day, it is necessary to allow them the time to confer, develop a consensus, and receive direction from above. Allow it all to sink in. You may also take some of this time to continue the bonding process.

STRATEGY

A clue to selecting the best forum in which to establish a relationship with others is to identify what is special about their culture. What is the culture noted for? In France, it is fine food. In England, it is elitism and aristocracy. In Italy, it is opera. In Austria, it is music. In Texas, it is ranches. So, in France you entertain over a lavish meal. In England, you entertain at an exclusive club or event. In Italy, you take a client to the opera. In Austria, you invite the client to a concert. In Texas, you really get to know someone over barbecue.

Protocol Challenge

In this culture, your best option for entertainment in the evening is most likely
a. dinner at the best restaurant in town.
b. the ballet.

We don't know much about the cuisine of this culture or the local interest in food, but we do know that the performing arts are highly regarded, so (b) is the correct answer. Move ahead to the next day.

You return to the office the next day at 10 o'clock. You shake hands with your host again and begin your second meeting. You discuss the action items listed the previous day. Your hosts indicate they are in agreement with you, and you begin to discuss a contract. You use a form you have brought with you to use as notes.

Protocol Challenge

Which of the following should *not* be included in your proposed contract?
a. an estimate of the time frame for achieving certain milestones, as well as a more detailed schedule
b. elements of the culture's commercial code
c. a complete description of the deliverables
d. standards to be used in performing the work
e. provision for arbitration instead of court ruling on subjects in dispute
f. simple language instead of American legalese
g. a detailed work plan showing the job tasks and decision points

The answer is that they should all be included. Any contract they propose will be vague. It is up to you to provide clarity, especially on points that are most critical. Don't make it so complex that they either cannot understand it or get lost in the paperwork. Give explanations of your intent as you review each topic. Be sure they understand each point.

STRATEGY

After discussing each contract point, allow them time to consult with others in the company before signing the contract. They have difficulty saying no, giving negative feedback, or admitting that they do not understand something. Give them an out. Arrange a later time at which you will pick up the signed document. Offer to make any changes necessary. Try to have the document signed by both parties during this trip, but don't push the time element. Don't be too anxious.

Your good strategy blasts you ahead to your last step: establishing a working relationship. This is the toughest part of the game, because it can be full of obstacles representing key cultural differences. You must negotiate this obstacle course in order to reach your goal that lies just beyond.

OBSTACLE COURSE

LOOSE ORGANIZATIONAL STRUCTURE
You clear it by establishing a clear
hierarchy with job descriptions.

NONACCOUNTABILITY
Clear this by explaining your system of
accountability and indicating
consequences.

FEAR OF TAKING RISKS
Clear it by encouraging openness and setting up a
safe structure for creative thinking. Reward creative
contributions and improvements.

THE CULTURE GAP
Clear obstacle by fostering a family
atmosphere at work. Show mutual
support. Share results. Include them in
your group by keeping them informed of
your office happenings. Bridge the gap
by visiting as often as is feasible.

You have cleared the final obstacle and made it to the finish. You have achieved your goal of hiring a new subcontractor.

The example used in this chapter represents a real country, but with some missing elements. It is Russia, without the influence of communism. Anyone who knows anything about doing business in Russia today will know that nobody stops for lunch. This and other important details will be covered in the true Russian game, in Chapter 4.

KEY POINTS

The game proceeds by the following.
1. Knowing the playing field
2. Learning the governing principles for that area
3. Developing a player portrait
4. Defining your objective
5. Devising a strategic game plan
6. Advancing through the game by applying your game plan strategy and rules of protocol in responding to challenges
7. Incorporating strategy and etiquette techniques to help you toward your goal
8. Negotiating an obstacle course—which may appear at any time—so you can approach your goal
9. Winning when have you taken all the steps necessary to achieve your goal

4

Major Games Played Around the World

In this chapter you will play the game of global business in five major cultural arenas: Western Europe, Latin America, the Arab world, the Pacific Rim, and Central and Eastern Europe. Within each of these playing fields are many countries with many similarities, but also many differences. Countries within a particular global arena have been chosen based on both their importance to international trade and their relative cultural impact on the region.

The premise of this book is that if you understand the underlying dominant cultural forces in a regional sense, then you will be able to deduce the rules of behavior for a particular country without having to memorize specific details. By this approach, no country is left out. You will have enough information to interact effectively anywhere in the world—and under any circumstances.

For each game, we have already chosen an objective. The objective will set certain variables, such as how many people are likely to attend a meeting and the organizational level of the person you will be dealing with. Certain points of protocol will not be needed under the specified objective, so anything of importance to other possible objectives will be covered at the end of the section in a list of supplemental notes.

THE WEST EUROPEAN GAME

Although most Americans claim some common ancestry with Europeans and therefore assume that European customs may be more familiar, there still is just enough difference for Americans to get into trouble. In fact, taken as a whole, Europe is the most culturally diverse area in terms of our three-culture model of the world. In the north the culture is heavily pluralist. In the south it is strongly tribal.

Central and Eastern Europe combine tribal and collective influences. Some nations show a transition from one culture type to another within their borders.

Because of the diversity of Europe, we are going to limit this game to Western Europe, which is essentially everything not included in the former Soviet bloc countries, with the exception of East Germany. Countries such as Ukraine, Hungary, Czech Republic, and Poland—basically the Warsaw Pact countries—experienced the domination of communist ideology for more than a generation, which severely altered their traditional cultural patterns. The old culture will resurface, but at present these countries cannot be discussed without factoring in the influence of communism. This will be covered in the next chapter. Turning now to Western Europe, let's look at the playing field.

The Playing Field

Figure 4.1 shows a culture map of Western Europe. We see pluralistic culture in the North, transitioning to tribal in the South. If we think about cultures in proximity, it is reasonable to expect a certain amount of mixing across borders. Much of this was the result of one culture's conquering another, then being pushed back across the original borders. In Europe, this was done on different occasions by monarchs, emperors, and tribes during one period, and by the Roman Catholic Church and Protestant reformers at another time, all resulting in a blend of cultural norms. Dominant values, however, are always retained.

Notice in Figure 4.1 that cultural boundaries don't always coincide with national boundaries. This is a very important point to remember when playing the game: where are you on the culture map?

Because more than one culture is represented, the governing principles for this large playing field will vary as well. However, these cultures do share a belief in animism— the belief that spirit is contained in all things in nature. From Celts and Teutons in the north to ancient Greeks and Romans in the south, religions were not monotheistic, but pantheistic. They all personified these spirits in some way, separating the humans from the gods. It was the interpretations of these spirits that differed. Greeks, and later Romans, attached specific gods to specific functions of nature. Demeter was the Earth goddess; Poseidon, the god of the sea. They each had their job to do, with Zeus, the patriarch, outranking them all. Celts and Teutons did not differentiate their gods by function. Some gods were more powerful than others, but their power was derived by their accomplishments. For Teutons, what was most impressive were their accomplishments in battle.

What is especially revealing—from a cultural viewpoint—is that one of the major differences between the Celtic and Norse gods and the Mediterranean gods was that those of the northern cultures were not immortal. Celts believed themselves descended

**Figure 4.1
Culture Map of Western Europe**

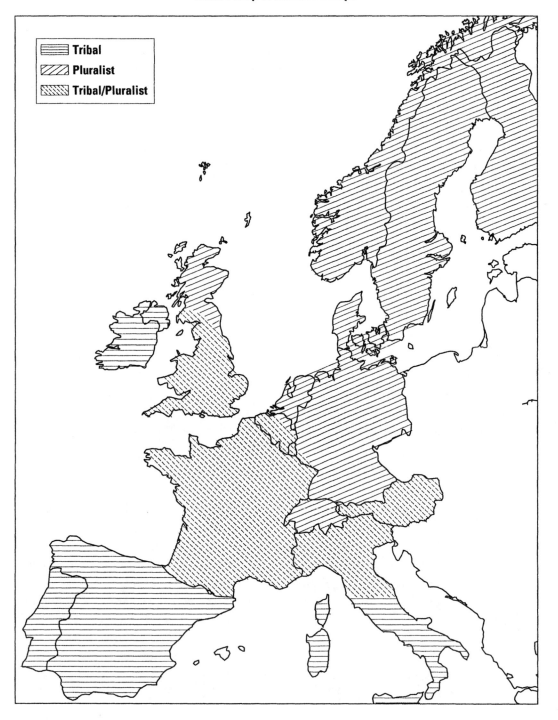

directly from gods. Norsemen believed that their gods were restored to youth through magic, but otherwise that those same gods could die just like human beings. What this meant to culture was that the northern cultures reflected the belief in equality in their cultural institutions. They valued accomplishments in themselves as they valued them in their gods. They believed that their gods could become angry with them and that consequences would ensue. They learned the meaning of cause and effect. They believed that nothing happened without a reason. They believed that by modifying their behavior, they had some control over what happened to them.

By contrast, in the south, Greek and Roman gods were more mischievous and fickle. Events were believed to happen at random, by will of the gods. What could a person do? There was not a sense that man controlled his own life. Man tried to get away with what he could and hoped the gods weren't looking. Roman Catholicism was later adopted, which fit that philosophy, providing for confession and absolution—guaranteed. The hierarchy and the patristic tradition were continued in the church as well. Before Christianity, the Roman father was also priest in his home. The concept of Pope was easy for them to accept.

At the other extreme, the Celts had set up a society that reflected their egalitarian beliefs. They were ruled by an elite group of priests, called Druids, who were non-authoritarian judges and teachers. Druids settled disputes by consensus and provided the ritual environment of the Celtic people. Celts were organized in clans. This sounds tribal, but their ways were anything but tribal. Consider the following concepts.

- Every man must marry outside his clan.
- There was a system of fosterage, in which a child was raised by another family until reaching adolescence.
- Clans were limited to four generations, at which point the property was divided and new clans were formed.
- There was no automatic succession from father to son in clan leadership. Women had full equality with men and could own property.

All this ensured that no one got to be too powerful. Each clan had complete autonomy. Regional decisions were made democratically.

Curiously, in Ireland, Celts believed that the gods resided in clans. The clans were constantly warring, struggling for power. There was belief in a paradise ruled by deities. All this showed a strong predilection for a power hierarchy, which naturally led to acceptance of the Catholic church and its ecclesiastical hierarchy. The family clan is the primary interest of the Irish. The Protestant north remained in line with the beliefs of Great Britain.

The Celtic traditions in England and France became overlaid by the strong patristic hierarchy of the Romans, remained for 400 years, altering the perception of class structure and power hierarchy. When the Romans left, the Roman Catholic Church appeared to fill the void. Christianity in the form of Roman Catholicism had pervaded Europe by the 12th century. By the early 16th century, those countries that had not been heavily assimilated into the Roman system returned to their inner cultural roots of self-determination. In the early 16th century, the Reformation sent the power hierarchy of the church back to Rome. The main difference between Rome and Martin Luther was the belief that all man has to do to be saved is to have faith in God. Luther disagreed. He believed man is saved according to his good works. Here we see a strong difference in the value of action. The strong work ethic of the north is a reflection of the fundamental belief in action and accomplishment to please God.

Where Rome held on, areas retain a tribal orientation, although not completely. France had a strong Celtic society, and the principles of "Liberty, Equality, Fraternity" still hold today. As the result of a Celtic background in a Roman Catholic country, the French are strongly individualistic, but their focus is on their home life. Again, geographic considerations mean that the north of France leans more heavily toward pluralistic culture and behavior, and the south is far more tribal.

Similarly, in Austria—a Germanic country with a Teutonic and Celtic heritage—there is a strong sense of power hierarchy. This is because the Catholic church held on to Austria with the help of the Hapsburg monarchy. There is a blend of customs here that also extends into the more Catholic southern Germany.

Defining the playing field has given us the governing principles that operate in the entire region. Our next step is to devise player portraits for each area. But before we move on to that next step, let's get an overview of this game: what is our objective and what is our plan of attack?

Objectives and Plan of Attack

Here is your scenario: You are an American manufacturer of equipment used for the production of metal parts all over the world. You have a new design that will allow manufacturing plants to increase the speed and quality of their production of those metal parts. Your business plan is to sell the new equipment to one manufacturer in each country of Europe.

You plan to start in Germany, proceed to Switzerland and Austria, and then go on to Denmark, Norway, Sweden, and Finland in the North. After Scandinavia, you will fly to Great Britain and Ireland, then across the channel to the Netherlands, Belgium, and Luxembourg, then south to France, Italy, Spain, and Portugal. Now take a look at the culture map in Figure 4.1 on page 67. You notice that you just happen to have arranged things so that the beginning of the trip is spent mostly in the pluralist countries, working through the transition cultures, which show influences of both pluralism and tribalism, and on to the tribal Mediterranean countries. This suggests the following approach.

1. Construct a player portrait for the first pluralist country.
2. For each subsequent pluralist culture, note only those aspects that are different from the previous one.
3. Do the same for the game plan: construct the first one; then note variations for countries with similar traditions.
4. When there is a large change in cultural behavior, construct a new player portrait and game plan.

Now that you know your objective, you also know that you will be dealing with both management and technical people, probably high enough in the company to have strong input into decision making, if they are not decision makers themselves.

The survival of your company, not to mention your job, depends on your successful performance. Good luck.

Germany

THE GERMAN PLAYER PORTRAIT

What does he believe is a person's responsibility?
Personal achievement, independence, self-control.

What does he expect of others?
Integrity, performance, competence.

How does he interact with others?
Very formal style, and precise communication.

What impresses him? What does he respect in another?
Intelligence, personal authority, perfection, organization.

What is his attitude toward foreigners?
Cautious, nonhostile.

Why is he in the game?
He lives to work.

What is his main objective?
To climb the ladder of achievement into a position of power.

How does he define winning?
Improving. Getting what he wants. Zero-sum is OK.

What is his business environment (physical and hierarchical)?
Closed doors, better executive offices. Strong hierarchy.

How does he conduct business?
Direct, organized, formal. Information is power and is communicated only to those who need to know. Secretive.

How does he learn?

Detailed data, independent analysis, text, data, graphics.

How does he give feedback?

Direct, specific, objective, impersonal.

How does he make decisions?

Independent analysis and verifications, decisions made at the top.

What is his attitude toward time, schedules, plans, and change?

Punctuality extremely important. Plans and schedules must be detailed and realistic.
There must be a good reason for him to make changes.

How does he approach problem solving?

Problems are addressed quickly and rationally. If adequate planning has taken place,
nothing should go wrong. Information is tightly held.

The German Game Plan

Germans prefer the power position of being on their own turf. Before you go, you should become as familiar with the physical layout of the city and transportation options. You should identify and stay in the best hotel. Germans are proud of their local hotels. Avoid American chain hotels. Most important, you should know everything you can about the company you are going to visit. This may not be easy, because information is tightly held. Germans are very insistent on good preparation. If you ask questions that can be answered easily elsewhere, you will not make a good impression.

A third-party introduction is a must. There are two methods for finding introductions: through bank references or through lawyers. If your business is industrial, you would use a bank reference. Contact your local bank to see if the bank can assist you in connecting with a local German bank. If your business involves professional services, a reference from a German attorney is the best approach.

There is an alternative to the referral method, and that is by attending trade fairs. Germany organizes trade fairs for almost every conceivable industry. All German businesspeople attend trade fairs, including upper-level management. This is the best place to become educated about your industry in Germany and to meet agents and company representatives.

Even though many Germans speak English, it would be a tactical error to assume that meetings will be conducted in English. German is a very precise language. Miscommunication may result if both parties are not fluent in German. Bring an interpreter. Also have all presentation materials translated and printed in German as well as English; this includes brochures.

Accept the German style of business interaction, which is very formal. Germans are formal even with coworkers they have worked with for many years. Do not try to, or expect them to, address you informally. Don't joke around or generally behave in a relaxed manner. Germans interpret such style as a lack of seriousness and commitment to your work.

Do not brag about your company's accomplishments or competitive standing. Use this information in your presentation material matter-of-factly. You should not exaggerate or make claims that seem unprovable.

The first price you offer should be competitive, but there should be some room for negotiation. Germans double-check all figures, so be prepared to back up your figures. They will not be impressed with you if you appear weak, so don't let this look too easy. Rework your numbers.

Compliments are highly suspect. Germans will offer a compliment only if something is truly outstanding. Be careful that your compliments do not sound insincere. Germans place high value on intelligence. Subtle comments regarding their ideas during a meeting will have an effect. Complimenting others on the questions they ask is a good tactic. To Germans, a good question indicates an intelligent observer. Use phrases like, "That's a very good question" before you give the answer, or, "That idea has a lot of merit, but consider this idea" before continuing with the solution you would like to see implemented. Listen intently to what they say, and support their view even when offering another opinion. When using an interpreter, never look at the interpreter; always look at the person who made the remark or to whom you are addressing your remark.

You must be very convincing as to how Germans will benefit. Specifically, this means how you can improve their performance. They consider quality to be more important than price. You must show them how you will improve their quality, or you must show them how you will decrease production time and costs while retaining their current quality. Statements will not suffice. You must prove it to them.

One more word about Germany: the word is *engineering*. Remember this word in all that you do. Germany is an engineered society. Everything is planned, in good working order, neat, punctual, and precise. They've even engineered a dog, the Doberman pinscher. The people they look up to most are engineers and scientists. This reflects their strong belief in man's ability to control his world and himself. They carry it to an extreme. Think like an engineer, and you will probably win the game.

You are now familiar with the playing field and its governing principles, you have the first player portrait and game plan, and you know your objective. Let's begin the game.

Protocol Challenge

You have identified the company that you wish to contact.
A referral came through your German agent at a German business fair. Your letter to ask for an appointment begins
a. "Director of Operations"
b. "Gentlemen"

The custom is to send an open letter so that those at the company may decide who the best contact would be. You may have addressed your request to an inappropriate person or to someone on vacation, and no one will answer his mail for him.

Protocol Challenge

A reply comes, inviting you to Germany for a meeting. The letter is signed with two signatures, both illegible. How will you respond?
a. Ignore the signatures and confirm the meeting.
b. You notice a reference number under the letterhead. You send another letter to the company requesting the identification of this code number.

Clever. They include all the information, but use their signatures to maintain their privacy. Typing the names below their signatures would be too personal and revealing. The code indicates who sent the letter. Two signatures are common, representing the two functional groups involved in business transactions: management and technical. They are treated as equally important.

You reply to the invitation with your travel itinerary and the hotel you have chosen. You have researched the area and chosen the best local hotel. You now move on to the next phase of your game: the first meeting.

Protocol Challenge

You arrive a day early to recover from jet lag and to locate the place of your meeting the next morning. You get to the office building early, knowing that traffic is difficult in the morning. You arrive at the secretary's desk at precisely the prearranged time. You then
a. take your coat off and drape it over a chair in the outer office.
b. shake hands with the secretary, introducing yourself, then give the secretary your card so that she can announce you.

The secretary moves to the closed office door, so you chose the right move: (b).

Etiquette Technique

Herr Burger, the operations director, does not leave you waiting long. The secretary holds the door open for you and asks you in. You enter the office. Herr Burger offers his hand. You shake firmly as he says, "Burger." In return, you say

a. "Fred Draper. Call me Fred."
b. "Draper."

The starkness of the last name alone sounds rude to American ears, but it is just the opposite in Germany. Your easy offer of friendship comes cheaply and is insulting to the German. You appear insincere. Business should always be conducted with formality. Unless Herr Direktor understands American ways, selection (a) will result in a difficult uphill battle. Notice the use of the title *Herr Direktor*. Germans love this. It elevates them, recognizes their accomplishments, gives them their due. Either use the last name with *Herr*, or *Frau* for any woman over 18, or *Herr* with the professional title. Note that women's professional titles are not so easy, because they are usually addressed by their husband's title. Dr. Schmidt's wife would be Frau Doktor Schmidt. It's best to stay with *Frau Schmidt*. You likely will not meet many women in high positions in Germany. Note that secretaries are addressed by the title *Frau*. No woman over the age of 16 should be addressed *Fraulein*.

You know to shake hands firmly and give your last name. The shake is a precise connect, one firm shake, and disconnect. Do this with all people present and anyone you might meet during a plant tour.

You handled the introduction well, so you move forward toward your goal. Your host helps you with your coat, which you make sure has no missing buttons. Image is incredibly important. Things are not in order unless they *look* in order. Your host makes a mental note of your professional presence and is impressed. The conservative dark suit, the white shirt and subdued tie (stripes might have been too bold), and the polished shoes all indicate to him that you mean business. Without knowing it, you just cleared a major hurdle.

Etiquette Technique

With your coat properly hung, you

a. take a seat near your host.
b. wait for your host to offer you a seat and ask you to sit down.

You allow him to lead, to orchestrate the group on his own turf, and you choose (b).

Protocol Challenge

Once are seated, you

a. open your briefcase, take out your business cards, and distribute them.

b. make brief remarks about the city or a current sporting event—nothing personal or important until the host closes the door.

The door is closed for privacy and indicates the time to get down to business. Not only have you waited for this signal, but when it is time to begin, you distribute your presentation material, which has your business card clipped to it. Your presentation is highly professional, well organized, and detailed, with reference and support data. All information is impressively packaged. Information is provided in both English and German.

STRATEGY

During the presentation, be prepared to answer questions in detail. Know where to find supporting documentation in your text. Prove your case. A hard sell will not work. Your presentation must be rational, and results must be achievable. Ask intelligent questions of your own. Good questions are a sign of intelligence, which Germans respect above all other qualities. If you can, give someone in your party, or over the phone to your office, an order to carry out. This makes you appear more powerful. Look as old as possible. Germans trust seasoned executives, not whiz kids. Speak with a strong, confident, but unemotional voice. Your voice should never be hesitant. Be in control of your body at all times. Be at attention. Keep hands still and out of pockets. Use language, not gestures, to express your ideas.

Protocol Challenge

After you have finished your presentation and answered all questions, you
a. ask your host if he agrees with your proposal and would like to do business.
b. say that if there are no more questions, you will allow them to review the information and you look forward to their response.

The Germans, being so meticulous in every detail, will want to pore over your proposal before coming to a decision. The final decision on any major transaction in a large business is usually made by an executive committee consisting of functional experts. This is called matrix management. The proposal is studied from all perspectives important to the company. It takes some time, so allow them time and do not push for an answer. After a few days you could send a letter asking if they require any additional information.

You correctly answered (b) so move on. You rise to leave. Your host helps you on with your coat, which you allow (and reciprocate if he is leaving, too). While you are taking leave, you invite him and his wife to dinner that evening. You have already researched the city and found a special restaurant. Of course, this is only proper if your host is of comparable professional stature to you. You would also invite others at the meeting if they have similar professional status. Remember to shake hands with the secretary upon leaving.

Now it is time to think about business entertainment. German dining can be a real obstacle course. Germans spend a great part of their childhood learning to act appropriately at the table. Manners are very important to them. You meet at the restaurant and the fun begins.

OBSTACLE COURSE

WHERE TO SIT
You are the host, so you seat your guests. The most honored guest is seated to the right of the host. In this case it is the manager's wife. If spouses are not invited then the most honored guest is seated to the right of the host.

DRINKS BEFORE DINNER
If you have a cocktail before dinner, the guests will defer the first sip to the host. You may either propose a formal toast or say a simple *Proost*, in which you raise your glass to mid-chest level, look your counterpart in the eye, nod mildly, drink, lower your glass to chest level, then set the glass down. White wine glasses are held by the stem, so as not to heat the wine. Don't clink glasses unless it's someone's birthday. Women should not toast men.

ORDERING
Before ordering, ask your German guests for their recommendations of local specialties. Allow the guest to your right, Frau Burger, to order first. You should order last. Be sure to order a German wine with your dinner.

USE OF UTENSILS
Germans eat Continental style. (Chapter 9 covers
this in detail.) Your fork stays in your left hand,
tines down, and your knife stays in your right hand,
never switching to put food in your mouth. Use the
knife to push food onto the fork. Imitate your
German guests if you're not sure.

HAND PLACEMENT
Hands are always shown, never resting in your lap.
Rest your wrists on the table, even if you are not
using both hands.

CONVERSATION
This is not a time to discuss business unless your
host leads the discussion. This will rarely happen.
This would be rude. Avoid discussing politics,
religion, World War II, and personal subjects. Never
discuss money or possessions. Germans value
intellectual discussions, and your image will be
enhanced if you are able to discuss philosophy and
German culture.

COMING AND GOING
Whenever a woman leaves the table or returns to
the table, all men stand for her. (This is why
women go to the ladies room in groups, so that
the men are not continually jumping up and down.)
This is in a social setting—not in business.

LEAVE-TAKING
On leaving, all members of the party help each
other with their coats. All shake hands with each
other upon leaving. Shake the woman's hand first.
Do not shake across others who are shaking
hands. Do not shake hands across a threshold.
Always remove your gloves before shaking hands.

You mastered the obstacle course brilliantly. You now leave the German players to
discuss your proposal as you proceed to the next arena of the game, Switzerland.

Supplemental Data: Germany

Shake hands when meeting and leaving. Be sure to include the secretary.

For Germans, relationship building comes after business. At the end of business discussions, a German may ask you to stay and share a brandy with him. Do not refuse.

At a party or business meeting, wait to be introduced by a third person.

Never say anything negative about soccer or the local team. Germans take the sport very seriously.

It is not customary for a woman to thank a man when receiving a compliment.

Men should allow people of higher status to walk through a door first; in social situations, women proceed first. But when entering a restaurant, a man should walk in front of a woman. During business a woman should let one of higher status enter first, but in social situations she should enter first.

Never eat with your fingers—not even a sandwich.

Never use your knife to cut potatoes, pancakes, or dumplings. It implies the food isn't cooked right.

Finish everything on your plate, even in restaurants, or make an excuse.

The guest makes the first move to go. If you are visiting someone and your host does not refill your glass, it is an indication that you should take leave.

Don't ask for coffee with a meal. It is served afterward.

A businesswoman will be perceived as not having authority to make decisions. Make it clear what your corporate authority is. Have your CEO send the Germans a letter introducing you as the company representative and outlining the decision-making authority you have.

Any gift should be small and simple. Large, expensive gifts are considered tasteless. If you are sending flowers to a hostess, never send red roses. They mean love. Avoid chrysanthemums also. Send an odd number, but not 13.

Switzerland

Because southern Germany is marked in Figure 4.1 as a transition area, one would think that Switzerland would bear similar treatment. The more Catholic southern part of Germany softens the approach somewhat. People there are not quite so stern or formal. They are more regionally focused. We will again see this effect when we move into Austria. But Switzerland is as fiercely pluralist as northern Germany. There would be little, if any, change to the player portrait. However, the Swiss are not German, and it should not be implied that they are. They are made up of people from France, Germany, and Italy, combining the independent nature in each of those cultures into a contiguous set of provinces called cantons. They are insistent on their own identities and self-determination. They believe in national unity, but not uniformity.

This part of the playing field will be a quick stopover.

Protocol Challenge

You are making initial contact with a Swiss company. What will be your approach?

a. Reference to a third-party introduction, request for a meeting, text translated into German.

b. Reference to a third-party introduction, request for a meeting, text of letter is in English.

Most Swiss in larger businesses understand English, so (b) is correct. It is not right to assume that German will be the language preferred in the southern and western cantons. If you know for certain the language of the party you are contacting, use that language. Otherwise, a letter in English from an American company is proper.

Your meeting is scheduled long before you departed for Europe, and you have reconfirmed your appointment while you were in Germany. You now observe the formal style of business as was done in Germany. We call this high business decorum. You will be safe in most pluralist business cultures assuming such an approach. If anything, it is best to err on the side of formality. The German model is the most formal.

Supplemental Data: Switzerland

When you write to a Swiss company, address the letter to an individual, but address the envelope to the company.

Business cards should include titles in English. If your company is quite old, list the year it was founded.

Be prepared to answer questions about your competition.

Hand your card to the receptionist when you arrive.

Business lunches are more common than dinners. Dinner is purely a social occasion.

Appropriate gifts include whiskey or brandy, food products from your home state, and coffee-table books.

Denmark

You conclude your presentation in Switzerland and move on to Denmark. You have confirmed your meeting in Denmark a day ahead. Before you arrive, you review the player portrait for Germany and make the following changes:

DANISH PLAYER PORTRAIT

What does he believe is a person's responsibility?

Cooperation, doing your job well.

What does he expect of others?

Cooperation, honesty.

How does he interact with others?

Formal style, but not stiff. More relaxed than German, but first names are not used.

What impresses him? What does he respect in another?

Contentment, having one's life in order.

What is his attitude toward foreigners?

Open, nonhostile.

Why is he in the game?

He works to live. Family life is equally important to work life. Having both aspects in
  balance is his goal.

What is his main objective?

To be content doing whatever work he has been given to do.

How does he define winning?

Win-win.

What is his business environment (physical and hierarchical)?

Open, practical. The comfort and convenience of the employee are important. Most
  companies have in-house day care centers. Power hierarchy is not strong.

How does he conduct business?

Direct, practical, less secretive than Germans due to lower power motive. Information
  is handled cooperatively.

How does he learn?

Organization and rational approach are important. Use text, data, graphics.

How does he give feedback?

Direct, specific, objective.

How does he make decisions?

Managers make decisions but rely heavily on input from those to whom they delegate
  responsibility for analysis.

What is his attitude toward time, schedules, plans, and change?

Punctuality, schedules, and planning are important. Change is resisted.

How does he approach problem solving?

A cooperative approach.

Changes to the game plan result primarily from the sense of equality, cooperation,
and practicality that is natural to the Dane. One of the strong influences from ancient
Danish governing principles is the profound sense of destiny. One cannot escape one's
destiny. Everyone has a specific purpose in life and cannot change who he is meant to
be. This is not the same as fatalism, in which no matter how one behaves, things will
happen as they will. It is more a framework for living on the earth. You relate to the

world through the abilities that you were given at birth. Your responsibility and source of joy are to live according to your abilities and aptitudes. This reduces anxiety in the Danish world. People are not consumed with trying to become better than someone else or with trying to achieve goals that seem unattainable.

Third-party introductions are not as critical when doing business in Denmark, but as is true anywhere, they will always help. It is most appropriate to use English in all business dealings. Danes recognize that they are a small nation and their language does not travel far. Be sure to treat them as equals. Do not compare your American standard of living with theirs. They will not be impressed by your wealth, material possessions, or status.

In elevating your Danish counterpart, be aware that he is Danish and not "Scandinavian." This goes for any country in Scandinavia. There is strong national pride in each of the five Scandinavian countries, and past political rivalries, now replaced by commercial rivalry, cause them to insist on separate identity.

In presenting the benefits of your proposal, emphasize the gain to Danes in efficiency, simplicity, and cost savings. How will your product work into their current system? Will its introduction cause upheaval in the production design? Be sure that the change you are proposing has minimal impact on operations while it is being introduced.

Etiquette Technique

You arrive at the business office on time. Your host greets you outside his office by
a. gesturing to you to enter his office.
b. offering you a firm handshake, pumping once or twice.

Danes are more casual than Germans, but not that casual. Handshakes are always in order when meeting anyone. A firm grip is a must. A weak grip is confusing.

Protocol Challenge

The manager ushers you into his office and introduces you to others who attend the meeting. You shake hands with everyone. Then your host offers you a seat. What happens next?
a. Those present seem quiet and put off a bit. There seems to be no reason for this. You dressed in your best three-piece pinstripe suit, you addressed them all by title, and you have begun your presentation with a strong forceful voice.
b. You sit comfortably, but not casually, unbuttoning your navy blazer. You talk moderately with your new acquaintances about their town and their company, the weather, and local sports. This does not go on long. You distribute your business

card and presentation materials to everyone in the group, then begin your presentation in a moderate voice. You use good eye contact, speaking to every member of the group.

If you chose (a), be reminded that Danes are not Germans and they do not adhere to such formality in business. Their power structure is not as strong as the German power hierarchy, so they allow themselves to be less personally competitive. Presenting such a severe image makes it look as if you are asserting power, which causes them to pull back and be defensive. You do need to maintain a certain air of formality in your behavior, but it can be more relaxed. Choice (b) moves you forward.

Protocol Challenge

Your morning meeting has come to its logical end. You allow them to consider your proposal. You neither ask for an immediate decision nor give them a deadline. At this point you

a. ask them all to lunch at a restaurant.
b. take your leave by shaking hands with everyone.

Be warned that there are not many places to go out and have lunch in Denmark. If the company you are visiting is not in a major city, a good restaurant might be located 50 miles away. Most companies have very good cafeterias. If your meeting ends near lunchtime, your host will probably ask you to lunch at the company cafeteria. Do accept.

Etiquette Technique

Which of the following would you *not* do at lunch?

a. Eat Continental style.
b. Talk business.
c. Allow your host to lead the way to the table and show you where to sit.
d. Direct all your conversation to the highest manager.

Managers are not elitist, so (d) is not done. Danes may socialize with those they manage. Everyone's place in society is respected; everyone is doing what he was born to do. All are equal and important, so talk to everyone in the group. Incomes do not separate people very much. Because the tax structure reduces a high salary to moderate levels, everyone makes a more or less comparable income.

If you had been asked to someone's home for dinner, you would never go empty-handed. A small gift of something made in the United States, some candy, or flowers would do. Always stay for conversation after the meal. Conversation should avoid remarks about one's personal life.

At the conclusion of lunch, you take your leave by shaking hands with all those you have met.

At the airport, take time to reconfirm your meeting in Norway for the next day.

Supplemental Data: Denmark

A handshake is as good as a contract. If you agree on something and shake hands, you had better perform.

Shake hands on meeting and leaving.

Don't comment on someone's clothes, even with a compliment. It is too personal and considered odd.

Feel free to introduce yourself in a group.

Don't drink until your host makes the first toast. Before drinking, raise your glass and look around at everyone present. Do the same after drinking.

American businesswomen will have no trouble in Denmark.

Appropriate gifts are liquor, products from your area, and coffee-table books. Gifts are not expected in business.

Norway

Moving to the top of the playing field, you remember that Norway was once ruled by Denmark, and then Sweden. Norwegians are arguably the most fiercely defensive and nationalistic of the Scandinavians, but they share a common culture. Begin your approach to Norway by making any necessary changes to the player portrait and game plan of Denmark.

NORWEGIAN PLAYER PORTRAIT

What does he believe is a person's responsibility?
Self-determination.

What does he expect of others?
Self-determination, competence.

How does he interact with others?
Informal, but reserved. Communication is direct.

What impresses him? What does he respect in another?
Concurrence with Norwegian opinion.

What is his attitude toward foreigners?
Superior to some, envious of others.

Why is he in the game?

He lives to work and works to live. There is a duality of private life and work life.

What is his main objective?

To gain influence and subsequent power.

How does he define winning?

Zero-sum. If you are a foreigner, he always wins.

What is his business environment (physical and hierarchical)?

Open plan, glassed-in offices. Not an obvious power hierarchy, but it exists.

How does he conduct business?

Direct, organized, egalitarian.

How does he learn?

Detailed text and graphics.

How does he give feedback?

Direct, strong opinions.

How does he make decisions?

Technical analysis, management decision.

What is his attitude toward time, schedules, plans, and change?

Punctuality is important. Plans and schedules are detailed. Change does not come
   easily and is initiated internally.

How does he approach problem solving?

Problems are addressed rationally.

The game plan must be altered in light of the national attitude in Norway. Because Norway used to be under the domination of Denmark and Sweden, Norwegians are continually trying to assert their sense of important national identity. This has spawned much protectionism, which results in attitudes that normally run counter to the otherwise pluralistic Norwegian culture. The government officially rigs all contract bidding, favoring Norwegian contractors and suppliers. The only way for you to sell something in Norway is if you have a joint venture with a Norwegian company, if the product has Norwegian content, or if you are the sole supplier of something Norwegians want. Price is never a determining factor. If it costs more, it is written off against taxes, and the government ends up paying the difference.

Another neutralizing factor that is prevalent in all Scandinavian countries is the enormous tax burden. After taxes, garbage collectors make about the same as top managers. There is no rich upper class. Therefore, because money is not a motivating factor, Norwegians have learned to value power through influence. Whom you know is very important. This is still a culture with deep roots in the ideal that the individual is most important, even though the sense of equality has been legislated into an equality of conformity.

Protocol Challenge

You arrive at the office punctually. You introduce yourself to the manager of operations using your whole name (Fred Draper). Your host introduces himself to you as Carl Lund, and you shake hands firmly. Thereafter you refer to him as
a. Mr. Lund.
b. Carl.

First names are all right. But it is generally more proper in any Western culture to wait until you are invited to use a first name. This may very well happen during the first meeting.

Protocol Challenge

You are invited to sit down, and after a brief discussion of winter sports you move on to your presentation. Your approach is the following.
a. "In America we have found that this machine cuts our production costs."
b. "Our technical consultant, who by the way is Norwegian and studied in Trondheim, convinced our management that this equipment would be of great value to the Norwegian manufacturing industry."

If you chose (a) move on to Sweden and don't make the same mistake there.

STRATEGY

Norwegians are not interested in what Americans think. Try to find (or manufacture) a Norwegian opinion to carry with you. Cost is not a motivating factor. Making a noticeable and risk-free contribution to the company operations will increase the manager's clout. This is the game he plays. Show him how to get more power, show him how to get past the Norwegian content stipulation, and show him that a Norwegian thought of it. All this constitutes "laying down your arms" and "paying homage" to your opponent.

You sense that you are making a crack in the wall of resistance. You think of sweetening the proposal with a more social encounter.

Protocol Challenge

Unable to locate a decent lunchtime restaurant on your premeeting reconnaissance of the town, you
a. invite Carl, the technical specialist with whom you also met, and wives to dinner at a lovely restaurant.

b. invite Carl and the technical specialist to dinner at an expensive restaurant.

It is not improper to invite wives out to dinner, but it is rarely done, is not expected, and may cause a raised eyebrow. This is because every restaurant is expensive in Norway. The only people who can afford to eat in them are businesspeople on expense accounts. The implication is that dinner is an extension of the business that is being done.

Etiquette Technique

Which of the following is *not* true?
a. Norwegians eat Continental style.
b. Business may be discussed.
c. The host gives the first toast, or skoal, to the visitor. The guest should reciprocate. Always look the other directly in the eye. Skoals toast an individual, not a group.
d. If you have driven to the restaurant, one person does not drink at all.
e. Refrain from using the word *Scandinavian.*
f. Dropping names of famous people you know will impress them.

They are not impressed by famous people unless it is someone with power whom you can influence, such as the president of the United States. Note that item (d) is very important. You will go directly to jail if you are caught driving a car with any amount of alcohol in your blood. Norwegians don't fool around about this. They take a taxi, walk, or designate a driver.

You may have possibilities here in Norway, so keep a channel of communication open. Do not press for an answer. Move forward to Sweden.

Supplemental Data: Norway
   Shake hands when meeting and leaving.
   Never speak in a loud voice.
   Women will not have difficulty being taken seriously in Norway.
   Liquor is an excellent gift, for it is so expensive there. Buy it in the duty-free shop.

Sweden

Similar to Denmark and Norway, Sweden has turned its natural sense of independence and equality into a legislated equality by economic conformity. Swedes are strongly capitalistic, though, and not as protectionist as Norwegians. Like the Danes and Norwegians, Swedes highly value intelligence and education. Unlike the Norwegians, Swedes have a history of strong and adventurous monarchs. Their historical focus was on the East, whereas Norway's was on the West. Their power hierarchy is stronger than Norway's, but not as strong as Germany. They are formal in their manners, but casual in their forms of address. First names are commonly used. It is good to invite someone to use your first name, as you would wait for them to invite you to use theirs.

Supplemental Data: Sweden

Shake hands when meeting and leaving.

Upper-class Swedes address each other in the third person, as in, "How is Mr. Nordstrom today?" instead of, "How are you?"

Businesswomen will be taken seriously and can invite men to business lunches without feeling awkward.

Finland

Since Finnish customs are similar to Norway and Denmark, you get a free pass to Finland. Finland is a Scandinavian country, but as a nation it is looked down on by its neighbors. Sweden once ruled half of Finland and helped to unify its tribes. Russia also ruled parts of Finland. Today Swedish and Finnish both are the official languages. One might expect that Finland would show strong influence from its more tribal neighbor, Russia, but it has taken on more of the Swedish influence in its social systems and customs. Finland is aggressively involved in international organizations. It has a small business elite that tends to be Swedish in character.

There are two concepts that you should keep in mind when doing business in Finland. Like Denmark, contracts can be verbal. If you make a verbal commitment, Finns expect you to fulfill it. They do not anticipate treachery. The second point is that Finns are more contentious than you might expect. They will aggressively assert their opinion, right down to complaining about the location of their table in a restaurant or scolding you for whistling off-key, which shocked one American businessman. They are formal in style, casual in address, and precise in communication. Noting the similarities once again, you skip ahead to Great Britain.

Supplemental Data: Finland

You should shake hands when introduced and when leaving.

It is a sign of arrogance to stand with your arms folded.

At a meal, the host and hostess toast their guests. They never receive toasts from their guests.

Don't leave food on your plate.

An invitation to a sauna is the equivalent of an invitation to an American golf course. But such an invitation is unlikely if you are a woman dealing with men.

Foreign businesswomen are accepted.

An agreement is usually celebrated by a long lunch.

Before you leave Helsinki for London, you take time to call the German, Swiss, and Danish companies you visited to see if there is any additional information that they need. You also say when you will be back in your office. And you add that you will check back with them as a courtesy before you leave Europe.

England

On the flight to London you rework the player portrait and game plan. In Figure 4.1 on page 67 it is shown that England has a combination tribal/pluralist culture. Although the foundations of English culture are extremely individual oriented, there is a strong overlap of tribal values from both the Roman and Holy Roman empires that leaves England a predominantly tribal society. Note and remember at all times that Great Britain comprises England, Scotland, and Wales. Scotland and Wales are not part of England, and they happen not to be tribal. They have retained their independent pluralistic outlook. The Roman empire did not extend into Scotland; it stopped at Hadrian's wall. The United Kingdom is composed of Great Britain and Northern Ireland.

The English derive their identity from their family and its place in society. There is little if any change in one's position except by birth or marriage. When Britons ask, "Yes, but who *is* she?" they mean "Who are her people?" Britons are extremely class-conscious at all levels of society. The power hierarchy in business is not a meritocracy. One does not derive identity or satisfaction from work. Britons work to live. More than that, it has always been ungentlemanly to work for pay. One could volunteer or go into the civil service in the service of the monarch, but one never worked to get paid. Working was a disgrace. Anyone with social standing who did work in commerce, should be a manager. Management is not viewed as a science or a skill. Management is based on wisdom and character. Management is stewardship. A manager is lord of the manor.

England is a nation of managers. At one time the English ruled one-quarter of the world. They conquered through cliency, an old Celtic custom. They exchanged work for protection. England no longer has the luxury of an overseas foreign labor pool. The English must now reeducate their culture to cultivate a work ethic that gives value to achievement, not only to family tradition. They are making some progress, but ancient values are hard to change. You will probably not meet in heavy industry any managers from upper-class families. Gentlemen do not go in for commerce. If it is a large, state-owned company, the situation may be different. Then it is considered a position of national stewardship.

The player portrait looks like this.

ENGLISH PLAYER PORTRAIT

What does he believe is a person's responsibility?
The Archbishop of Canterbury suggested, "God first, others second, self last."

What does he expect of others?
Form first, deference second, competence last.

How does he interact with others?
Formal, reserved, gracious.

What impresses him? What does he respect in another?

Family stature, self-control.

What is his attitude toward foreigners?

Inwardly snobbish, outwardly gracious. This is a nation of cultural supremacists.

Why is he in the game?

Outwardly, to serve the queen; inwardly, because the inheritance doesn't pay all the bills. He works to live.

What is his main objective?

To uphold tradition and benefit the common good.

How does he define winning?

Appearance of zero-sum.

What is his business environment (physical and hierarchical)?

Closed plan. Closed office doors. Strong power hierarchy with little movement up the ladder.

How does he conduct business?

Correct behavior. Detailed information not widely disseminated. Secretive. Companies must form coalitions to receive government support.

How does he learn?

Strongly verbal.

How does he give feedback?

Negative feedback will be worded so as not to be offensive. He will be honest, but not uncivil.

How does he make decisions?

Decisions are made at the top with input from appropriate departments. Decisions that need government approval will take a long time.

What is his attitude toward time, schedules, plans, and change?

Punctuality is important. Schedules and plans are precise and adhered to. Change is resisted. The English face backward in time. They value the past more than the present or the future.

How does he approach problem solving?

Problems are delegated, but ultimately addressed.

The English Game Plan

Stay in a nice hotel. Do not attempt to drive in Great Britain. You will always turn the wrong way at a traffic circle (called a roundabout in Great Britain). Arrive for the meeting on time.

The more prestigious a third-party introduction, the better—especially in older, more traditional businesses. Third parties rank in the following order: aristocracy, government civil service, professional, and commerce. Anyone who attended Eton, Oxford, or Cambridge will also be useful.

Showing humility is most effectively carried out by deferring to the English superior knowledge of decorum. Image is everything to them. They take pleasure in crossing up Americans in the area of etiquette. They are so detailed and precise in their knowledge that you will have a hard time keeping up. You will be able to do well, though, but accept a small defeat now and then. Play their game. Do not brag about America—or anything else.

Elevate their sense of self-worth. In most tribal societies, this would be done by complimenting the host's family or his family's power. However, compliments or comments about one's stature, power, or financial status are very rude. Personal compliments in general should be avoided. You elevate your hosts by playing their game of decorum, and not by considering them your equal. As an American, you are a poor relation, with no social standing.

Pose benefits as improvements to the functioning and well-being of the group. Appeal to their rational side and their sense of maintaining tradition.

A general word before you begin this leg of the journey: image is everything. You will likely not have a name of importance or status in terms of the English aristocracy, so appearance, demeanor, and behavior befitting the upper class is important to your success.

Protocol Challenge

Your first letter to the company should be
a. very brief, simply requesting an appointment.
b. detailed, so that the right person to handle your request is assigned to reply.

The detailed letter is the right approach. When you do receive a positive reply, it is proper to call the writer to confirm the meeting and to be sure you reached the correct area of responsibility.

Your first meeting is important. First impressions are hard to change, so you will experience this as an obstacle course.

OBSTACLE COURSE

PUNCTUALITY
As in all northern European countries, be at the office precisely on time.

APPEARANCE

Dress conservatively in a traditional business style, choosing a subdued, dark color. A white shirt is best, but not a button-down. The tie should be classic as well, without attracting attention. Don't wear a tie with stripes. Each school has its own color-striped tie. It acts as a flag, indicating a particular school. Take off your overcoat when you arrive at reception. Leave an umbrella in the stand by the door.

INTRODUCTION

You are met at reception by either your contact or his secretary. Shake hands using a slightly firm grip. The secretary will introduce you, or you should introduce yourself. Use your full name.

NAMES AND TITLES

Always use Mr. or Mrs. with the family name. If a hyphenated name is given, such as Vyner-Brooks, use both names.

SEATING

Wait to be invited to sit down. It is not necessary in business to rise when a female secretary enters the room. Do rise to introduce yourself whenever someone new enters. Always stand for women in social settings.

OPENING REMARKS

Start with small talk about the weather or the office view. The visitor should be the one to get down to business after an initial icebreaker.

PRESENTATION

Be organized. Give your contact a professional-looking document supporting your proposal. Use a moderate tone of voice.

BODY LANGUAGE

Control of the body means to the English that you are in control both mentally and emotionally. Do not use gestures. Men sit upright with legs together or crossed, one knee over the other knee—never with an ankle resting on the knee. Keep your hands still. Use good eye contact.

REFRESHMENTS

Coffee may be served during a morning meeting. Don't ask for it if it is not offered. An afternoon appointment may run into teatime. Knowing you are American, you will probably be offered coffee, but be prepared for tea.

TEATIME

Tea is served loose in a common pot. Allow your host to pour. You should place the tea strainer across your cup to catch loose leaves. Use the sugar that is provided; it is usually colored. Don't pull a packet of sugar substitute from your pocket. Use milk, never cream.

CONCLUSION

The guest initiates leaving. Don't sit waiting for your host to conclude the meeting. When you are done, summarize your remarks and confirm action items. Present your business card before leaving. The English do not shake hands when leaving, but your counterpart may know that Americans do. Let him offer his hand first. If a morning meeting concludes anytime after 11:30, invite your contact to lunch. If your counterpart is in upper management, make a reservation at a good restaurant before the meeting. If not, ask him to suggest a restaurant, which will probably be a local pub.

STRATEGY

The British don't like the concept of selling. It seems undignified. Don't sell them; reason with them. Managers will be looking for the wisdom in your proposal. What you propose must be solid, reliable, and conservative in approach. The English will not take risks with their stewardship. Novelty is not exciting to them. There must be a good reason to make a change. Try to relate the idea of using your product to some element of tradition. For example, "Your company has always been known for (whatever quality). Our equipment will allow you to continue that tradition by making (some operation) more efficient or making your company more financially secure." Talk security, tradition, low impact, low risk. Reserve some noncritical information for an opportunity to follow up several days later.

Your invitation to lunch has been accepted.

Etiquette Technique

Which of the following should you *not* do at lunch?
a. Eat Continental style.
b. Ask your guest his ethnic background.
c. Ask if he is from London originally.
d. Answer your cellular phone after first saying "excuse me" to your tablemates.
e. Have beer or wine with your lunch.
f. Discuss business.

Actually, there are several things you should not do. Never take your cellular phone to a restaurant. If it is with you, turn off the ringer. It will save you incredible embarrassment. It is good to ask others what towns they are from originally, but you will show ignorance if you ask whether they might be a Scot or a Welshman. Everyone can tell by the way one speaks what country one is from and what social class one occupies. Do not discuss business unless it is brought up by your guest.

If you scheduled the meeting for late morning, it will be assumed that you are paying for lunch. When taking leave of your contact, don't shake hands unless he does, say you enjoyed meeting him, and add that you look forward to his reply to your proposal. Do not say, "Have a nice day." You may now move on to Ireland.

Supplemental Data: England

Shake hands only on meeting. Always wait for a woman to extend her hand first. Say "how do you do?" rather than "hello," and expect the same reply. No answer is expected.

If you say something is "quite good," you have not given a compliment. In general, remember that British English and American English are not the same. Many of the words that are common to both have different meanings. It is best to consult a book on British usage before you begin spending a lot of time in Great Britain.

To get a waiter's attention, use eye contact. Don't wave.

Businesswomen might find men condescending, depending on the women's age and the type of business.

If during the course of working together, you and your English counterpart agree on action items for each side, don't make changes to the plans unless you get together again. He will feel that you are usurping his power if you do anything not agreed on.

Wait for a British businessperson to offer the first invitation to lunch. You should reciprocate when possible.

Don't offer business gifts.

Ireland

Ireland is not a part of the United Kingdom, but it shares heavily in the cultural history that formed the British isles. It had strong Celtic beginnings, although the clans in Ireland were more contentious and, culturally, more tribal than those elsewhere. The Roman Catholic Church has maintained its dominant position in Ireland since the fifth century and even today shapes the life of the Irish. Divorce is still illegal in Ireland. Northern Ireland is not part of Ireland. It is predominantly Protestant and is under British rule. When we speak of Ireland, we are not including Northern Ireland.

The Irish are predominantly tribal in nature. Their extended families are the center of life. They have a more relaxed attitude toward business than other northern Europeans. This is the only northern culture in which punctuality is not required, although it is wise to be on time for business meetings. Although the Irish appreciate manners, it is unlikely that you will offend anyone by a faux pas. The Irish are very tolerant of foreigners. Keep in mind that they are not very demonstrative and will be made uncomfortable if you are.

In business, the Irish are generally more reserved than Americans. Be slightly more formal than you would at home, and dress conservatively. First names are used after a while, but when you first meet someone, use last names. The Irish shake hands upon greeting and leaving. As with all tribal cultures, expect some time to be spent in establishing a relationship. This will likely happen more quickly than in Latin American or Arab cultures, but don't neglect an attempt to socialize. Business lunches are more common than business dinners. The Irish enjoy spending time in pubs talking. It would be impolite not to take your turn buying a round of drinks for your group. Refusing a drink should occur only for medical reasons.

Supplemental Data: Ireland

Business cards are not commonly used in Ireland. Bring them with you to leave with a secretary if the person you want to see is out.

Keep gestures to a minimum.

Wear tailored clothing, even for casual wear. Dress warmly.

Gift giving in business is not done. If you go to someone's home, don't go empty-handed. Flowers (not roses, not red or white, not an even number, not 13, and not wrapped), candy, cheeses, and wine all make good hostess gifts. If someone gives you a gift, open it immediately.

Wait for a woman to extend her hand first.

At a large party, introduce yourself. In a small group, wait to be introduced.

When the Irish describe someone as plain, it's a compliment.

When offered a drink, raise your glass before you drink, and say "cheers."

At dinner, the small plate next to your dinner plate is not for bread. It is for the peelings that you are supposed to remove from boiled potatoes. Bread is rarely served at dinner.

When ordering beer at a pub, women are expected to order half pints, but a man ordering less than a full pint will have his masculinity questioned.

There are few Irish businesswomen, but American businesswomen will be taken seriously.

Your stay in Ireland was brief, and it is now time to jump the channel for the Netherlands.

The Netherlands

The Netherlands is the correct term. *Holland* refers, more or less, to the northern part of the country. The Netherlands is perhaps the most pluralist of all societies. Every conceivable interest group, from gardening to political action to bicycling—has a well-planned, structured organization. Each organization is associated with an ideology. There is a garden club for Protestants, for Roman Catholics (mostly in the south), for socialists, and for unaffiliated people.

This natural aversion to chaos and the affinity for self-organizing systems form the foundation of Dutch egalitarianism. The Dutch are so completely open to outside influence and so tolerant of new ideas because they have a social structure that allows them to absorb new influences in nonthreatening ways. They encase the new influence in structure, which controls and immobilizes it.

The Netherlands is a bourgeois country, a country of the middle class. The Dutch are thrifty and practical. They are said to worship reality. Although 37.5 percent of the Dutch population is Roman Catholic, they are the most rebellious Catholics in the world. They are antiauthoritarian and believe in self-determination. The player portrait looks like this.

DUTCH PLAYER PORTRAIT

What does he believe is a person's responsibility?
To be productive, to respect others' rights.

What does he expect of others?
Equal treatment, consideration, self-control.

How does he interact with others?
Direct and respectful.

What impresses him? What does he respect in another?
Personal accomplishments, global perspective.

What is his attitude toward foreigners?
Ready acceptance.

Why is he in the game?
He lives to work and works to live. His identity comes from many associations. Work
    is one of them.

What is his main objective?
To reach his goal, to make progress.

How does he define winning?
Win-win.

What is his business environment (physical and hierarchical)?
Open access to individuals, but privacy is important. Not a strong power hierarchy.
    Management can be horizontal.

How does he conduct business?
Direct and pragmatic style. Information flows freely, and input is requested.

How does he learn?
Text and graphics, independent analysis.

How does he give feedback?
Honest and blunt, but not contentious.

How does he make decisions?
Input comes from many, and the final decision is made by the top manager. Less
    important decisions may be made at lower levels in the company.

What is his attitude toward time, schedules, planning, and change?
Punctuality, precise planning, and scheduling are very important. Change is not
    threatening. New ideas will be absorbed into a study and implementation group.

How does he approach problem solving?
Problem solving is a cooperative effort. The Dutch are realistic and deal with problems
    straight on.

The Dutch game plan is rather simple. Be honest, be practical, do what works, and respect everyone as equals. The Dutch appreciate good manners but are more relaxed. Form is not as important as content. The Dutch are outward looking. They enjoy new ideas and personal expression. Be nonconfrontational. Be clear on your own political and commercial opinions; you will be asked for them. In presentations, emphasize the usefulness of your product.

While in England, you called ahead to confirm your meeting with Peter Van Embden. He is the director of the company to which you wish to sell your equipment. You met him in the United States at a trade show. He confirms the meeting and says he is having a cocktail party at his home that evening; he asks you to come. You accept.

Etiquette Technique

Later that evening you arrive at his home. There are many people present. Peter greets you at the door. You
a. return his firm handshake and wait for him to introduce you to the other guests.
b. greet him with a firm handshake and use first names; after you offer a few words about your trip, he must attend to another guest; you enter the large group and introduce yourself, using your full name and shaking hands with each person.

You will be expected to take care of yourself in a large group. Everyone is welcoming to outsiders, although they will try to learn enough about you to classify your ideology. Move forward toward your goal.

Protocol Challenge

You are standing, talking in a group with your host, glass in one hand. You should *not*
a. put your free hand in your pocket.
b. discuss politics.
c. talk business.
d. ask about a person's interests.

As in all northern European countries, self-control is a virtue. Control of the body indicates a disciplined mind. Hands in pockets, casual posture, and gesturing with the hands are signs of disorganization. Asking people their interests is good, but don't invade their privacy.

The next day you send a note of thanks and an odd number of flowers (not roses) to Peter's wife. Then you get to your meeting precisely on time. The meeting proceeds as follows. Decide whether or not you believe the meeting has gone well.

The Meeting

You have dressed in a traditional, understated business suit, not too formal. The tie blends with the outfit, but may be more fashionable. Personal expression is OK, but ostentatious dress or a show of affluence will not leave a good impression.

You shake hands with Peter once again, and call him Peter if he has previously asked you to do so. Never use nicknames, like Pete for Peter, or Jim for James. Always use the exact first name.

Others from the technical staff join the meeting. You introduce yourself to each and shake hands with all. You get clarification of who does what and what expertise each person has.

You wait for Peter to show you where he would like you to sit. When you are seated, you take out your presentation and get down to business.

Your presentation contains the same information you presented to the Germans, except that here you hand out only the English version of brochures and performance data. Your presentation is logically structured. You show cause and effect, give concrete information, and discuss specifically why this equipment will be useful to them. Point out cost savings with specific examples. You direct your technical comments to the person who specializes in that area. You encourage questions.

The entire time your voice is moderate, you maintain strong eye contact with all members of the group, and you do not gesture or move around in your seat.

At the end of your remarks, you allow time to let your audience think. Price will be negotiated. You make a small concession only after logically considering it. Don't make a concession sound as though they have won and you have lost. Make it work for both of you. "We can reduce the price if you allow us to ship next month." Don't say the concession will kill you, but indicate you want to make a deal.

You initiate your leave-taking, saying to Peter that you would like them to seriously consider your proposal and that you will call before you leave the Continent. Tell him when you expect to be back in your office and whom he can contact there if he needs information quickly. You know that the group will need to discuss the merits of the purchase among themselves before coming to a decision. You shake hands with each person, beginning with Peter.

Did you make any mistakes? No. Everything went well, even though you didn't make a definite sale. You will follow up in a few days. France is next on your itinerary.

Supplemental Data: The Netherlands

Shake hands when meeting and leaving. As you are introduced, repeat your last name. Always stand when being introduced.

If you don't introduce yourself before speaking, the Dutch may be offended by your casual behavior.

Be prepared to discuss world politics with the Dutch.

Don't offer compliments until you know someone well.

Before drinking, all in a group raises their glass simultaneously and say *Proost*.

Don't get up during a meal, even to go to the bathroom. It is considered rude.

When entertaining at a restaurant, the host usually chooses and orders for the whole party.

Women are treated as equals in business.

Business dinners are more popular than business lunches.

Invitations should not be spontaneous.

France

When you get to Paris, you take the time to construct a player portrait and game plan for France. France is a complex country that exhibits a unique social style. On the culture map, you see a shift from individualism, or pluralist tendencies in the north, to tribal tendencies in the south. The Celtic influence was enormously significant in shaping the behavior of the French. Equally so was the influence of the Roman Empire and the Roman Catholic Church. Recall that at one time this strongly independent country relocated the seat of the Pope from Rome to Avignon. Today France is thought of as a secular Catholic country. Most believe that religion is for the poor.

France is striving toward pluralism. The French are insistent on the values of equality and liberty, but they also seem to draw their identity from their family structure. This feeling is stronger in the more tribal south. There seems to be general confusion about how Frenchmen derive their identity. They do not live to work, but work to live. Their business institutions are organized to stress the importance of the individual in some aspects, yet there is a strong power hierarchy that tends to be based on seniority and influence, and not merit. Academic affiliation is also very important. If you attended one of the most prestigious schools, you have a better chance of advancing. The French are very title conscious, especially with regard to academic titles.

One of the major differences between the French outlook on life and the American perspective is the pronounced French cynicism toward mankind as opposed to the American tendency toward optimism. The French seriously doubt the perfectibility of mankind through his own works—an attitude that is echoed in Catholicism. This leaves the French valuing individuality, but not personal achievement. This sentiment summarizes the basis for French behavior in business: static individuality versus dynamic accomplishment. From that guiding principle we can construct the player portrait.

FRENCH PLAYER PORTRAIT

What does he believe is a person's responsibility?

None.

What does he expect of others?

To know their place in society. They also expect antagonism.

How does he interact with others?

Superior, formal, closed, adversarial.

What impresses him? What does he respect in another?

Power and wealth.

What is his attitude toward foreigners?

It is a hardship to deal with foreigners.

Why is he in the game?

He works to live and lives to eat.

What is his main objective?

Maintain nonaccountability and minimize work stress.

How does he define winning?

Zero-sum.

What is his business environment (physical and hierarchical)?

Closed plan. Strong power hierarchy but well camouflaged.

How does he conduct business?

Formal style. Information is tightly held. Secretive.

How does he learn?

Logic, text.

How does he give feedback?

Internally critical, but criticism is withheld in negotiations. In a working relationship, criticism would be direct.

How does he make decisions?

Centralized at the top. Decisions based on rational process as well as power implications.

What is his attitude toward time, schedules, plans, and change?

Punctuality is important. Schedules are maintained, and plans are implemented. Change is not welcome. Time is not money.

How does he approach problem solving?

Solutions are discussed rationally. Implementation is a problem. This suggests accountability.

The French Game Plan

Bring an interpreter with you. Translate all documents into French. If you can take the time to learn French fairly well, it is highly recommended. This will elevate you somewhere above barbarian status.

The French do not like dealing with foreigners. A prestigious third-party introduction may be essential to getting in the door unless you work for a major multinational company. Use contacts that are high in social standing. The French are very status conscious. A person who attended one of the best universities in France is also recommended.

Appear humble, but not like a country bumpkin. Show some sophistication. You are naturally humble because of the fact that you are not French. Do not attempt to find common ground. The French do not want to relate to you. Generally, the French don't care to know anything about you.

Your proposal must be compelling. Keep an eye on the points you do not want to give up. Do not trust words. Get a contract. Appeal to their self-interest. Point out that your product will cause noticeable improvement and reflect well on your opponent's judgment.

Protocol Challenge

Your appointment has been set for several weeks. You had met a French diplomat of some stature who gave you an introduction to a company outside Paris. Your contact gave you the name of someone else to contact, which you did. A meeting was scheduled, to be followed by an invitation to lunch. Your concern is

a. that it might not be the right person in the organization; there was no job title attached to his name.

b. that he might be of a higher level—one far above your relative status.

c. who pays for lunch?

All of these are appropriate concerns. It is difficult to find out a person's functional responsibility. Try to get information through an affiliate or from your intermediary. The question of status is difficult. Manufacture a title for yourself if your host turns out to be a high-level executive and expects you to be as well. If he has invited you to lunch, he, as the host, will pay. You may wish to reciprocate at a later time. Do not give gifts. Gifts are considered a personal expression, which is inappropriate.

When you arrived in Paris, you reconfirmed the meeting. You arrive at the office right on time. How will you handle the following?

Protocol Challenge

The secretary asks you to wait. You take a seat near her desk. After 20 minutes you
a. ask the secretary about the delay, for you begin to get irritated.
b. continue practicing your meditation technique, knowing that it will probably be another 20 minutes.

Time is not money; time is power. The delay is a manipulative device, meant to show superiority. It constitutes an element of control. Some think French executives are just disorganized. This is not so. They understand the value of time in their own terms. Your patience has paid off.

Etiquette Technique

Your host finally appears. You rise and
a. extend your hand to introduce yourself.
b. wait for him to offer his hand.

Answer (a) would seem natural, but this is France. He may not want to shake your hand. This is another technique to humble you, put you down, and otherwise throw you off balance. He does offer his hand, and you shake moderately—and with a slight nod if he is very much your senior. The obstacle course is in his office.

OBSTACLE COURSE **STOP**

ADDRESS
Always use last names and *Monsieur.* Never attempt to be familiar.

SEATING
He shows you a chair. You sit without further invitation.

BUSINESS CARDS
If there are others in attendance, you need give your card only to the host.

LANGUAGE

Everything has been translated into French. You
have brought an interpreter, whom you ignore.

OPENING CONVERSATION

Break the ice with some petty conversation about
France—nothing personal and nothing about
yourself.

APPEARANCE

Forget the subdued, traditional business suit.
The French appreciate elegance and chic. Don't
be trendy, but be fashionably businesslike—and
on the formal side.

BODY LANGUAGE

Body movements should be subdued. Use very
little gesturing. Use your face to express meaning.

SPACE

Keep your normal business distance. It shows
respect for a person's private space.

PRESENTATION

Use the same organized, professional, detailed
presentation that you have used in every northern
European country so far. Stress performance,
quality, financial benefits, and low risk.

RESPONSE TO FEEDBACK

The French way of expressing opinions always sounds
critical. Don't become defensive. Try to hear the underlying
concern, and ignore the negative tone. Respond calmly to
challenges to your credibility. Prove your assertions.

Excellent effort! You almost lost your temper over the negative-feedback obstacle;
however, you responded with composure.

STRATEGY

The French disdain the concept of selling. They believe that if a product is good, buyers will come to you. You should not need to sell. Try to present yourself as a nonsalesman. You are not here to sell, but to inform them of this new product that they probably have not had the opportunity to learn about. Use the soft-sell approach. Become an ally as a user yourself: "I have been using this equipment with 'X' results." Frenchmen don't really care about your results or anyone else's, but it might make you appear less like a salesman and more like a knowledgeable user. Don't focus on money.

Your next challenge is to respond to the French use of time. The French have the following ideas about time.
a. Historical perspective; they value the past.
b. Time is power, not money.
c. Taking time is prudent.
d. Stability over time is impressive.

You counter those obstacles by:
a. Giving your product a historical perspective.
b. Patience.
c. Using a step-by-step progression of decision points and action items.
d. Not projecting results too far into the future.

You feel that you need more information about the company with which you are dealing—specifically about production quantities and annual growth. The management does not comply with your request for information. What is the most likely reason for the resistance?
a. Control of information secures the company's power.
b. Maintenance of privacy.
c. Protection against the discovery of tax evasion.

All three are correct. Tax evasion is the French national pastime. Be aware of this in terms of financial negotiations. French businesspeople may have some strange requests, which ultimately allow them to hide income.

Protocol Challenge

Your host expresses interest in a possible purchase and shakes your hand. You interpret this to mean

a. he is seriously interested and all that is required is management's signature on a contract.

b. He may recommend the product, but he has no power and there's no telling what the top man will decide.

Unfortunately for you, (b) is the correct answer, even after you've made an excellent presentation. Power is tied to individuals. Decision making is central and lies with the man in charge. Those who work for him are not necessarily aware of his motivations. To increase your chances for success, involve the highest-ranking individuals that you can early in the process.

Now it's time for lunch. Be aware that dining is a focal point of French life. Lunch takes about two hours. The pace is very leisurely, and the conversation is not about business. A substantial amount of wine is consumed. The French demand good table manners as a complement to the cuisine. They eat Continental style. For your information, if you use the good American table manners that your mother worked so hard to teach you, you will be doing everything exactly wrong. See Chapter 9 to avoid embarrassment.

Supplemental Data: France

Shake hands with a quick, light grip when meeting and leaving. No pumping.

When entering a room, greet everyone in it.

Be careful not to speak or laugh loudly. The French speak more quietly than Americans.

Don't drink until your host proposes a toast, after which everyone will say *santé* and then drink. Your host will continue filling your wine if your glass is empty. If you don't want to drink much, take small sips.

Place your bread on the table next to your plate. There are no bread plates.

Finish everything on your plate.

Businesswomen will be more accepted in the north than in the south of France. Businessmen have been known to treat women flirtatiously, but not condescendingly. Businesswomen should give special attention to their dress. They must be fashionable and elegant.

Contracts are written in precise detail, but they tend to be advisory. The French may not honor all contract points. As a method of updating their concurrence from time to time, stress often the points that are most important to you.

Business lunches are more popular than dinners. Don't expect to talk business. Lunch could last two hours.

If you are the one hosting a meal at a restaurant, be sure you get a menu that has prices. Some restaurants give the prices only to the host. If you are a guest and are given a menu without prices, either let your host order or ask what he recommends.

The best gifts are those with some intellectual or aesthetic appeal instead of logo gifts. Don't give a gift until you have met someone several times.

It would be wise to know something about California wine. The subject will probably come up over a meal. The French love to discuss wine. Don't expect to know as much as they do on the subject, but be able to offer some opinion.

Belgium

You also are considering approaching companies in Belgium. The culture map in Figure 4.1 notes that Belgium is a transition country, combining both French and Dutch influence, with Dutch predominant in the north. Brussels is more French in its culture. Playing the French game will help you on your future trip to Belgium.

Supplemental Data: Belgium

Shake hands on meeting and leaving. Shake quickly with a light pressure. When being introduced, repeat your name.

Be sure to shake hands with secretaries when arriving and leaving.

At a large party, let your host introduce you. You don't have to shake hands with everyone.

Belgians value tact and diplomacy over blunt honesty.

Don't discuss language differences in Belgium.

Don't use the same business contact in both French and Flemish Belgium.

If you translate your materials, provide both French and Dutch.

The first meeting is usually for getting acquainted. Belgians lean to the tribal side on this point. In the Flemish north, such will not always be the case.

Schedule business entertaining for lunchtime. Belgians like to spend the evening with their families.

An American businesswoman who wishes to entertain a Belgian businessman should arrange payment in advance or say that her company is paying. He won't allow her to pay otherwise.

Italy

Italy can be extremely perplexing. The north is pluralistic and the south is tribal. Oddly enough, in a small area there is not much in the way of transition between the two cultures. It is a good bet that you will be doing business in the north. Italy is really made up of two countries: the affluent, industrial north, and the impoverished south. Rome is the seat of government, not industry.

Let's assume your target company is in Milan in the north. Your approach would be to use the player portrait and game plan for Germany. You should modify it slightly by decreasing the level of formality. Dress can be more fashionable, for Milan is the fashion capital of Europe, if not the world. Do not make the mistake of assuming that because you are dealing with Italians, gesturing will be appreciated. The northern Italian people value self-control as much as those in any of the northern European countries. Our stereotype of Italians comes from those who emigrated here. Most of them came from southern Italy to escape the poor conditions at home.

Supplemental Data: Italy

Shake hands when meeting and leaving. Exchange business cards with anyone you haven't already met.

In the south you may encounter more physical contact during greetings, like a hand on the shoulder.

Don't drink until your host does. Take small sips, or your glass will be refilled. Women should not pour wine.

When eating spaghetti, don't cut it or twirl it against a spoon. Twirl it against the rim of the dish.

Even though you are the one who has invited people to a restaurant, there will be fighting over the check. You must insist on paying. A businesswoman has almost no chance of picking up the bill unless payment is arranged ahead and she explains that her company has paid.

A woman will be taken seriously in business, but if she is traveling with a man, she will be taken for his secretary. Women must dress very formally and expensively to give the signal of being a person of some authority. Always have academic degrees and titles printed on your business card.

On arrival in Italy, send a fax to confirm your appointment. The phones are not reliable.

Don't discuss business or hand out business cards in a social setting.

When you invite an Italian businessperson to a meal, ask which colleagues should be included in the invitation.

Spain

Spain is the first Western European country you are in that is truly tribal. Now all the rules change. Motivating factors are different, power structures are different, the pace is slower, and the entire feeling of the game will change.

Spain's history is dominated by Roman, Islamic, and Catholic rule. Each influence was resident for centuries. All three cultural powers were tribal, with strong authoritarian power structures reflecting man's separateness from his divinity. The early gods of this area were mischievous. Their behavior was random, and human beings could only react to the whims of the gods. Man tried to get away with what he could. Man's accomplishments meant little. Family structure mirrored early beliefs in the distribution of power. This was carried on by Islamic law, which clearly defines the complete authority of God. Catholicism continued the tradition.

Spain's mode of operation consisted in progress by coercion. Productivity was not stressed. The family's power was derived from its possessions, its wealth. To increase one's power over one's neighbors, one came to possess more. This is a form of materialism not rooted in personal satisfaction but in its symbol of family stature. How one's family appears to others is important. It defines the pecking order in society. There is little trust between tribes, or family groups, and therefore the more power one had, the more certain the survival of the group. All members of the group were dedicated to its survival, because they each drew identity from membership in the group. The resulting player portrait follows.

SPANISH PLAYER PORTRAIT

What does he believe is a person's responsibility?
Allegiance to the family group.

What does he expect of others?
To protect their interests.

How does he interact with others?
Courteous but cautious.

What impresses him? What does he respect in another?
Wealth and status.

What is his attitude toward foreigners?
Outgoing but protective.

Why is he in the game?
He works to live.

What is his main objective?
To better his position.

How does he define winning?
Zero-sum.

What is his business environment (physical and hierarchical)?
Strong power hierarchies require definite differences between hierarchical levels.
    Small offices at the bottom; large, sumptuous offices at the top.

How does he conduct business?
He must control the interaction. Relationships are important, and he decides when to
    move forward. Communication is closed, limited, and personal.

How does he learn?

He is not a linear thinker. Cause and effect must be clearly shown. Use visual representation and analogy.

How does he give feedback?

Indirectly. Body language and attitude may communicate opinion. He avoids conflict and accountability.

How does he make decisions?

Decisions are made at the top. They are not necessarily a direct result of persuasive presentations. Decisions can be subjective and based on emotion or hidden agendas.

What is his attitude toward time, schedules, plans, and change?

Time moves forward, but not necessarily in a linear fashion. He is not influenced by time. Plans tend to be general, and schedules advisory. He resists change and has low tolerance for the unknown.

How does he approach problem solving?

Everything resolves itself in time. Do nothing. Wait for solutions to develop.

The Spanish Game Plan

Don't assume the person you are meeting speaks English. Have materials translated, and bring an interpreter. You will not often get in the door without some form of introduction. The Spanish conduct business through agents. Such commercial agents can be located through Spanish trade missions. They are almost essential to your success. They know the local customs and attitudes and can act as interpreter.

Spain is a poor nation compared with its European neighbors. Spaniards are sensitive to their shortcomings and are trying to catch up. Do not make comparisons between Spain and other nations. Defer to the Spanish way of doing business, and be tolerant of a process that might seem cumbersome to you. The Spanish love to bargain. Bring a lot of negotiable points.

Ego is strong in tribal countries. Your counterpart's honor is paramount. Compliment him with regard to his country, his city, his company, and his office. Show him how he will benefit and how his group will benefit. Reduce risk.

Expect a long process of relationship building. He will not do business until he reaches a certain level of comfort with you. Be sure you have approached the right person and at the appropriate authority level, or you will waste a lot of time.

Well before you began your trip, you hired a Spanish agent. Your first order of business is to make contact with him. Meet with him first, and be sure he understands your objectives. He has arranged the first meeting with your prospective customer.

Protocol Challenge

Your first meeting is
a. at the customer's office, scheduled for mid-morning.
b. at a café after work hours.
c. at a good restaurant.

You do not want to select (a). The other two options depend on the level of the person you are meeting. If he is a top executive, a fine restaurant is in order. If he is middle or lower management, he will feel uncomfortable in a fancy restaurant. Remember that people do not move into positions of authority by merit. These are posts reserved for members of the social elite.

Your agent will accompany you and provide your introduction. He will attend other meetings if you need translation service. He is also valuable in deciphering body language that you may not be accustomed to.

Protocol Challenge

At this first meeting your goal is
a. to establish an agenda for business discussions the next day.
b. to let the Spaniard find out who you are, measuring what kind of person he might be doing business with.

First meetings almost never accomplish any business purpose in your terms. In the Spaniard's perspective, he is accomplishing a great deal. The only way one can be assured of contract performance in this culture is if there is an element of friendship between businessmen. He must be sure his position is safe before exposing himself during negotiations.

If you ended up at a restaurant, you notice everyone eats Continental style. Table manners are not extremely important, but under no circumstances become inebriated. Your manners are slightly formal, but do not be subdued; it would be assumed you are uninterested.

Etiquette Technique

First impressions are important, so you
a. shake hands firmly when introduced.
b. address Carlos García Méndez as Señor García.
c. share a drink with your host.
d. avoid talking about business.

e. wear a good-quality dark suit and black leather shoes.

f. give your host a gift.

You know that gifts might be misconstrued as bribes, so you choose (a) through (e) and move ahead to the next day's meeting.

Protocol Challenge

When you arrive at the office, you expect

a. to get down to business.

b. to be kept waiting.

Always be on time for appointments, but never expect a Spaniard to be. If you are very important, he will not keep you waiting long. Don't expect to get down to business just because you had a drink together last night. He may talk about business in general, but let him make the turn to business. Once he is comfortable, he will initiate the discussion. After a moderate wait, move on.

Protocol Challenge

You are asked for your presentation. You conduct the presentation as follows.

a. You give the same presentation as you have been using throughout Europe. Your posture is good and you avoid gestures. You speak in a moderate tone.

b. You give the same presentation, but highlight benefits for the Spanish market. Your manners are formal, but not stiff. You use your body, especially your hands, to emphasize points. You speak forcefully and with animation to project sincerity. You use good eye contact.

You have made a good impression with (b), even though throughout your presentation there were interruptions and your customer tended to get off track. You managed to gently guide the discussion back to your presentation.

S T R A T E G Y

Be very clear in your presentation. Use visual aids and repetition. Emphasize the most important points. If your presentation is complicated, it would be wise to have another employee in the meeting. The reason is that Spaniards will not admit that they don't understand something; they don't want to appear unintelligent. Even if you encourage questions, you may not get honest feedback. The danger is that your prospective customer might just let the deal drop if he doesn't understand it. Try to anticipate problem areas. Tell him that others usually are confused about (something technical) or that you are often asked about (some detail). If another person from his organization is present, the two of them may be able to work out the confusion in private or they may say the other person didn't understand.

You don't push for closure on the deal, but instead suggest meeting again tomorrow to discuss prices. This gives them the opportunity to digest your presentation and figure out how your proposal fits into company and personal priorities. Business lunches are not held until after a few meetings. The next day you return to the office on time.

Protocol Challenge

Several things happen that give you an indication you are being successful: He doesn't keep you waiting as long, he puts a hand on your shoulder when shaking hands, and he sits closer to you during discussions. After negotiations are complete, he shakes your hand in agreement and suggests you both have lunch. What do you expect will happen next?

a. He will write a letter of agreement for you to return home with.

b. He will let you know the head of the company's final decision at some later date.

Remember that all decisions are made at the top. You are halfway there, but anything can happen during the decision process. The handshake is not considered binding, as it is in Denmark and parts of Latin America. Enjoy lunch and continue building rapport, but talk only about personal matters if your host brings something up for discussion. Consider this leg of your trip a success, and move on to your last stop, Portugal.

Supplemental Data: Spain

Shake hands on meeting and leaving.

Older people and people of high rank may address you by your first name. Don't take this as a signal to use theirs. Use their surname until invited to do otherwise. If a person of high rank asks you to use his first name, precede it by *Don* as a sign of respect.

Beware of casual U.S. gestures. Some of them are offensive. Use the whole hand to gesture, and not fingers.

Dressing well at all times gives the impression of accomplishment.

Businesswomen must project a professional air. Dress elegantly, but conservatively.

Don't be flirtatious in any way. Men may make comments to women as they walk by. Be sure not to react or acknowledge them in any way. If you return the gaze of a man, he will think you are interested in him.

Correspond with a Spanish company in formal English. Do not have letters translated into Spanish. The translation will probably not be sufficiently formal, flowery, and poetic, and might therefore offend.

Be careful in gift giving. Wait until you have formed a relationship. Products or artwork representative of your home state are appropriate gifts.

Portugal

The Portuguese represent a more subdued version of the Spanish, but they don't like to be thought of that way. By the 16th century, Portugal had a huge overseas empire. The Portuguese have a strong national identity separate from Spain in spite of their size and proximity. They have traditional ties with England and feel comfortable emulating English behavior. They are certainly tribal, but without the modifying influence of England's strong Celtic character. Business procedures would be more like those in Spain as far as need for security and relationship building, but more formal and reserved in style.

Supplemental Data: Portugal

Shake hands on meeting and leaving. Shake hands with everyone present.

Business cards need not be translated, but plan on bringing an interpreter to meetings. Exchange business cards at the beginning of a meeting.

The Portuguese respect professional women. Dress elegantly, but conservatively.

Portuguese tend to be somewhat unreliable in meeting deadlines.

Give gifts after you have begun business dealings. Ask your contact if there is anything he would like from America. He may appreciate access to technical products like computer programs, books, or CDs.

Dinner is always social. Do business at lunch only.

Finish everything on your plate. Never eat with your hands. Keep your napkin on the table, or you will be offered one continually.

You should now be able to play the game of global business in Western Europe. You have not signed contracts yet, but your follow-up from your home base will certainly produce results. When you return to America, remember the cultural differences when speaking with someone on the phone. Sometimes when we are physically situated in our own cultural surroundings, we forget to be "on their turf" when speaking on the phone or communicating by fax. Keep cultural motivations in mind when closing the deal from a distance.

Figure 4.2
Latin American Map (Central America)

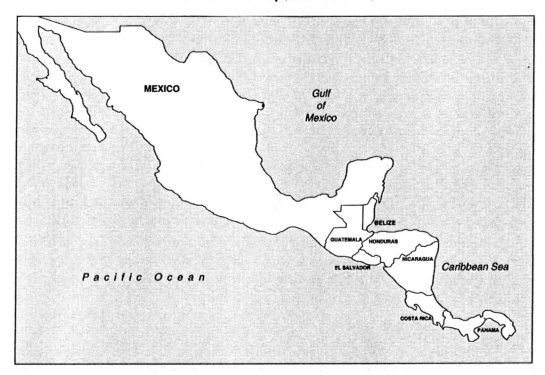

THE LATIN AMERICAN GAME

You might have noticed that in Western Europe you were interacting in primarily pluralist cultures. The behavioral differences between countries were a matter of degree. Germany is the most disciplined enforcer of individual recognition. England is one of the least appreciative of personal expression. France is having an identity crisis between pluralist and tribal culture. Other countries are in transition from tribal to pluralist within their borders. Spain and Portugal are the only truly tribal nations in Western Europe, but that will probably be modified in the decades ahead as membership in the European Community causes the two to restructure themselves in order to keep with member standards.

The legacies of Spain and Portugal can be found in Latin America. Tribalism is clearly the operating system in both South and Central America. The Hispanic countries and Brazil have kept the Spanish and Portuguese social system intact for almost 500 years. There is such a remarkable homogeneity of culture spread over such a vast area that one might speculate it has remained unchanged due to its isolation from other cultural systems. Mexico, sharing a border with the United States, has the so-

Figure 4.2 *continued*
Latin American Map (South America)

ciety perhaps most apt to be affected by proximity to a pluralist culture. And yet, doing business in Mexico is essentially the same as doing business in any other Latin American country. Mexican businesspeople are probably more experienced in doing business with North Americans and are aware of the differences in style, but this has not caused them to change their own style.

Although the similarities between Latin American countries are remarkable, there certainly are differences. Whereas in Europe the differences were a matter of degree, in Latin America the differences are a matter of attitude.

The Latin American game will be played in one hypothetical country that will be representative of the characteristic Latin American culture. The subtle differences that exist in each individual country will be covered by a set of supplemental notes that highlight information necessary for business travelers.

It doesn't take much convincing for most people to accept that there are major cultural similarities shared by all Latin American citizens. Spain and Portugal began colonizing this part of the world in the early 1500s. Portugal ruled Brazil, and Spain held everything else. Brazilians speak Portuguese, not Spanish, but otherwise share the same tribal tendencies. Although Latin America was ruled by two nations, it was also ruled by only one religion: Roman Catholicism. Even today the church dictates behavior in many Latin American countries.

The Hispanic countries received their culture from Spain, but received their independence thanks to Napoleon. When Napoleon overran Spain in the early 1800s, the Spanish colonies declared independence rather than be claimed by Napoleon. After Napoleon's defeat they retained their independence. Brazil took a slightly different route to independence. Napoleon invaded Portugal as well, but the monarchy there fled to Brazil and set up shop with Rio de Janeiro as the new capital of the Portuguese empire. After they returned to Portugal, the Brazilians did not want to return to subordinate status and so declared independence.

Once independence was achieved by the Latin American countries, they progressed on similar paths. Their pathway included:

- an unstable economy.
- an unstable government.
- a small, wealthy, and elite class of families that held most of the land and all of the power.
- corruption at all levels of society.

These all are understandable by-products of the tribal culture. As an aside, please remember that the first rule of the game is not to judge other cultures. The foregoing list seems to contain only negatives, and they are to most North Americans. In our system those outcomes would be unacceptable. They are not consistent with our guiding principles as a pluralist culture. But the values of a tribal society are different: The highest value and motivating principle is the good of the family, or tribe. If the economy within the family is stable, the members of a tribal society are satisfied. If the government within the family is stable, they are also satisfied.

If their family is one of the landowning power elite, they are satisfied. And—remarkably to us—even if their family is not, they tend to be satisfied. This is because they accept the premise of destiny. Poverty and wealth constitute destiny. If you are born into a poor family, it is your fate. Some of the tribal guiding principles are that man does not have control to change things to benefit himself. He does not believe in perfectibility and progress. His religion states he has no responsibility to reach his full potential or to improve himself in order to be saved at the end of his life; he merely has to have faith in God and accept God's will for him, which, translated, means that if he is poor, it is God's will.

What we view as corruption is not of great concern to the tribalist. The tribal person is the most honest, generous, selfless, responsible, upright citizen on the face of the earth. He is the most moral of all people—*within his tribe*. Remember that his universe centers on his tribe, his family. He will defend the honor of every member of his family to the end. But outside his tribe, morality is of little concern. To us, Latin American Catholics are hypocritical. To them, they are Christian where it counts: at home. That kind of value system has major implications for doing business in Latin America, as you will see.

For the businessperson the most important aspect of tribal culture is the family power hierarchy. People who are in positions of power in business are there as a result of their family's power. One does not rise in the company through merit, but through connections and seniority. Only family ties determine success. Nepotism is common practice. To Latins, nepotism is logical and moral. It perpetuates their value system. Consequently, the business elite is small and consists usually of the direct descendants of European colonists.

Accompanying the perpetuation of family power is the bias against those who have intermarried with members of the local native culture. There is a strong color bias: the whiter the skin, the better the family and the greater the power. Even in countries whose population has a majority of mestizos (European and American Indian mix), as in Bolivia and Paraguay, the business ruling class is still the very small percentage that are of pure European descent.

Fatalism notwithstanding, those who make up the underclass have begun to reject the traditional power balance, if for no other reason than that their family is often forced to give up its standard of living when asked to do so by the power elite. This causes hostility, when the good of the tribe is threatened, and this is where conflicts arise. The solution is often to take what you want—a course of action programmed into Hispanic cultures, whose very existence is founded on the model of the conquistadors. The Spanish explorers simply took what they desired from the local Indians, claimed the land as theirs, and increased the wealth of their family tribe back home as a result. Perfectly justifiable. They were acting for the good of their tribe. This zero-sum approach to business still reigns.

South America gives us the perfect opportunity to point out the merits of the approach presented in this book. Several South American countries have substantial populations of Europeans other than Spanish. There are also large numbers of Japanese in São Paulo, Brazil, and in Peru. The general case that will be used for the game in this section must be modified when you know you are dealing with an Italian, German, English, or Japanese businessperson. One set of rules per country does not always work for everyone you will encounter. You must understand the native culture of your counterpart as well as the culture in which he is conducting business. This book gives you the information necessary to apply protocol strategically in any situation.

With this background on the Latin American playing field's governing principles, we can construct a player portrait and game plan.

LATIN AMERICAN PLAYER PORTRAIT

What does he believe is a person's responsibility?
To support his family. To obey the rules of his family tribe.

What does he expect of others?
Mutual support and absolute loyalty within the tribe.

How does he interact with others?
With strangers he is formal and aloof. With those he trusts he is warm and welcoming.

What impresses him? What does he respect in another?
Power and status.

What is his attitude toward foreigners?
Cautious, formal, defensive, distrustful.

Why is he in the game?
He works to live.

What is his main objective?
To increase his power, which increases the respect he receives from others.

How does he define winning?
Zero-sum.

What is his business environment (physical and hierarchical)?
Strong vertical hierarchy. Sumptuous offices for top management; simple, open plan for lower-level workers. Management is inaccessible and privileged.

How does he conduct business?
He must be in control of meeting content, pacing, and decision making. Things are done on his terms or not at all. Correspondence is limited and controlled, and communication is subjective.

How does he learn?

Communication must be visual as well as verbal. Content should be more concrete
than abstract. Generalizing data, coaching, and repetition are helpful, but must be
done without any condescension.

How does he give feedback?

He avoids criticism and accountability. Feedback is subjective and general in
nature.

How does he make decisions?

Decisions are made at the top. Decisions are influenced by personal issues, pride, and
emotion rather than by the objective merits of a proposal.

What is his attitude toward time, schedules, plans, and change?

He is not goal oriented. Time is not money. He tends to become absorbed in the
process while losing sight of the goal. Plans and schedules are not detailed and can
become fluid. He resists change to the ways things are done. He is not a risk taker.

How does he approach problem solving?

Admission of the existence of a problem is avoided. Blame is assessed. Problem
resolution is delegated.

The Latin American Game Plan

Go to the offices of the tribal player. This is very important because it allows the tribal
player to feel in control by remaining in his own surroundings. He finds it hard to
defer to another person's culture without feeling as though he has humbled himself
and lost power. You, however, know that deference does not mean weakness and can
use his need to appear in control to achieve your goals. Going to his camp also means
communicating in his language. He may speak English fluently and be proud of this
sign of intelligence and worldliness. But he will be pleasantly surprised to find your
willingness to accommodate him. You don't have to carry the whole presentation in
Spanish. Even a few memorized phrases would be appreciated. Bring an interpreter,
and have all text translated into Spanish. Beware that there are certain differences between Latin American Spanish and the Spanish spoken in Spain. Argentina, for example, has incorporated some Italian influences. Tell the translation service for which
country you are preparing your presentation.

To gain access to a tribal player, it is extremely important to approach as a friend.
The tribalist's primary mode of operation is defensive. He lets no one in without trust.
This is so important in business that every Hispanic country, including Brazil, has established the profession of *enchufado*, an agent that helps in establishing contacts between foreign businesses and local companies. In Mexico this person is called a *per-*

sona bien colocada, meaning *well-connected person*. In Brazil your contact is called a *despechante*. *Despechantes* are invaluable in getting you to the right person in the right company. They are, predictably, well connected. Such an agent can be found through a country's embassy or trade mission to the United States.

Accept your host's way of doing business. Be patient with his use of time. Be understanding of his need to size you up. Be sensitive to his need to establish trust and friendship. Be prepared to make many trips to his camp, and be prepared for long-term gains, not short-term advances.

He may use time to manipulate you. Keeping one waiting shows greater importance in tribal culture. In pluralist cultures, it is merely considered rude. Offer this act of humility by being punctual but not expecting your counterpart to be anywhere near on time. He may keep you waiting as long as an hour. When he finally greets you, you can take the opportunity to note that he is a man of great importance to be kept so busy.

Show him deference by maintaining formality until he chooses to relax his style of interaction. Do not treat him casually as you might an equal in the United States. This includes your manner of dress, which should be formal and subdued. It includes your posture and general body control. You should use gestures sparingly and keep distances until he chooses to bridge the gap. Your posture should show attentiveness, and not casual disrespect. Never stand with your hands on your hips, for it implies a challenge. Never put your feet on the furniture.

Your goal here is to appear humble but not weak. You should show that you are a person of status. Image is very important in achieving this distinction. Your clothing should be elegant, with high-quality accessories such as shoes, belt, and briefcase. Women should minimize jewelry, however. Where you stay and how you travel are important. Stay in the best hotel and hire a driver instead of using taxis. Assuming you are the highest-ranking person on your team, be sure others defer to you and don't interrupt, contradict, or embellish what you say. You are the person that the Latin American businessperson is interested in, not your subordinates. You must show that you are in charge, that you are powerful in your own "home."

Your greeting upon first introduction is important in this respect. You should meet his firm handshake and, especially important, maintain good eye contact. Most likely you will be given an *abrazo* (hug or embrace). An *abrazo* is exchanged same gender at first meetings. If you are highly acknowledged, you may receive a double *abrazo*. Men, when given an *abrazo* do not back away. It is an insult to do so. Looking away implies you have something to hide. Americans may have difficulty maintaining eye contact and standing very close during an introduction. It would be a good idea to practice this so you will feel more comfortable at it. Any sign of pulling back to increase the distance would be interpreted as a sign of rejection. Allow him to stand close and touch your shoulder, your lapel, or your forearm. Shake hands each time you see people and when you leave. In a group, shake hands with everyone individually.

The Latin American is happy with a zero-sum game. He is not especially interested in what you lose as long as he achieves his purpose. He should always be allowed to better his position, so do concede something substantive. However, do not concede easily. An easy win shows you to be weak or stupid in his eyes. He also interprets compromise as a sign of weakness—on his part and on yours.

Elevate your counterpart's sense of self-worth. This is very important and very easy to accomplish. Continuing with the first introduction, respect is shown by using titles when addressing your counterpart. Professional titles are used along with the last name. In most countries, anyone with a college degree may be referred to as *Doctor*. Engineers are *Ingeniero*, architects are *Arquitecto*, lawyers are *Abogado*, and teachers are *Profesor*. These may vary slightly from country to country, so check the supplemental notes. Those who do not have professional titles are referred to as *Señor* or *Señora*. Hispanic names include the father's and the mother's family names. The father's precedes the mother's and should be used as a term of address. For example, Carlos García López is Señor García.

The person your company sends to meet Señor García is considered a reflection on him. If he is the head of his company, he will feel slighted if he is sent a middle manager. Your company should send the highest-ranking person available, if not your chief executive. The first meeting should be between highest-ranking officials—the "head of the household," in tribal terms. Subsequent meetings and actual negotiations are carried out by subordinates. It is the initial meeting that is crucial.

Business entertainment should take place at the best restaurants. Spare no expense, but be understated and dignified in your demeanor. Act like you've been there before. Use excellent manners and the proper dining form, which is Continental (see Chapter 9). Be aware that gift giving in the early stages of the relationship will not elevate his ego and might be mistaken as a bribe. Save gifts for later, as an expression of friendship, once friendship has been established.

Make your purpose their welfare. He will insist on this. If a proposal does not benefit his tribe, or his personal needs for status and power, you don't have a chance of success. Market share, monopoly, power, and wealth all are benefits than can be invoked. You must be sure that, coming from the United States, you don't give him the impression of being the stronger partner in the deal or that you have only your own self-interest in mind. Don't tell him how you will benefit; tell him how he will benefit. Always assure him the risks are minimal, and prove it.

Your first meeting will probably begin in his office but conclude over a long lunch. A normal lunch in Latin America takes at least two hours. Expect to take all afternoon. Remember that your purpose is not to discuss business but to let him get to know you. Therefore, do not ask personal questions, especially about his family, and particularly about wives and daughters. Discuss what he wants to discuss, whether you know anything about the subject or not. You should prepare for this lunch as you would a presentation. Study subjects that might be of interest to him, like soccer, or opera, or current events that may be affecting his country.

You may feel you are wasting your time during this meeting, but quite a lot is being accomplished. He is evaluating you. Can he trust you? Do you act superior? Are you obnoxious or abrasive? Will your authority conflict with his? Are you weak? Can he respect you? Are you worthy of friendship and loyalty? Sometimes this evaluation period may get out of hand. One American businessman making his first visit to Brazil was taken on an excursion to a nearby island for a day in the sun followed by a day of deep-sea fishing and several lavish dinners. It would be appropriate after a day to start steering the discussions toward business. Your counterpart may merely be taking advantage of the company expense account with you as an excuse.

Be aware that if you have established a business friendship with someone, should your company then change its representative, that new person will have to start the process all over. The Latin American businessperson has accepted you, not your company. His trust is personal, not generic.

The other topic that must be addressed in your game plan—which no other book on the subject of business in Latin America has been honest enough to bring up—is the subject of sex. You will certainly come face-to-face with the subject, no matter which gender you are, and your response must be prepared. It is common practice for a host to offer business guests the company of a woman for the evening. In Brazil there is an entire motel industry that accommodates businessmen and their guests. Several Americans being entertained by a high-level businessman were surprised to be taken on a tour of Salvador's best motels. The Brazilian proudly pointed out that this motel is where you would take your best girl, but this other one provides women for you. The Americans mumbled among themselves in the back seat, not knowing if they would offend their host if they declined. Let's stop right here so you can be reassured that it is perfectly all right to decline. They know you are American. But if you are traveling to Brazil, do not make a reservation at a motel. There are no tourist motels. Tourists stay at hotels.

Sometimes, a Latin American businessman might send his wife to your hotel to seal a deal. This is more delicate to deal with, but may also be declined. Be aware that if you invite a man to dinner and include his spouse, he might bring his mistress instead. This is another good reason not to discuss family with him. If you give a gift to his secretary, which might be useful in getting communications through, be sure to tell her it is from your wife. Never make it look like you are personally interested in the man's secretary.

Keep in mind that the macho tribal male will protect his family, and, assuming that others think as he does, he is not likely to invite you to dinner at his home until you are a close friend. In his culture any woman, married or not, is fair game unless she is a member of his tribe or of the tribe of his close friend. If he doesn't know you well, he will feel afraid that you will try to seduce his wife or daughter, and therefore he will not risk exposing them to you.

The flip side of this is that he will consider an American businesswoman fair game as well. He will further assume that a woman traveling with men is sleeping with them. A businesswoman traveling alone may be interpreted as a gift from her company. You can see how difficult it is for an American businesswoman to succeed in Latin America. It takes a powerful, no-nonsense image, and lots of credentials for a woman to have a chance. This is discussed further in Chapter 6.

There should also be a note here regarding race. Latins are is very color conscious: the whiter the skin, the more status one has in society. An African-American businessperson will have to work hard to bridge the prejudice gap by proving himself or herself worthy of their respect.

This is a challenging game—more so for some than for others. You won't be able to change the way they think, but you may be able to overcome obstacles by using protocol strategically.

For this game, let's assume you want to make an agreement with a new distributor. Say your company makes computer hardware. The company you have identified is the leading distributor of computer hardware in that company's South American country. You will need to convince the distributor to carry your brand, even though your brand competes with a brand it currently carries. Now, begin the game.

You have already made contact, through a well-connected agent, with the company you are targeting. The agent has set up a meeting for you. Although you had requested a meeting in early February, the agent suggested you wait until March. The seasons are reversed in South America, and many people are on summer vacation in January and February. You would also want to avoid the time around Carnival, which is the week before Ash Wednesday—usually in February or early March. Seasons in Central America correspond to those in the United States.

Protocol Challenge

The day before you leave for your trip, you call to reconfirm your meeting.
You do this because
a. the person may not have noted the appointment or may have changed the time without notification.
b. the person may have agreed to the appointment as a courtesy, never intending to keep it.

Latin Americans never dishonor anyone by refusing a courtesy. They do not like to say no to your face and often will seem to be in agreement, only to have a final reply come back negative. More than likely, the reply will not come at all if it must be negative. Answer (b) is correct, but then so is (a). Time and schedules are not well kept. Several requests might have been received, and conflicts in schedule arise. For any reason, it is wise to confirm your meeting.

Etiquette Technique

You arrive at reception and give your card to the secretary. The secretary announces you and gives your card to Señor García, director of the company. You are kept waiting for about 20 minutes, and then he greets you. You return his greeting with a

a. firm handshake, a hand on the shoulder, and a gregarious *"Buenos dias!"* (or *"Bom dia"* in Portuguese)
b. casual, low-key greeting; you offer him your right hand, left hand remaining in your pocket.
c. formal but friendly handshake, your other hand remaining at your side; you use his professional title and make good eye contact.

The eye contact was the giveaway. Answer (c) is correct. Eye contact is very important. It indicates your sincerity and your self-confidence. The firm grip in (a) is fine, but, although Latins tend to touch more than North Americans do, they usually keep their distance until a relationship has been formed. Don't force a relationship by your breezy greeting. A low-key, more subdued approach is better, but hands should never be in the pockets. This is considered very rude. Your goal during a greeting is to be formal, subdued, self-confident, and respectful. Move ahead to the meeting.

Protocol Challenge

If interested in receiving your proposal, he will

a. escort you to his office, point out a chair, and take his seat behind his desk.
b. escort you to a well-appointed conference room and sit close, but facing you.

Positioning himself behind his desk as in (a) is defensive. It puts distance between the two of you. He is probably not terribly interested in what you have to say. If he wants to do business with you, he is more likely to take you to a conference room, which is more prestigious, unless he has a reception area in his office. He has taken you to his large, well-appointed office, where he shows you to a comfortable chair. He pulls one up and sits opposite you. You move on.

Protocol Challenge

During this meeting you discuss
a. no business.
b. your company.

Although the first meeting is to get acquainted, it is all right to introduce your company without getting into the specific details of your business. You should point out your position in the company (which should match his) the number of employees, the area you are located in, and some specifics about the company. Try not to sound as though you are bragging, and do not try to discredit your competition. Be matter-of-fact and give general information so he forms in his mind a picture of your company.

You have also turned the conversation to his company, without asking very detailed or pointed questions. You have now shared your "families" in a sense. Move ahead to lunch. He suggests a very nice restaurant nearby.

Etiquette Technique

Your late-morning meeting was brief. You go to lunch to continue your discussion. You know not to bring up business at lunch unless he does. The conversation turns to *futbol* (soccer). You respond,
a. "I never could get interested in that game; now, have you ever watched the Dallas Cowboys play football?"
b. "I enjoyed watching the World Cup matches when they were played in the United States."

If you answered (a), go back to square one. You have insulted his culture and shown that you are interested only in yourself. Even worse, you have implied that the U.S. sport is better than the South American sport.

STRATEGY

Anywhere you go in Latin America, soccer is a good topic of conversation (if you avoid discussing the violent subplots). Be prepared for this subject. Do a little research. In a society strong in machismo, sports will be a common point of reference. As in America, often it is sports that forms the basis for communication and camaraderie between father and son. This comfortable association is carried throughout life, and it continues as a source of friendship for adult males. Try to identify with your Latin American counterpart by attaining some understanding and appreciation for his national sport. This strategy applies not only to Latin America but also to any culture in the world.

Other good topics of conversation are the local cultural offerings, the beauty of the country or city, world travel, and the history of his country. Keep it noncontroversial. Restrain yourself from attempting humor. Humor is usually culturally based, and the punch line will probably miss its mark. All this conversation is going on while you maneuver the obstacle course of the dining table.

OBSTACLE COURSE   STOP

UTENSILS
The Continental style of dining
is used in all of Latin America.
See Chapter 9 for details if
you need help.

USE OF THE HANDS
The hands never leave the
table. Wrists, not elbows,
should lean against the edge
of the table. It is rude to keep
even one hand in your lap.

DRINKING
Latin Americans drink at lunch. Your job is to join in,
but make a glass of wine last all afternoon. It is
terribly rude to get drunk. Do not order imported
liquor if you are the guest. It is very expensive
there. Do order it if you are the host, if you want
your guests to do the same. Do not pour wine if
you can help it. There are certain taboos, such as
never pouring wine with your left hand and never
pouring it backhanded, for all of these have
meanings. It is polite to wipe your mouth before
and after each sip.

EATING

There may be certain spices in the local foods that will be difficult for you. Try to taste everything on your plate. It is offensive to leave food on your plate, so finish if you can. Otherwise, make some plausible excuse.

THE BILL

Do haggle over the bill, as they will, even if you have been invited out. If you intended to host and have run up a generous tab, be sure to win. If you want to be certain to win, arrange with the restaurant captain ahead of time for payment. Do this if you are a woman, or you will never be allowed to pay the bill. Be sure to explain that your company is paying.

You managed the course well and move ahead to the end of the meal (before the subject of the bill has arisen).

Protocol Challenge

After coffee is served, your host may

a. begin to talk business.

b. suggest a time to meet again the following day.

He might do either. Either is a good sign, meaning that he accepts you as a business associate. With further meetings planned, you might now invite him to dinner one evening. Keep in mind that Latin Americans dine very late. An invitation for 9:30 P.M. means eating at 11. Be prepared to linger and stay out until easily 3 A.M. Business should not be discussed. Spouses can be invited, but it is not expected. If you are invited to your host's home for dinner, which is a great compliment, be at least an hour late. One business traveler invited to dinner at 8:30 found his hostess was in the shower at 9. Dinner was served at 11. For now, move on to the next day's meeting.

Etiquette Technique

The next day, you arrive at the office and greet him,

a. *"Buenos Días,* Don Carlos."
b. *"Buenos Días,* Doctor García."

Don't assume that because he has accepted you as a business associate, he will become an instant friend. Remain formal. Do not assume that first names are to be used until he suggests the idea. Even if you are asked to use his first name, if he is your senior, you should address him as Don Carlos. *Don* is a term of respect.

He invites you into his large office and, after a friendly conversation, turns his attention to your proposal. It has not been mentioned up to this point, but you have been accompanied on your trip by one of your sales managers who will carry on the work once an agreement has been reached. It is a good tactic to have more than one person from your company at an initial meeting. This gives your Latin American counterpart an option should he want to do business with your company, but he doesn't care to do business with you personally. He could choose to establish a relationship with someone else from your company and communicate through that party.

Etiquette Technique

During your presentation, you reprimand your subordinate for an error in one of the graphs. The effect of this on Señor García is

a. positive; he respects you for showing your authority.
b. negative; one should never publicly criticize or humiliate anyone, causing them to lose face.

Honor is very important to this culture. One would never discredit another person. Latin Americans can't even criticize you if you ask for their honest opinion. They will find a way around criticism.

Protocol Challenge

At the end of the presentation, you ask for feedback. You ask direct questions requiring a yes or no answer. You ask whether he agrees with you proposal and will commit to representing your product. He says yes. You are being given

a. a contract.
b. a brush-off.

Most likely, (b) is the right answer. You've given him no room for consideration; you've not allowed him to consult with others; you've imposed your decision-making time frame on him. When pushed, he will say no, by saying yes. It is probably the last communication you will receive. Yes means yes only if it is in writing in legal contract form.

You aren't doing very well, are you? Let's consider a different ending.

Protocol Challenge

You have finished your presentation. Señor García responds by saying he will give your proposal to a subordinate to review. This means
a. a brush-off.
b. positive progress.

This might sound like a brush-off, but actually the real work is done by the technical support staff. Once the head man agrees to do business with you, it is up to the technical people to review and comment on the proposal. The rest of the deal will be worked out between subordinates, with final approval coming from the company head.

Let's leave the game on this positive note and look at supplemental notes for specific countries.

Argentina
The global approach is most effective in this country. Eighty-five percent of the population are of European descent, including Italian, Spanish, German, English, French, and Russian. Be cognizant of the person's background, even if he speaks Spanish as his first language. There is likely to be a cross-cultural influence.

Learn to keep your hands still. Many of the gestures we use are offensive or have different meanings in parts of Latin America.

Argentines might make personal observations about you. This just means that the person is comfortable with you.

Opera is a good topic of conversation in Argentina, as is sports.

Bolivia
Bolivia is an isolated, landlocked country that still maintains a navy just in case it ever gets its coastline back from Chile.

The population is 50 percent Indian, 30 percent mestizo, and 15 percent European.

Machismo is very strong.

Bolivians believe that seeing a black person is good luck.

It is OK to talk business over lunch, but not over dinner.

Our hand gesture that means so-so (palm down, rocking the hand back and forth) means no in Bolivia.

Brazil

Brazilians are better at abstract thinking, but still they make decisions based on feelings and personal interests.

Look for German and Japanese influence in São Paulo. This city operates more like northern cities. Expect a faster pace.

Brazilians seem very different from their Hispanic neighbors. Their attitude is very light and optimistic. They have good expectations for the future. This feeling of optimism isn't carried over in the other countries of Latin America.

When thinking, don't absentmindedly rub your fingers under your chin, as some men with beards do. It means you don't know the answer to a question.

Central America

The smaller nations of Central America have historical ties with the United States, good and bad. The United States has been involved militarily in Nicaragua since the latter's early days as a nation. As a result, Nicaraguans have strong and negative sentiments about the United States.

Costa Rica is unique among Central American countries in its ability to have maintained a fairly stable government and a dynamic capitalism. There is a strong work ethic, although Costa Ricans are not completely goal oriented. They paradoxically believe in equality, machismo, and the class system. The population is 95 percent European, which is unusual for Central America. Costa Ricans are the most punctual of all Latinos. Women tend to be accepted in business.

Note: Throughout Central America, the handshake is rather limp, not firm as in South America.

Chile

Chile's population is 95 percent European, primarily Spanish, German, and Italian. Use global protocol when meeting someone from Chile.

There are more professional women here than in any other Latin American country. This is the best place for a businesswoman to work, although it is still very difficult.

The northern European influence in Chile results in a strong desire for progress and advancement through education. There is a significant middle class.

Avoid aggressive behavior.

Don't raise your right fist to head level. It is a communist gesture.

For best results in Chile, try to overcome the Chilean sense of physical isolation by making frequent trips and keeping in contact.

Business gift giving is not customary. If someone gives you a gift, open it immediately.

Colombia

The population is 58 percent mestizo, 20 percent European, and 22 percent Indian.

The only professional title that is used is *doctor*.

Be sure when meeting someone that you drag out the act of greeting. Don't be in a rush. Chat for a minute.

Gifts are not opened in front of the giver.

Women are restricted from some aspects of business.

Leave small amounts of food on your plate to indicate that you are done and don't want more.

Ecuador

The population is 65 percent mestizo and 25 percent Indian. There are few pure Europeans, but they are the power elite.

Business is somewhat less formal here, especially along the coast.

Theirs is a more self-centered form of tribalism. Ecuadorans show more personal interest.

There is a strong work ethic, but Ecuadorans are not goal oriented.

Women do not drink hard liquor.

Don't use head motions to indicate yes or no. Use words.

Mexico

The population is 60 percent mestizo, 30 percent Indian, and 9 percent European.

Be careful not to make comparisons with the United States.

In price negotiations, don't start with a very high price, expecting to bargain. This is insulting to Mexicans. Leave a little room for movement, but don't expect them to be ignorant of the marketplace.

There are three distinct regions in Mexico that impact the way business is conducted: sophisticated Mexico City, where the government is located; Monterrey, which is entrepreneurial and industrial; and Guadalajara, the largest and most important business center, known as the Silicon Valley of Mexico.

Paraguay

The population is 95 percent mestizo.

Formal titles are used, but someone with a university degree is referred to as *licenciado* instead of doctor, which is reserved for medical doctors and those with a Ph.D.

Don't wink. It has sexual connotations.

Peru

Peru was the seat of the Incan civilization, overthrown by the Spanish in 1532. The population is 45 percent Indian, 37 percent mestizo (European and Indian mix), and 15 percent European. The business class consists mostly of the European minority. There are also a significant number of Japanese and Chinese businesspeople in Peru.

Unlike in other South American countries, men should not cross their legs one knee over the other, but placing one ankle on the other knee is all right.

Peruvians use lots of hand gestures when they speak. Be careful of your own.

It is best not to discuss ancestry or politics in Peru. There is an extremely strong caste system in Peru based on ancestry.

If you are invited to a home, bring the hostess flowers. They must be roses, or you will be considered cheap. Avoid red, which means love.

Uruguay

Uruguay is the most secular of the Latin American countries. Uruguayan population is 88 percent European, mostly Spanish and Italian.

Uruguayans have a reputation for being pessimistic and opinionated.

There are more professional women than men in Uruguay, yet men still are dominant and women's rights are restricted.

A little known fact: At the time Uruguay was under military rule, the country's economic advisers trained under Milton Friedman at the University of Chicago. In the mind of Uruguayans, this financial procedure was unsuccessful. If you attended the University of Chicago it would be wise not to disclose that fact.

It is common to be invited back to someone's home for coffee after dinner in a restaurant. Don't stay very long.

Venezuela

The population is 70 percent mestizo, along with Spanish, Italian, Portuguese, Arab, German, African, and Indian making up the balance.

A businesswoman going out at night with a businessman will be misconstrued.

Announce your full name when shaking hands.

Businesswomen should not give gifts to their male counterparts.

THE ARAB WORLD GAME

Certain terminology must be discussed before we begin the Arab world game. The Arab world is closely linked with the Islamic religion. The term *Arab* refers to a culture, not a race or religion. For instance, there is such an entity as a Christian Arab. The Arab culture had its birth in Arabia and expanded its influence during the seventh century to include North Africa and most of the Middle East. Several of the predominantly Islamic nations are not Arabic. They include Afghanistan, Azerbaijan, Indonesia, Iran, Pakistan, Turkey, and Turkistan. Indonesia will be included in the Pacific Rim game.

Since culture-based behavior in the Arab world is dictated largely by Islamic beliefs, there is a great deal of similarity in customs among all Arab countries and between

Figure 4.3
Arab World Map

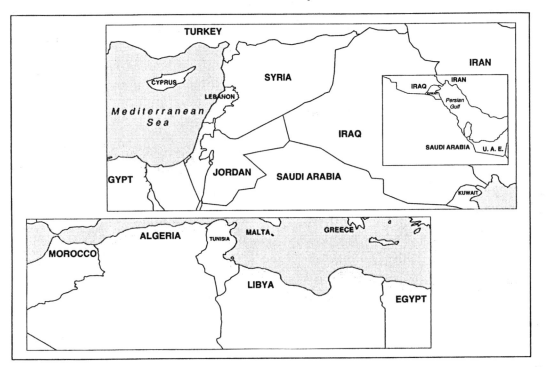

Arab and non-Arab Islamic cultures. Therefore, this game will consist of doing business in a representative, hypothetical Islamic country. The game will be applicable to those countries (other than Indonesia) that are dominated by Islam. Differences in customs for all Islamic countries will be reported in the individual supplemental notes. One more explanation of terms: *Islam* is the name of the religion; a Moslem, or Muslim, is a follower of Islam.

Now that we have defined the playing field, we turn to the governing principles. The only way to understand the Arab mind-set is to understand some of the basics about Islam. *Islam* means "submission to the will of God." *Moslem* means "one who submits." The Koran is the bible of Islam, containing God's laws as revealed through his prophet, Mohammed, in the seventh century. Moslems consider Islam to be the final act in a three-act play, beginning with Judaism, continuing with Christianity, and ending with Islam. They believe in the same God that Jews and Christians believe in. Judeo-Christian religious history is included in Islamic religious texts.

Like the Jews and the Christians, Islamic reality is perceived as a separation from God. God is in complete control of all events. The individual does not participate in the external workings of the world. Actions are not important. Faith is all that matters. Islam is based on God's laws. This understanding is reflected in an extremely strong social power hierarchy. Islamic culture is strongly tribal in nature. The individual is subject to the authority of the tribe, finding personal identity in the hierarchy of family structure.

The reduction of the individual to an element of the tribe requires that the individual form his identity outside himself. He is constantly using others' perceptions of him to reinforce his identity. Perhaps it is helpful to think of Islamic society as analogous to a mirror. All reflect one another by giving feedback, which must be positive to ensure the good of the individual and therefore the good of the tribe. Moslems know themselves by looking at others.

One person's behavior toward another is also a reflection of that other person's image. Disrespectful behavior tells the recipient he is not worthy of respect. One American found this out in a most surprising exchange. He had been negotiating quite extensively with the head of a Saudi Arabian company. They had come to terms and were ready to sign the contract. The American left for Riyadh a day before his meeting, dressed for comfort in jeans and tennis shoes. He had packed his formal business clothing in his suitcase. As does happen, his luggage was lost. He had arrived on a holy day when the shops were closed, so he couldn't buy new business clothes. He knew this was a difficult situation, but because he had already established a relationship with the Arab, he felt that if he went to the meeting and explained the mishap, the Arab would overlook it. After the American explained and offered his regrets for his poor dress, the Arab asked for the contract. The American handed it to him. Glancing at it, the Arab tore it in half, saying he never again wanted to see the American or do business with him.

The mirror shows an image. It is important to understand that one's image is everything. How you appear to others is what you are. You are known by your reputation. The motive behind all action in Arab society could be summed up in the question, "What will the neighbors say?" The family tribe brings great pressure to bear on each member to conform, because each individual's reputation affects the reputation of the entire family. If the tribal unit is discredited, its place in society is severely diminished. And since, in Moslem belief, a woman's misbehavior can do more damage to the family honor than a man's misbehavior, women are severely restricted in their activities. Islam claims these restrictions are for the protection of women, but in truth they are for the protection of the family's reputation.

Reputation is so critical that the failure of an individual is not allowed to be acknowledged. Arabs choose their own reality. When something they have done is too painful to accept, it simply didn't happen. Moslems remove it from their consciousness. But when confronted by evidence and accused directly in front of a witness, there is nowhere to hide.

Failure has extreme negative repercussions on the tribe. In ancient times, a person's failure could cause the demise of the entire tribe. A shocking modern-day example of this concerns an American employee's troubleshooting a mechanical problem on an oil installation in Saudi Arabia. Finding the source of the problem to be human error, the American reported it to the supervisor. The supervisor called in the technician responsible and, in front of the American, shot the man. The American was horrified, quit his job, and never returned to engineering.

As a strongly hierarchical culture, Moslem society is stratified into a rigid class structure. The ruling families and wealthiest families are at the top. Merchants and landowners form the middle class. The peasants and the poor form the lowest class. Because God is believed to control everything, there is a strong sense of fatalism. One is born into a certain class, and one accepts one's family position in society. People do not expect to move up or down on the social ladder. Along with class level comes expected behavior. Those of the upper class never do manual labor, not even so much as getting another person a glass of water. They are very careful to show their wealth and dress their best whenever they go out in public. Foreign residents are given upper-class status. You are expected to behave as such.

What the neighbors think is important, but it is also important for you to know that to the tribal Arab there are two kinds of people: neighbors and strangers. Neighbors, or members of other tribes they might come into contact with, can reflect and judge their behavior. Strangers are of no consequence. Therefore, although Arabs pride themselves on their friendliness, good manners, loyalty, and hospitality, they behave this way only with their own tribe and neighbors. There is often much pushing and shoving in lines at the airport, and drivers take no note of other cars on the road. If you want to change someone's rude behavior, simply say something such as, "Please don't push me if you can help it." Speaking to him makes you a reality in his social consciousness, and he must then watch his behavior around you.

In general, outside that certain sphere of influence, decorum goes out the window. Arabs visiting America might totally cut loose and behave in ways that would be scandalous at home. But the Americans are outside the Arabs' sphere of influence, and the Arabs' behavior will not affect their social standing. There is also an Arab proverb, "A sin concealed is two-thirds forgiven."

It is very important to your efforts in business that you establish personal contact. Arabs acknowledge others by interacting with them. Bringing you into an Arab's consciousness requires his interacting with you physically and intellectually. He needs to see you, hear you, touch you, smell you, share food with you. This is the evidence that you are a factor in his life. But he doesn't claim to know you until he knows your family. No one exists apart from his family. You are the product of your father, your grandfather, your mother, and all of your other relatives. Your spouse and your children reflect upon you.

In America one is proud to admit being a self-made man, that one's parents were poor immigrants, and that today one is a multimillionaire. To an Arab, such an American would be accorded low status because the parents were of humble origin. Arabs would not feel comfortable doing business with such a one by crossing class lines. It wouldn't even matter if the American were CEO of a major multinational corporation. After several generations, perceptions change, and some movement in social class can be made. As an American, it is best not to talk about your family if your ancestors were of humble origin. Likewise, it would not help you to discuss your child's drug problem, or that your wife divorced you, or any other family problem. You are a composite of family behavior. Show Arabs only what you want them to use as evidence of your worthiness. Their own social status is the sole determinant of their success.

All business is conducted with friends. You must first be accepted as a friend before an Arab will do business with you. Only friends can be trusted. But more than that, friendship comes with a contract for mutual support and assistance. Once you are accepted as a friend, it is expected that you will give help and do favors to the best of your ability. Your Arab friend will do the same. Etiquette requires that you must never refuse. But there is a loophole.

In Arab culture, words speak as loudly as—if not more loudly than—actions. It is the intent that is important. If you are asked to do something that is illegal, too difficult, or impossible, do not refuse. Say that you will do your best. It is the positive response that is important, not the result. After all, people can't control an outcome; they can control only their intentions for a good outcome. If you don't perform, it won't be mentioned. Your Arab friend would not want to embarrass you by bringing up your failure.

Words have a great deal of power to an Arab. Words are often sufficient to preclude action. Arabs may make threats, venting their emotions. But they don't have the need to follow up a threat with action. Saying the words has solved the problem. No action is required.

Arabs feel most comfortable in groups and in close proximity to others. It gives them a sense of security. Their choice of physical space illustrates this preference. They seem to be attracted to other humans as if they were magnets. When an American enters an elevator that already has one person in it, the two rearrange themselves so that they are standing at opposite sides of the elevator, giving each other maximum personal space. An Arab who entered would probably stand right next to or directly in front of the other person. This behavior often confuses and annoys Westerners. Arabs don't like to be alone. The best translation of the English word *privacy* is the Arab word for loneliness. As a result, most homes have communal rooms and few partitions. Offices are open plan. Even the separate offices of high officials do not provide privacy, because they hold conferences with many individuals at one time.

People are of greatest importance to Arabs. They are the resource that makes up their tribal structure. They have a list of priorities that begins with family, then adds friends, and then adds neighbors; work is somewhere further down the list. You may be in a meeting with an Arab executive and be constantly interrupted by his family and friends making requests of him. He will not delay responding to them simply because you traveled from the United States to meet with him. Loyalty to his family will always take precedence over personal needs.

Hospitality is a duty and a privilege to an Arab. When entertaining a guest, an Arab must spare nothing for the comfort of that guest. His generosity shows both his willingness to provide for his friend and his ability to provide for his family. His self-worth is enhanced by the guest's acceptance of his largess. It is the duty of a guest to praise the host. But guests should refrain from complimenting their host on any personal object. If you admire something, your host will feel obliged to give it to you. Declining can be awkward. Although he will insist you take it, he may reciprocate (retaliate?) by admiring something of yours of equal value. Of course, you would give it to him.

The Arab concept of time is not linear. Arabs are not goal oriented; they tend to do many things at the same time. Time is a gift from God, and they savor it. It is interesting to note that the Koran is not arranged chronologically. Cause and effect is difficult to perceive. Time may also be used as language. Withholding it can mean lack of interest. Delaying can be a power play and tell you that the one who delays time is your superior. It can also be a test of character. Patience and persistence are highly valued. Many Western businesspeople have been kept waiting for appointments, not only for hours, but for days or weeks. You may have an appointment, arrive on time, and be escorted into a room where others are doing business with the one you have come to meet, and he may never get around to talking with you. You may be asked to come back tomorrow. This may have nothing to do with his interest in you, but other priorities come up and time goes by. There is always tomorrow.

The Arab use of language is not highly precise. Much sensate imagery is used. Arabic is very poetic and very spiritual. Rational thought often gives way to emotion. Scientific evidence is not as important as faith. Decisions are made according to human needs and are not necessarily based on the objective merits of the proposal.

One of the pitfalls for American businesspeople is to assume that because an Arab dresses in Western fashion, speaks fluent English, and has been educated in the West, he is like us. He will still think and behave like an Arab. Certainly there have been Western influences affecting Arab civilization, and some social change has occurred. Many of the younger generation and people who do business with Western companies find a duality of culture in their lives: one at work and one at home. Islamic fundamentalist groups have been on the rise in recent years to stem the flow of Western influence on Arab culture. They perceive Western ways to be a threat to their way of life.

In some Arab countries, a trend toward modest liberation of women has begun. Saudi Arabia is the most strict of all the Islamic countries and maintains tight restrictions on women, but Iraq, Tunisia, Lebanon, and a few others are increasing their literacy rates and allowing women to work and vote. Pakistan has elected the first female prime minister of a Moslem country. More women are entering the labor force each year. The women are not especially prepared for liberation, and most are comfortable with their traditional roles, but progress in a Western sense is being made.

Western businesswomen can be successful in Arab countries if they are prepared to become a third sex. (The concept of businesswomen as a third sex will be addressed in Chapter 6.) Western women just don't fit into Moslem society. There is no place for them. Islamic laws forbid them to act in many of the ways that are necessary for them to conduct business. Most Arab countries recognize this and don't require foreign women to obey all Islamic law. If a woman must be alone in the presence of men, she is given the status of *honorary man*.

Arabs are inherently religious. They do not comprehend atheism. They respect all who practice their own religion, no matter what that religion is. Faith is the Arabs' strongest value. They believe that God controls everything and that prayer must be directed only to God, not to an intermediary. That belief is reflected in secular life as well. Society provides many laws, as does religion. Although obedience is required, nothing is absolute. One can always appeal to a higher power. A well-connected person can make a personal plea to a high official and be able to circumvent cumbersome commercial laws.

With this background we are now prepared to construct the player portrait and game plan for the Arab world game.

ARAB PLAYER PORTRAIT

What does he believe is a person's responsibility?
Obedience to the will of God and to uphold the honor of his family.

What does he expect of others?
Mutual support and courtesy.

How does he interact with others?
With those he knows he is warm and personal. With strangers he is defensive and
   closed.

What impresses him? What does he respect in another?

Status and wealth.

What is his attitude toward foreigners?

Complete disregard. Defensive when approached. They are low on his list of priorities.

Why is he in the game?

He works to live.

What is his main objective?

Social interaction. Positive feedback.

How does he define winning?

Zero-sum if you are a stranger, win-win if you are a friend.

What is his business environment (physical and hierarchical)?

Open plan, with impressive offices for upper management. There is a strong vertical power hierarchy.

How does he conduct business?

In a nonlinear fashion. Many things are done at once. Personal responsibilities are mixed with business priorities. Information is restricted to those who need to know.

How does he learn?

Through the senses. Use of imagery, analogy, and graphics. Repetition is important and shows sincerity.

How does he give feedback?

Feedback is always positive, spontaneous, and frequent. Negative feedback is often handled through intermediaries and is always indirect, never fixing blame on a person.

How does he make decisions?

Decisions are made at the top. Criteria are rarely objective, rational, and concrete, but more likely emotional and socially useful.

What is his attitude toward time, schedules, plans, and change?

Time is flexible and nonlinear. Schedules are not closely followed. Plans are not detailed and may be altered spontaneously. Change is resisted.

How does he approach problem solving?

Denial and amelioration. If blame must be accepted, the consequences are harsh. Problems are rarely caused by people. They are probably the will of God.

The Arab Game Plan

In Arab culture, it is essential that you go to them. If you are not present, you do not exist. At most, you are of little consequence. Arabs are used to seeing their friends frequently. Three days is a very long time between visits. The initiation of business must certainly be done at his office. You must change your status from stranger to neighbor and then from neighbor to friend. Your business will not succeed otherwise. In most business circles, the top managers speak English and many have been educated in the West. Translation is probably not necessary. Rely on your local agent for advice.

Most Arab countries require a foreigner to be represented by a local agent. Agents do not like the term *agent*, and prefer to be called a service representative. These people are well connected and can identify and obtain meetings with the right people in your industry. They are aware of the local permits required of foreign businesses and can advise you on local customs and language requirements. You should also use the service representative as an escort as much as possible, for getting around Arab cities can be difficult and hazardous. Service representatives can be located through the country's embassy or possibly through your banking and professional contacts.

Humility shown by a man of stature is well regarded by the Arabs. It shows that you are powerful yet sensitive to the needs of your tribe and your friends. It demonstrates that you are a servant of God. There will be many humbling experiences for a Westerner immersed in Arab business culture. What we regard as disrespectful behavior toward an individual must be tolerated as their way of doing business. The first instance of this concerns time. There is no concept of wasting a person's time. A person does not own time such that it can be wasted. Appointments cannot be confirmed until the person is in town. Even confirmed appointments require endless hours of waiting and being delayed possibly for days on end.

Our concept of respect includes paying attention to the individual. It is humbling to be ignored, which is exactly what will happen during group sessions with Arabs. Even though you are admitted into an office, there are many meetings going on at once. Your Arab counterpart may speak with you for a few minutes, then move on to someone else, returning to you at a later time. Whichever topic is of greatest priority to him is where he will focus his attention. The term *focus*, is used loosely. Humble yourself to accept this form of interaction. Do not demand to be treated as you would treat others in a pluralist society. You are not in a pluralist society. If you choose to do business in another culture, you must accept its ways of doing things.

Negotiations require numerous and costly trips. Decisions can take months in coming, with no progress reports. Your needs will not be taken into account. You are completely irrelevant to the decision-making process, unless you have become a close friend, with all the duties and obligations that the relationship entails. Never try to push for a decision. Never criticize anyone for the way that person conducts business.

Arabs love to bargain, but they are not stupid. A highly inflated price will insult them. There is a fine balance between leaving enough fat in a contract to cut out during negotiations and presenting a competitive bid. Your bid must be reasonable enough to attract the Arab's attention. Price, however, is not the primary decision factor. Most of all, an Arab must like you and your company. The Arab's personal needs come next. Technical merit might be third, and price is last. Avoid uncertainty and obvious risks in what you are proposing.

It is absolutely critical to spend time elevating the Arab's ego. You do this by your behavior as much as by your words. Both are important. Praise and appreciation must be verbalized often. Your own good manners and respectful behavior reflect the quality of the person you are doing business with. Your conservative dress indicates your respect for the other person. The better you dress, the greater your perceived status. This reflects well on the Arab, as it shows to others that he is worthy of attention from a person of high position.

Make his welfare your purpose. Even if you don't, he will. There is no reason to do business with you if it doesn't solve a problem for him or make him look better. His family and friends are his primary concern. Business is an inconvenient necessity. Find a way to show him how he will benefit, now and in the future, from doing business with you. Be careful not to give him expensive gifts as a tactic. It is appropriate to give a gift on first meeting, but keep it small, as a gesture of your desire for friendship.

For the Arab world game, our objective is to sell services to a new customer. You own a construction company and have decided to bid on a job to construct facilities for an Arab company. You have contacted an appropriate service representative, you have met with him before, and he has succeeded in obtaining bid documents for you. Your proposal is ready and your agent has convinced the director that he should hear your proposal. You have been granted a meeting. The date and time are not precisely known and cannot be confirmed until you arrive in the city. After you arrive, you check with your representative. He schedules a meeting for sometime the next day. You wait to hear from him regarding the time of the interview. You wait all afternoon. Finally, he calls back and says the meeting is confirmed for the day after tomorrow. You patiently wait for the meeting. Be aware that Thursday and Friday are the Moslem days of rest. There are also many holiday periods that should be avoided. During the extremely hot summer months, most businesspeople are on the Riviera.

The meeting is scheduled for 10 A.M. You are there precisely on time and asked to wait. Now the game begins. What follows is a typical Arab business encounter. However, you may be doing business with someone who has adopted the Western style of doing business. It is best to be prepared for the traditional approach. Be careful on encountering what seems to be a Western approach; do not assume that all aspects of the meeting will be conducted like in the United States.

Protocol Challenge

After 30 minutes you are ushered into an office. As you enter you notice four or five other people having conversations among themselves and with the director. What do you do?

a. You find the director and interrupt his conversation to introduce yourself. He asks you to take a seat and turns back to his conversation. After a few minutes, you speak to him again to ask if you should come back at another time.

b. You announce yourself, sit down, accept any refreshment that is offered, and wait to be asked your business.

Remember that at this point you are still a stranger with no standing in the Arab's mind. There are others before you—meetings that might have been spontaneous, but granted because a personal request was made. Do not rush your host to receive you, and don't expect privacy during the first meeting. The Arab feels safer in a group. While waiting, you may introduce yourself to others in the room and speak quietly. You are being observed, so refrain from appearing agitated. Cultivate patience. Expect to be ignored, and it won't come as such a shock. This is just the beginning of the game.

Etiquette Technique

The director finally comes to you. He says to you, "I am Rashad Abdullah Asad." What do you do?

a. You bow and say shalom.

b. You shake hands with a limp grip and without pumping, hold the grip throughout the introduction, say good morning, and refer to him by title and first name.

If you chose (a) return to Israel, where you must have thought you were. When you shake hands with an Arab, the grip must be nonconfrontational. Arabs touch much more than Americans, so be prepared to clasp hands for several minutes while you might be asked about your health and the well-being of your family. You may do the same, but never ask an Arab about his wife. If you do not know someone's professional title, use *Sayed*, which means *Mr.*, along with his first name. The other two names are his father's and grandfather's names. Some countries have required people to use surnames, and Westernized Arabs use their family name until better acquainted. Ask your local representative for advice.

When you are sitting or standing, be careful of your posture. Poor posture is disrespectful. Never slouch, drape yourself over a chair, sit on a desk, cross your arms, or stand with hands in your pockets. And above all, never ever show the soles of your shoes to anyone. This is a severe insult. Be careful when crossing your legs that you never cross an ankle over a knee, exposing the bottom of your foot.

Protocol Challenge

You have now gotten the ear of the man you came to see. What do you expect to accomplish?

a. You hope to establish friendship.

b. You hope to get a second meeting.

It is true that no substantive business will take place until some level of friendship has been established, but that doesn't happen at this first meeting. Your purpose at this point is (b), to give your host enough information to interest him in your proposal. If he is interested, he will grant you a second meeting alone when you can present your proposal in detail.

Protocol Challenge

After a few minutes, your host moves on to another supplicant. He has not told you to come back for another meeting. What should you do?

a. Pick up your briefcase and go.

b. Sit down, have more coffee, and wait for him to return to you.

Answer (b) is correct. Just because he leaves you with no resolution does not mean he is not interested. He puts your words into his mental processor while he greets another businessperson. Time and processes are not linear in the Arab world. Arabs can do several things at once. If he comes to have a good feeling about your proposal, he will return, ask you to come back the next day at a certain time, and shake your hand. Expect this next meeting to be more formal. You are now free to leave. Shake hands with others you have met as you leave.

Protocol Challenge

You shake hands with your host and greet him as you did the previous day. He directs you to a chair, usually to the right of his desk—the seat of honor. You take a seat, and after a few minutes chatting about your health, a servant comes in and serves coffee. At that time you

a. drink your coffee and put your cup down, then begin your presentation.

b. drink your coffee and talk about your family, when he asks.

The first choice rushes things too much. You are not taking advantage of your host's hospitality. It is not polite to have fewer than two cups of coffee or more than three. Business is not discussed until after the refreshments. During this time your host will want to get to know you. You assume that he wants to talk about your education, your profession, and your personal interests. This is not so. He wants to hear about your *family*. He knows a person by way of the person's heritage. Tell him of your roots, unless they are not flattering. He does not want to hear that you endured a difficult childhood and rose to the top. This will not gain his respect. After family has been discussed, subjects of common interest may help form a bond, such as sports. Find out about his local and national sports. Be sure to maintain eye contact while you are conversing.

When you are offered coffee, or handling anything, always accept an object and hand an object with your right hand. The left hand is used for hygiene. Never eat with your left hand, even if you are left-handed. Coffee is not over until you give the proper signal to the servant. He will continue to refill your cup if you put it down or hand it back to him without first shaking it from side to side. In some places, the signal is to twist the cup quickly a few times in your hand. Beware that the bottom of the cup is full of thick grounds. Sip the coffee slowly, leaving an inch in the bottom of the cup. Note that during the month of Ramadan (approximately September on our calendar), coffee will not be served. Arabs are required to fast between sunrise and sunset, and even the display of a coffee cup in their presence is very rude.

You may now move forward and discuss business, but don't enter the subject too abruptly. The Arab considers good manners to be the best gauge of a person's character. Being sincere is very important. Don't rush the pleasantries.

Protocol Challenge

The best way to present your proposal is through
a. a linear, detailed, logical approach, supporting each point with facts and calculations.
b. a general approach at first, highlighting the human aspects of the project, such as jobs created, the work space that will be provided, and the positive effect of the finished installation on the community and the employees; you will use many visual support data, including renderings, graphs, blueprints, and material samples.

The second approach will be the most persuasive. Do not talk money at the beginning, but interest him in your technical proposal first. If the benefits are clear, then you will enter further negotiations. Don't expect any sort of decision the first few meetings.

Your goal will be accomplished only after many meetings. This shows your interest, sincerity, and ongoing friendship. You must show a commitment. It is wise not to tell the Arab at what time you are scheduled to fly home. He may leave things to the last minute and get concessions from you in your hurry.

Your style of presentation is also important. Be very careful not to let casual swear words creep into your speech. Omit the offhand use of "God," which is so common in casual American conversation. This is very offensive to a Moslem. Speaking with emotion shows your sincere concern for the outcome of your presentation. Consider practicing your presentation at home, because it is difficult for Americans to change their technical style of presentation. Repeat yourself often, especially on important points. Otherwise, Arabs will not believe you are telling the truth.

Protocol Challenge

Which of the following responses is positive?
a. Your counterpart praises you and compliments you on your proposal.
b. He suggests a counterproposal.
c. He promises to be in touch.
d. He hints that changes are needed.

None of the above—at least not necessarily. His response could be anything from high praise to "changes needed," but he will never say directly that he is not interested or that he doesn't like your proposal. Negative feedback is not polite. On the other hand, a noncommittal reaction might just mean that he needs to get approval from higher up, or he doesn't understand something he wants to talk over with his staff. Only time will tell what is going to happen. He may at some time invite you to negotiate price, or you may get no response. When it is time to bargain, be staunch. Allow some room for movement, but don't give anything away easily. Arabs will respect you for standing your ground.

Protocol Challenge

When do you know you have a deal?
a. When you shake hands.
b. When you sign the contract.

You can be sure you have a deal only when the contract is signed. Be careful not to offend by including in the contract every conceivable misunderstanding that might arise, as lawyers in America tend to do. Arabs will perceive you don't trust them and they may back out of the deal.

You have successfully negotiated the contract for the construction project, but before you can win this game you have an obstacle course to maneuver. At some time during the process, your Arab associate is likely to invite you to his home for dinner.

OBSTACLE COURSE

THE INVITATION

The invitation will probably be verbal and spontaneous. Never decline hospitality. Expect dinner to be late—between 10 and 11 P.M. Don't be too punctual, but plan to arrive about two hours before the meal. Conversation takes place before the meal.

DEPORTMENT

Use formal manners and good posture, and praise your host often. Do not admire any of his possessions. He will feel obligated to give it to you. Compliment him on his lovely home.

GIFTS

Gifts are not expected, but it is considerate to bring something such as a house plant. Flowers may be considered too personal and meant for the wife. Never give liquor or a candy made with liquor at the center. A coffee-table book about your home state is a nice idea. Gifts for the children are also appreciated. Present gifts with your right hand. Do not expect your host to open gifts in your presence. It is an insult to bring food items.

GREETING WOMEN

A man should always wait for a woman to extend her hand first. She may not offer to shake hands. It is correct to address her directly, but after your greeting, do not direct comments to her. Men always stand when a woman enters a room.

EATING

Generosity to guests is essential for a good reputation. You will be offered many courses. The amount of food may seem overwhelming. It is a compliment to the hostess to take second helpings. This must begin with a ritual refusal by the guest, three times, ending in acceptance. In most places, if you clean your plate, it is an indication that you want more. Leave just a little food on your plate to indicate you are done. Be sure to eat only with your right hand. Pass food only with your right hand.

AFTER DINNER

Tea and coffee are served after the meal. Conversation continues during coffee until it is time to leave. A signal to leave is when a tray of ice water is brought around. On the Arabian peninsula, incense and perfume may be offered instead of ice water. When you are ready to go, the host will ask you to stay. This is a ritual and may be declined, unless your host protests profusely. Be sure to offer extensive praise and thanks. Reciprocate the hospitality when you can.

One last note: Smoking is pervasive in the Arab world. It is considered the right of a male to smoke. An Arab will probably ignore you if you ask him to stop. There are no segregated smoking sections at restaurants. The only possibility for you to have an effect is if you claim a physical problem due to the smoke.

Supplemental notes for countries where Americans would likely do business are noted below, country by country.

Egypt

Do not use first names immediately. Wait for your host to offer.

Don't take any criticism of the U.S. government personally. Egyptians like Americans, but often criticize the government's policies.

Do not discuss bad news on a social occasion.

The U.S. gesture for waving good-bye means "come here."

Women should avoid direct eye contact with men and avoid crowds, where men may try to touch.

Finishing everything on your plate is considered rude. Leaving food indicates the abundance of the host.

Law requires that a company doing business in Egypt must have an Egyptian agent. Get separate agents for Cairo and Alexandria.

Political contacts do not have the same influence in Egypt as they do in other Arab countries.

In the cities, women will not have difficulty doing business. Entertain at hotel restaurants that are European style.

Morocco

Women should never make eye contact with men who are strangers. Men interpret eye contact as an invitation.

Moroccan bureaucracy is patterned after the French. Moroccans conduct business formally, a la the French.

Don't bother to use the telephones. It takes too much time.

Print business cards in both Arabic and English.

French is spoken by much of the business class. Use an interpreter.

Business is never done without serving tea first.

You will probably be invited to a home dinner. Men and women eat separately. The women get the leftovers.

Tunisia

Tunisia is the most Western-like of the Arab nations because of its long domination by France.

When greeting someone in business circles for the first time, use the French title *Monsieur.*

At a home meal, it is important to wash your hands in front of everyone. The servant will bring a bowl and pitcher.

Hire a French interpreter.

Give your business card to the senior man first, and then others.

Saudi Arabia

Saudi Arabia is the most strict of all Islamic countries. Western men will not meet Saudi women.

Whenever someone enters the room, always rise and shake hands.

Never enter the country with Western girlie magazines. The wife of a foreign businessman was deported for carrying a copy of *Cosmopolitan*.

Arabs usually wait to be asked more than once before accepting second helpings of food.

Whenever something is offered, refuse first, then accept.

Never send a woman to do business, even as a member of a team. There are strict legal restrictions on women's activities.

Print business cards in both Arabic and English.

Present a modest gift after meeting someone two or three times.

Immigrants do the paperwork.

The Gulf States (Kuwait, Bahrain, Oman, Qatar, United Arab Emirates)

When you see someone bowing and kissing someone's hand, do not feel that you must do likewise.

After any meal, leave when you have finished coffee.

Send your company's CEO to do all business. Sometimes decisions are made on the spot.

Suggest that instead of meeting at the man's office, you meet in your hotel lobby. There won't be so many interruptions—or so much Turkish coffee. Remember that you are now the host and must be generous in your hospitality.

When meeting with a group from the Arab company, the Arab who sits, listens, and says nothing is usually the decision maker.

Your meeting is over when coffee is served again.

Kuwaitis are very punctual. Don't be even 10 minutes late.

Don't send a woman to do business.

The British manage many Omani firms.

Never whistle in public.

Iraq

Use first names as soon as you are introduced.

When offered food or drink, refuse the first time, then accept.

Iraqis are much less formal than Arabs in other Arab countries.

Almost all business goes through the Iraqi government.

Iraqis don't like the excessive praise and flowery language used in other Arab nations.

Women have had equal rights for 20 years.

Never try to bribe anyone.

The best business gift is a book.

Jordan

English is Jordan's second language.

Address by the English titles Mr., Mrs., and Miss those people you don't know well.

Jordan is much less conservative than other Arab nations. Women may dine out with men.

Private businessmen are much more straightforward than other Arabs.

If a woman must do business in Jordan, she is given honorary male status.

Syria

Syria is officially a secular state.

Educated Syrians are cosmopolitan but conservative.

Lebanon

The Lebanese have had long contact with the West and know Western customs. However, they are Arabs and they share the perceptions of most Arabs.

French and English are widely spoken by the educated.

Non-Arab Islamic countries

(Iran currently has no diplomatic relations with the United States and so will not be included as a possible business destination.)

Turkey

Turkey is the bridge between Europe and Asia. It is the home of the former Ottoman Empire, which came to an end after World War I. It is a democratic, secular state. Ninety percent of the population are Moslem, and 85 percent are ethnic Turks.

Turkey is a tribal nation and, because of Islamic law, shares many customs with Arab nations.

One difference is that Turks do not shake hands again when leave-taking.

The form of address upon introduction is the surname preceded by *Bay* for men and *Bayam* for women.

Most entertaining is done in restaurants.

Pakistan

Pakistan was established as a separate Moslem state during the British partitioning of India in 1947. The government is a democracy. Urdu and English are the official languages. Note that the Urdu word for *yesterday* and *tomorrow* is the same.

Forms of address are very complicated, for there are many variations on Pakistani names. Ask how an individual should be addressed.

Pakistan conforms to Islamic law, so the tribal elements and customs largely remain the same.

Men should never wear a suit and tie from November through March. A jacket need never be worn except when meeting with government officials.

Never gesture with a closed fist.

Women are generally not well received in business, even though the prime minister is a woman.

THE PACIFIC RIM GAME

The Pacific Rim is dominated by Chinese culture. Every country in the Far East and Southeast Asia was populated to some extent by the ancient Chinese. Today, even though many countries have predominant populations of indigenous, ethnic people, such as the Malays, the so-called overseas Chinese control business as an elite minority. The key to understanding the motivations for behavior in Pacific Rim countries is to understand Chinese culture.

As in the Arab World game and the Latin American game, the entire Far East region is fairly homogeneous with respect to protocol and etiquette. This is not surprising, because all Asians have a common spiritual and philosophical background. They share a set of values that has remained unchanged for millennia. The nations that exhibit the greatest deviation from those otherwise common beliefs are Indonesia, Malaysia, the Philippines, and Japan. Indonesia and Malaysia are Moslem countries, and the Philippines is Roman Catholic. These are both tribal cultures overlaying the basic collective nature of the original culture. Japan remained isolated for centuries and so developed some aspects of culture that are uniquely Japanese. We will turn to China first, so that its culture can be used as a basis for understanding. All nations of the Pacific Rim and their particular points of protocol and deviations from basic Chinese culture will be discussed separately.

China and all original cultures of the Pacific Rim are collective cultures. Their underlying philosophy is nontheist; they do not believe in a separate, personified god. Reality is, therefore, seen as a continuum. All things are interrelated. All things are part of a continuous whole. No one thing in nature is of significance. It is the wholeness of nature that is important. This view of reality is portrayed in the language, which is very imprecise. Individual words or characters do not transmit exact meaning. Characters must be combined in such a way as to paint a picture representative of the intended meaning.

The guiding principles for this culture are harmony and continuity. These principles are observed in the laws of nature, for it is believed the divine is revealed in the laws of nature. For the human being, this means that no one person is significant. The col-

Figure 4.4
Pacific Rim Map

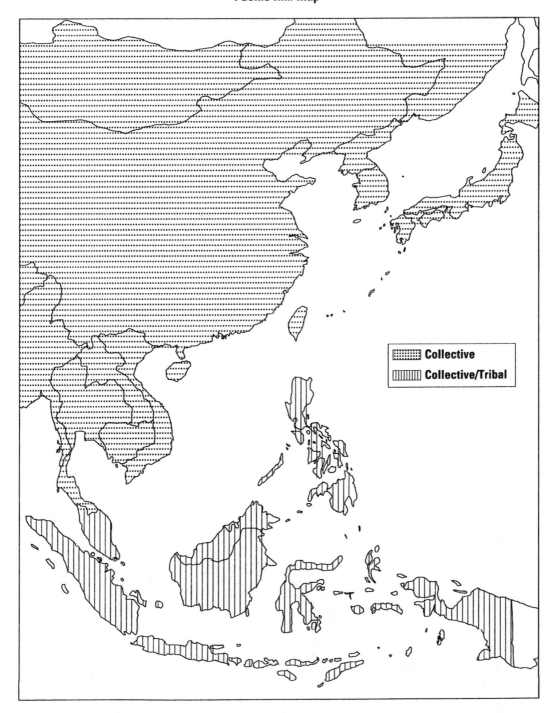

lective is the smallest unit that can survive. People cannot survive on their own. They have no definition outside the group. People in this society must conform for the good of the whole. It is as though the individual is a cell within a body. All the cells work together to maintain a healthy body. One bad cell can start a disease. Therefore, all cells must work in harmony and must work hard for the benefit of the body.

The Far Eastern collective group identity differs from the tribal group identity. Tribal culture is based on a strong perception of separateness. The family tribes are top-heavy authoritarian power structures professing the virtue of obedience, as opposed to conformity. They are similar in effect, but not in perception. In tribal society there is a sense of self as a member of the family. It approaches a sense of multiself, for the entire family enters into one's identity. In collective societies, there is only a very weak concept of self. In reality, collective identity is relative. It is relative to someone who is older or younger, or more or less educated.

This is such a true representation of the Asian perception of the individual that in Asian languages there are many variations on the pronoun *I*. You refer to yourself in one way if you are talking to an older person, and in another way if you are addressing a younger person. There are other pronouns to be used when you meet someone more learned than yourself, more powerful, less learned, and less powerful. The list goes on. Often, on meeting a person for the first time, Asians ask each other questions about each other before a formal greeting takes place. This is to determine the right pecking order, the proper use of pronouns, and how low one should bow in greeting. Until you know how you relate to someone, your identity and worth to society are not pinned down.

The desire for conformity and harmony might suggest that this is a culture that professes equality of all people. Such is not the case. All people are important to the collective, but some are functionally more important than others. Just as the cells of the brain might be viewed as more important than the cells of the skin, so there is a hierarchy of importance in collective society. Whereas tribal cultures have a power hierarchy, collective societies are organized as functional hierarchies. Everyone has a specific position in society and a specific job to carry out. Those at the top serve those below, as those below support the work of the top. There is, of course, recognition that those higher up are more important to the body, and worthy of high esteem. But those in power do not have free rein to lead the group into ill-advised plans. The position of authority comes with the burden of contribution to the group's well-being.

Each person is born into a certain position in life, but not a static one. The Asian view of position is similar to the Asian view of time. It is all a continuum, and as future flows into present, which flows into past, so the younger become older and as they do, their stature increases because identity and position are always relative to someone else. Asians carry with them the concept of improvability. Although they may not have control over the processes of life, they know that life is always changing and that one's position can improve. There is a reason to strive for a better place. It remains difficult, however, for a skin cell to become a brain cell or for a servant to become a leader.

Chinese culture has perpetuated these beliefs through the adoption and institution of the philosophy of Confucius. Confucianism is not so much a religion as a social doctrine. In a way, it is a religion in the same terms that communism is a religion. Confucian reality supported the belief that there was no self, but there was structure and dualism in the world. Confucian dualism recognizes that there is one older, one younger, one stronger, one weaker, one servant, one master. Dualism suggested position and status, and so society was organized into a highly structured and stratified organization of the whole. Duality suggested inequality. People are not equal, but all contribute to the good of the whole. What resulted was a strong authoritarian social structure with mutual cooperation among classes for the good of the group.

The cooperation between upper and lower ranks of society can be seen in the corporation and in government. In collective societies, employers and employees have strong commitments to one another. Decisions are made at the top, but they are decisions made through a consensus of information provided by lower-level managers. Usually, top management will not participate in specific decisions, but will keep an eye on the organization as a whole. Decisions are made by the next level of managers, consistent with the guidance from above.

Likewise, government takes a hands-on approach to business. Yet this is not an adversarial involvement as it can be in Western societies. Government plays a significant developmental and supportive role for businesses in collective society. Collective societies are concerned with the good of the whole on a larger scale: the nation. Westerners call this protectionism and brand it as unfair. But what is unfair about ensuring the survival of your collective? We Westerners should not judge the actions of a collective society based on our own values and definitions of fair play.

Following the precepts of its underlying belief in the natural order, Confucianism promotes harmony in all aspects of life. To be in harmony with each other is to treat each person with dignity and humility. Conflict avoidance is a must. No one should give negative feedback. Criticism promotes conflict, not harmony.

It is also necessary to emulate the structure of the natural order by showing respect to those who are superior. The structure of society is maintained by rules of protocol regarding the interaction between superior and subordinate, and also between men and women. Women have predetermined functions in society, and governing is not one of them. Men and women are a duality and, therefore, must be separated.

Time is a continuum to the Chinese way of thinking. Past and present are related. The present exists relative to the past. The flow of time is unbroken, but cyclical in nature, as are the seasons. There is a great reverence for ancestors and for the elderly, who are considered part of the larger definition of time. To collective societies, time is not money; time is harmony.

One of the most significant differences between the beliefs of Confucian societies and those of the more fatalistic tribal cultures is the concept of improvability. As we saw in the northern European pluralist cultures, belief in perfectibility, or improvability, is the only impetus one has for hard work. Why should one work long hours with great effort and take pride in one's work if there is no hope of gaining anything by the effort? One can be forced to work, but in that case the motivation is fear. Such a motivation is ultimately self-defeating as a long-term tactic.

The work ethic is ingrained in each culture as a result of basic beliefs about improvability. The attitude toward hard work can be grouped by culture-based religion in the following way: Confucianism and Protestantism promote hard work for improvement of the group and the individual, respectively; Islam and Catholicism promote a sense of fatalism and nonaccountability; therefore, adherents do only the work that is necessary to live.

Confucianism promotes hard work, but perceives achievement as being valid only in the context of the group. Confucian cultures hold education in high esteem as being the best means to foster achievement. However, to its believers, education is little more than facts. Everyone learns the same way. There is a rigid requirement of conformity in education as well as in other areas of one's life. Even though a collective society values education, it does not promote imaginative thinking. Collective cultures contribute best in group efforts, such as large-scale production.

As in tribal culture, concepts of ethics are relative. Within one's collective group, traditions of respect, honor, and dignity are upheld. There is little regard for others outside the group. If rules are sent down from power structures that are far removed from the collective, they will be disregarded.

With this background, we can now construct a player portrait and game plan that are applicable to countries in the entire playing field.

PACIFIC RIM PLAYER PORTRAIT

What does he believe is a person's responsibility?
Contribution to the welfare of the collective group.

What does he expect of others?
Cooperation; everyone in his place.

How does he interact with others?
Respectfully and properly. People outside the collective are not worthy of note.

What impresses him? What does he respect in another?

Status and education.

What is his attitude toward foreigners?

Defensive and inattentive. Foreigners are barbarians; they have no place in the
collective.

Why is he in the game?

He lives to work and works to live.

What is his main objective?

Harmony; a secure place within the group.

How does he define winning?

With those inside the collective, winning must be harmonious or have a win-win
outcome. With foreigners, it is a zero-sum game.

What is his business environment (physical and hierarchical)?

Those in top management have large, separate offices; lower managers and workers
share open-plan areas. There is a rigid, functional hierarchy.

How does he conduct business?

Business is cyclical rather than linear; subjects may reappear after they have been
dealt with. Many discussions can take place at once. It is assumed that all issues
will find their place in the order of the endeavor. Information is communicated along
functional lines.

How does he learn?

Facts, details, and especially, visual representation.

How does he give feedback?

Feedback must be positive. There is no criticism. When attempting to imply a
negative, he most likely will use body language.

How does he make decisions?

By consensus, with ultimate responsibility at the top.

What is his attitude toward time, schedules, plans, and change?

Time is harmony, and therefore punctuality is important so as not to inconvenience
others. Schedules and plans have a long-term perspective. Change is avoided.

How does he approach problem solving?

Denial and evasion. If a problem is not presented as an error, but as a change, then he
can deal with it logically and efficiently.

The Pacific Rim Game Plan

Asian strength is in the Asian collective group. It is almost impossible to get the attention of a businessperson in this culture if you are not present. You must go to them,

initially. Personal relationships are necessary before business can be done. This relationship does not necessarily mean friendship. Asians must have some reading on you as a person. They will try to locate you in a position relative to their society to see where you fit in. They will not deal with someone who is deemed unworthy of them. Large businesses and logo products gain easiest entry. Your top management should be present at the first meeting. Asians will be attempting to know you as a part of your collective group. Bring a group with you. The group should consist of functional division chiefs.

Almost all Pacific Rim countries have some requirement for entry into business circles in their country. Many require registering with a local agent or directing all business through national trading companies that regulate international commerce. It is best to work with a local representative, even if it is not legally required. Business is personal, and only friends do any business of substance. Always approach your targeted company through a representative who has personal contacts with the organization.

Humility is a required part of Asian life. One who is powerful shows his humility. This demonstrates his allegiance to the collective group and shows him to be a wise and beneficent leader. It also demonstrates he is ultimately no better than those who are his inferior. Humility maintains harmony. The humble but powerful man gains respect for his humility and not envy for his power.

The visiting businessperson must show humility as a sign of respect and yet must maintain an image of power, or the resident leadership will not perceive the visitor as a person worthy of doing business with. Humility must be demonstrated primarily by accepting Asian values of harmony, respect, and social structure. Applying the pluralist notions of time as money and objective decision making will cause conflict and dismissal. Your humility must be accepted because you are an outsider. Humility will gain you an invitation into the Asian orbit.

Negotiations will be time-consuming by Western standards. Many trips will be required to obtain a signed contract. The Asian pace must guide negotiations. Asians may discuss many aspects of a proposal at once or may return to points already settled. Your patience and cooperation are important.

With respect to outsiders, Asian businesspeople look for a zero-sum outcome. Once you are an accepted trading partner, the win-win approach is possible. It is always necessary for Asians to better their position. Improvability and progress are basic values. Asians look to make a gain. Bring something to concede in many areas. They are adept at determining your motivations and primary focus and will use these to make gains in areas away from the main subject under discussion.

In this society a person's self-worth is relative to his position in the group. A person's worth is acknowledged by treating him as is appropriate for his station in life.

Special attention is bestowed on to those who are older and those with advanced degrees. A teacher is more important than a doctor in most Asian cultures. Defer to another person's knowledge.

Never compliment a person directly. This makes him stand out. It separates him from others in his group and makes him feel uncomfortable. Be extra careful not to praise someone in front of his superiors. This threatens his relative position in society. It causes a subtle challenge to lines of authority and respect.

You should address a person's welfare by addressing the welfare of his collective group. This is often his nation, if he works in government, or his company, if he works in commerce. It is easier to buy from a collective group than to sell. Unless you are offering something the group needs and can't produce itself, or you have an interesting new technology, it is difficult to break in as a supplier. In some cases it is essential for your agent to be a friend of top management. Then the transaction becomes personal. The proposal will be believed to be of benefit to all within the group, because the proposal in a sense has come from within the group.

When considering game plans for the Pacific Rim, one must keep in mind the pervasiveness of strategic thinking within all business transactions. The Chinese culture has developed and transmitted a strategy for engagement in any competitive undertaking. It is called *Bing Fa* and is based on ancient military strategy. The basic concepts are described here.

The five essential components of victory
1. Know when to fight and when not to fight.
2. Obtain the wholehearted support of your troops.
3. Be well prepared to seize favorable opportunities.
4. Free yourself from interference by superiors.
5. When the time is right, act swiftly and decisively.

War is a game of deception
1. If one is able and strong, then one should disguise oneself to appear inept and weak.
2. When you are ready to attack, you must convey the impression that you will not attack.
3. When you are close, pretend that you are far, but when you are far, give the illusion that you are close.
4. One should bait the enemy with small gains.
5. If the enemy comes well prepared, strong, well trained, and secure in all areas, avoid direct confrontation.
6. Create opportunities for victory by arousing your opponent's anger and causing him to take foolish action.

7. Make your enemy grow proud and arrogant by your expressing humility and weakness.
8. When your opponent is inactive, give him no rest.
9. Destroy the enemy's alliances, leaving him totally alone.
10. Victory is determined before the battle begins: in the mind of the commander.
11. The opportunity for victory is provided by the enemy.
12. Use local guides.
13. Attack when the opponent is least prepared and least expects it.
14. When the enemy speaks peace, he is plotting deception.
15. Keep plans as dark and impenetrable as night.

Above all, the highest form of victory is to conquer by strategy.

These concepts are detailed in an excellent book: *The Asian Mind Game*, by Chinning Chu.

Before doing business in the Pacific Rim, look at your own game plan in light of these concepts. Know that this is what your counterpart will be working with, and you will be well prepared to play the game at his level. Before we proceed to the playing field, we must choose an objective. Let's assume you have a new technology that, if brought to a country, will enhance its export opportunities. You are selling and the businessperson in that country is buying, but is a very eager buyer.

You have secured representation through one of the nation's recognized trading companies. This was accomplished through contacts in the United States who acted on your behalf. Your proposal of a new technology has aroused interest with a major company, and an appointment has been secured with the chief executive. You are ready to begin the game.

Protocol Challenge

You arrive at the office punctually, and after reaching reception, you

a. shake hands with the secretary and hand her your business card; she walks you to your host's office immediately and announces you; you shake her hand as she leaves.
b. nod respectfully to the receptionist, giving her your name; she asks you to wait; after about 20 minutes, she escorts you into your host's office.

Answer (b) is correct. The sexes are not treated equally. Touching people of the opposite sex is taboo. If a woman is Westernized, she may extend her hand, in which case it is proper to shake gently. Notice that you are expected to be on time to appointments, but your host may leave you waiting. This is not often gamesmanship, but the predicament of an overworked executive. If your business is not deemed vital to his interests, you will not receive top priority.

You may be escorted into a conference room instead of an office, especially if your presentation is technical. Many functional experts will likely be present. Let's assume such is the case.

Protocol Challenge

As you enter the room you

a. greet each person present with a handshake and take a seat at the conference table.

b. determine who the chief executive is and approach him first to greet; you, being the senior person in your own delegation, make the initial greeting; you shake hands with a medium-firm grip and add a nod of the head; your eye contact should be at throat level; you address him by his first name, which is his family name, and yourself only by your last name.

Greetings must be made in order of seniority. Among the locals, bowing may take place. Don't try to copy this ritual, because there is a definite communication by the depth of the bow. Bowing too deeply to the wrong person or not deeply enough may cause an insult. A Westerner is not expected to know this ritual, so keep to a handshake and a nod of the head to acknowledge the local custom.

As the senior member of your delegation, you are responsible for all communication. Your team should follow your lead and defer to you at all times. Otherwise, you will appear weak. Introduce yourself by your last name to relieve your hosts of the effort in determining which name they should use. Begin introducing yourself with the most important information first: your company name followed by your title, then your family name. The next required act is the exchange of business cards.

Etiquette Technique

After greeting your host, you present your business card by

a. removing a pile of cards from your jacket pocket and handing them out to the group as though you were dealing a deck of playing cards.

b. taking one card from your pocket at a time and presenting it with your right hand and a slight bow; you have had your cards printed in English on one side and in the language of your host on the other side; you make sure to present it facing your host so that he can read it.

In America we pass out cards as a reminder of how to spell our names at a future date. In the Far East, the exchange of business cards is a symbolic ritual. A business card is an extension of the person presenting it. The collective individual is not well-defined on his own. He exists relative to a group. On that card is information about his group and his place in that group. His name, his title, his degrees, and his corporate responsibility will all be printed on that card. That is who he is. Treat your host's business card with great respect. Study it and remark on the education of the bearer. Never write on it or put it away in the presence of the offerer. Keep business cards in a man's gold card case in your left breast pocket.

By regarding your own card in the same way, you have a great opportunity to garner Asian's respect. Be sure to include on your card your academic degrees and your functional title. When listing a functional title, be sure to look up uses of business titles in the country you are visiting. A director in America may be a top executive, but in other places, a director is a lower-echelon manager. Never inflate your title to impress Asians. If you are found out, the deception will not be tolerated. Be sure to use high-quality printing and paper stock.

Protocol Challenge

A staff member arrives and offers you a cup of green tea. You
a. decline the offer.
b. accept the tea.

Hospitality is important to the Asian. Asian culture is very ritualistic, and hospitality is part of the ritual. Always accept an offer of hospitality. When it includes invitations, be sure to reciprocate as soon as possible. Reciprocity of hospitality is important, as it demonstrates mutual support and respect. You accept the tea and spend some time chatting.

More time is spent on relationship building in some societies than in others, and these will be addressed in the supplemental notes. With some businesspeople, several meetings will take place before substantive talks ensue. Generally, the more Westernized or capitalistic the country, the sooner your host will likely get down to business. Remember that even in these countries it is to your benefit to establish a relationship. Foreigners are never truly accepted into the collective, but can be accepted as useful and nonthreatening neighbors. Work on breaking down barriers by indicating your desire for a long-term business relationship.

STRATEGY

It is important to make a strong first impression. The best way to do this is by way of visual techniques. Models, demonstrations, and interesting graphics are highly recommended. Novelty is greatly appreciated. Beyond the visual effect, the content must be heavy on facts and data. Abstract concepts and vague remarks will miss their audience. Use a highly rational approach. Separate information by function, so that the chief engineer gets only engineering data on a separate piece of paper, the chief accountant gets a separate paper with only economic data, and so on.

In this culture, good manners are essential to acceptance. There are many subtle ways of demonstrating good manners during your meeting. This may seem like an obstacle course.

OBSTACLE COURSE

DRESS
Business attire is a "uniform" of conservative, traditional styling in subdued colors. The idea is not to visually stand out, but to show status by choosing clothing of high quality.

DEPORTMENT
A gentleman projects an attitude of quiet reserve. He is modest and shows other people respect. He takes care not to hurt anyone's feelings.

BODY LANGUAGE
Posture represents a person's self-control. If the body is controlled, the mind is disciplined. One should refrain from crossing legs. Posture should be almost rigid. One should never touch the head of another person, which is the most sacred part of the body, nor should the soles of the feet be revealed, they being the least sacred part of the body. Yawning is particularly offensive and should be stifled, not just covered.

THE HANDS
It is important that the hands always be visible and calm. They should not be used to point or gesticulate. Try clasping your hands loosely in front of you so they are visible, yet still. Never rest your hands in your pockets.

HUMILITY

Any act of deference to you as an honored visitor should be refused at least once before being accepted. This applies to taking a seat of honor (the chair in the middle of the table facing the door) or to the privilege of going through a door first. Graciously reject with sincere modesty any compliments you might receive.

SPEECH

Speak softly while directing your comments to each person. Important remarks or initial speeches should be directed to the seniormost person. Do not ignore an elderly attendee, and address your remarks to him as well, even if he does not speak English.

You may encounter another obstacle course. This one concerns your hosting a dinner for your Asian counterparts. Business entertaining is important and expected. This is the relationship part of the game. Lavish dinners, or banquets, are the norm.

OBSTACLE COURSE STOP

PREPARATIONS

Let your hotel make the arrangements. The staff there knows what is expected. It is usually assumed that women will not be invited.

THE BEGINNING

Often, guests are escorted to an anteroom or may be seated directly. Tea or drinks are usually served before the meal begins. When a group enters the dining room, the guest of honor should be allowed to go first.

SEATING

The guest of honor is seated to the left of the host in the middle of the table, facing the door, if possible. Proximity to the center of the table is by descending order of rank.

TOASTING

Toasting happens often. Always reciprocate a toast. Toast using both hands on the glass.

EATING
Collective cultures tend to use bowls for serving food. The guest of
honor, or the eldest and most highly revered is given the honor of
starting to eat first. This honor should be declined at first, then
accepted. Use your right hand to eat.

> **CONVERSATION**
> Business is never discussed at a dinner. Business discussion is often
> acceptable at lunch, but only at the end of a meal.

The next day you find yourself in the middle of negotiations.

Protocol Challenge

During negotiations, your hosts appear to dismiss a key point. You note this and
a. let your team person responsible for that issue restate the point to your host.
b. let it go.

Be sure your subordinates know that they should never speak out of turn. This will
shock the Asian listener. Subordinates should give you, their leader, information when
requested. You should speak for the group whenever possible during negotiations. It
is proper for the others to discuss issues among themselves. Answer (b) is correct because negotiations do not necessarily follow a linear path. Your opponent may have
chosen not to deal with that issue at the logical point in the discussion. Remember that
he has his own strategy, some of which might include making key points appear in-
significant.

Protocol Challenge

During negotiations, you request feedback. Your counterpart and those of his team
smile and nod their heads. This means
a. they agree.
b. they don't have a clue what you mean.

A general rule of thumb is, the bigger the smile, the deeper the trouble. Negative feedback must not be given. Usually a smile means lack of understanding, but a yes could
mean anything from yes to absolutely not. It usually means, "Yes, I understand you,"
but not, "Yes, I'll do it." The best way to understand is to have your local agent present. Locals are much better able to interpret signals, which usually consist in body
language that the foreigner cannot translate. In Japan, for instance, a quick sucking in
of air through clenched teeth is a very distressing signal.
Let's assume they agree.

Protocol Challenge

What happens after you reach agreement on all issues?
a. If the chief executive is present, a contract will be offered.
b. You wait.

Answer (b) always happens. Most businesses in Asian countries need the public sector's approval of major transactions. Business deals must be consistent with the direction of the state. It is useful at this point to have a person of status on your side to bring the project to high-level attention. The person should not be used to interfere with or unduly influence an official, but things do move slowly at the public level.

After a long wait and another trip across the Pacific, approval has finally come. In keeping with their language and approach to life, the contract they propose will be vague, by our standards. A written contract is a guideline to further negotiations. Be sure to nail down critical responsibilities, but do not overload it with detail, for you will appear distrustful. The best recourse you have lies in detailed meeting notes. Make the effort to take detailed notes, marking the date and time of key points of agreement, as well as who spoke.

Congratulations. Your technology is up and running in the Far East.

Supplemental Notes

The People's Republic of China

Establish contacts before you go. The U.S. Department of Commerce can help.
Everything shuts down between noon and 2 P.M.
Avoid colors in your presentation. Colors have symbolic meaning.
Bring at least 20 copies of your proposal. You will meet with many groups.
Relationships are important before a deal is closed.
At the end of a meeting, leave before the Chinese.
Reciprocate banquets, but never outdo your host in lavishness.
Spouses may be invited to banquets.
Guests arrive on time for banquets.
Wait for the host to eat or drink.
The host offers the first toast.
If you are greeted by applause, applaud back.
Never put your hands in your mouth.
Gift giving is technically illegal. Don't give anything expensive in front of others. A gift from your company to the Chinese company is acceptable. When giving or receiving a gift, use both hands. The gift is not opened in the presence of the giver. Chinese will decline a gift three times so as not to appear greedy. Keep in-

sisting. Never give a clock. It is associated with death. Do not give gifts until all business is concluded.

Everyone belongs to a work unit, which becomes the individual's collective. The work unit takes care of housing, medical needs, and vacation plans, as well as employment. The smallest unit of survival is the collective.

South Korea

All official Korean import-export traders belong to the Korean Traders Association, a very exclusive organization; this limited group forms the foundation of the Korean economy. There are also registered independent agents who belong to the Association of Foreign Trading Agents of Korea; they do not have as much clout as the trading companies.

Be punctual for all appointments.

Shake hands with a moderate grip, and add a slight bow. To indicate added respect, support your right forearm with your left hand.

The junior person should initiate the greeting and be the first to bow. The senior person extends his hand first. Women do not commonly shake hands. A businesswoman will have to initiate a handshake with a Korean man.

Do not introduce yourself in a group. Wait to be introduced.

Address a person by his family name, which comes first, along with his title or Mr. When writing, use the greeting "To my respected . . ." with the title and *full* name.

Relationships and hospitality are important, but Koreans are the most familiar with Western practices. In comparing them with the Japanese, one Westerner observes that they are less ethnocentric, less xenophobic, and less chauvinistic.

Although harmony is very important to Asian societies, Koreans are the most likely to express emotion and to be direct and even somewhat aggressive during negotiations. You, however, should remain calm.

Try to match the rank of individuals who are meeting. Age is an important determining factor in establishing rank.

Koreans often hold one-on-one meetings. This does not contradict their collectivist nature. The person you meet with is acting as an intermediary who must present your proposal to the entire company. It is important to establish a good relationship with this person.

Do not use triangle shapes in your presentation. They have a negative connotation. Remember that this is a culture that uses symbolism.

Silence can be a clue that you were not understood. Do allow some silence for thought, but follow up by rephrasing your last point.

Koreans are more likely than other Asians to say no, but they will still avoid it when possible.

If during the meeting the Koreans return to social small talk, it is an indication that they are through discussing business for the day.

Meetings begin and end with a bow. If the ending bow is deeper and longer than the opening bow, it is an indication that the meeting went well.

Never criticize your competition or admit that you do not know the answer to a question. Either will cause you to lose face. You may not care, but the Koreans will feel uncomfortable and lose respect for you.

Do not bring gifts from Japan or mention contacts or travel there. Koreans hold great animosity toward the Japanese.

Offer your business card with your right hand. Treat it with dignity. Don't put a person's card in your wallet and then put the wallet in your back pocket.

Do not write a person's name in red ink. It means the person is deceased.

Entertaining is done at night. Do not talk business over a meal unless your host does. If you are a man, you will probably be invited to a Kinaeng house or bar where lots of alcohol is served. The alcohol allows Koreans to drop barriers and be more direct. Be aware that you will be held accountable for anything said or promised. Such excursions are important for evaluating another person's character and establishing an informal relationship. Wives will not be included in the outing.

At the end of a meal, there may be singing. Singing is very important to Koreans, and you should not refuse when asked. Have a short tune prepared. Singing expresses harmony in a symbolic, extradimensional way. It is a form of controlled emotional release.

At a meal, do not finish everything on your plate. Finishing everything indicates that the host did not provide enough food and you are still hungry. Always refuse food twice before accepting.

Never blow your nose in public.

Eye contact shows sincerity for and attentiveness to the speaker.

Koreans may laugh when embarrassed.

When giving or receiving gifts, use both hands. Do not open a gift in the presence of the giver. Expect a gift you give to be refused at first; this is good manners. Reciprocate gifts and hospitality.

Koreans eat a lot of garlic, which can be detected as odor coming from their skin. They in turn do not like the way red meat eaters smell. Before a trip, you may want to change your diet to be less offensive to them.

Japan

The Japanese language is very subtle. There is much left unspoken, but to a Japanese, all is understood.

Use of an interpreter is recommended, even if the Japanese you are to meet say they speak English. Provide your own interpreter. The two languages require completely different thought processes, and your hosts will probably understand only half of what you are saying. When they respond to your remarks with a big smile, they have not understood.

Numbers should always be written on a piece of paper for clarity.

A negatively phrased question will be answered with yes if the listener agrees. This is one way to elicit negative feedback. Allow the Japanese to answer yes to a negative question.

Letters will not be answered if the sender is not known.

Foreign companies do not have to go through trading companies to do business in Japan. However, it is important to have an intermediary or agent to make introductions and set appointments, especially if you are a small company.

Use an intermediary to discuss bad news.

Be punctual for meetings. For social engagements, be somewhat late.

Greet a person by using with a weak handshake, if the Japanese person extends his hand, and a nod of the head. Do not attempt the bow.

Present your business card after shaking hands.

Address the person by his last name. Use Mr. and the last name. Foreigners should not use the honor term, *san*, after the name.

The smallest gesture may have great meaning. Keep your hands and face quiet.

Don't blow your nose in public, and never use a cloth handkerchief. Use a disposable one.

Gestures indicating a negative response are fanning the right hand in front of the face and sucking air.

When conversing, maintain greater physical separation between yourself and others than is normal in the United States.

Gift giving is very important to the Japanese. The ceremony is equally as important as the present itself. Business gifts must be given January 1 and July 15 (year-end and mid-year). Gifts are often exchanged on first meeting. Wait for your host to offer a gift first. Reciprocate with a gift of equal quality. Remember, image is everything. Logo gifts from well-known Western stores are appreciated. Never give an even number of anything; especially avoid the number four. Avoid giving anything predominantly white, which signifies death. Have gifts wrapped in Japan by a wrapping service or hotel service. The Japanese have their own notions of what is attractive. The wrapping is part of the symbolism. Bows are not used. Consult a local person for color suggestions.

Wear slip-on shoes because you will be removing them frequently. Slippers are provided for guests entering a home and in some restaurants. Be aware that there are special slippers to be worn in the bathroom. Change your slippers going in, and don't forget to change coming out, or you might be walking around with a pair of slippers that say "toilet" on them.

If you wear a kimono, or kimono-style wrap clothing, always wrap left over right. Only corpses are wrapped right over left.

Use visual aids whenever possible. This does not mean text on an overhead projector, but symbolic presentations like drawings and diagrams.

The term *manager* does not mean *the* manager, but is more likely one of many managers in a group. Be careful of Japanese corporate hierarchy, and use their title that best describes your status. Do some company research.

Unless the visitor is selling, your host will make the first invitation for evening entertainment. Entertainment is lavish and should be reciprocated. Keep parity of status in mind when initiating an invitation.

Evening entertainment includes large quantities of alcohol to "aid in the search for inner truth." Dinner is often followed by a trip to several bars, each with decreasing formality. It is not offensive to be drunk, unless you become abusive. Group seating arrangements at a restaurant are important (see Chapter 9).

During meetings, sit opposite the person who matches your rank.

Taiwan

Have written materials translated by a Taiwanese expert. Chinese characters are not the same in both Taiwan and China.

Local contacts are extremely important. The U.S. Commerce Department or an international bank can help.

In a group, sit according to rank, with the most important member at the center, the next important to his right, third important to his left, and so on.

Greet someone with a slight bow and a light handshake. If you are asked whether you have eaten, the correct response is yes, even if you have not.

Use the person's title or Mr. or Madam, with the family name, which comes first.

Do not point with the index finger; use your whole hand. Chinese indicate themselves by pointing to their nose, instead of their chest, as Americans do.

Gifts may be given on the first trip. If offered a gift, always decline three times before accepting. Avoid giving clocks or anything that cuts, like a letter opener. Avoid the colors white, black, and blue.

Evening business entertainment is very important. Dinner may be followed by entertainment at bars or clubs.

The guest samples the food first. Eat lightly, leaving a small amount of food in the bowl. There may be as many as 20 courses. If your bowl is empty, it will be refilled.

Thailand

Thailand is ruled by a cooperative, yet competitive triumvirate of bureaucracy, military, and commercial elite. Local influence is necessary to accomplish anything. Reputable agents are not always easy to find. The Bangkok Bank and U.S. Commerce Department can be helpful in locating a good agent. Expect a long-term relationship.

The greeting in Thailand is the *wai* (pronounced \why\). It is done by pressing your hands together as if in prayer, pointing the fingers outward. Elbows are held close to the body, and the head is lowered toward your hands. The higher the hands are placed, the greater the respect. Westerners may shake hands, but Thais appreciate the effort.

Titles are very important. Use titles plus the person's first name.

Thais are very proud that their country has never come under foreign rule, as has much of Southeast Asia. *Thai* means *free*. Ethnic Chinese make up most of the business community. Ethnic Thais are more likely to be found in government positions.

Be punctual.

Entertaining is done in the evening. If you are hosting, you may invite your counterpart's wife to a dinner. Some evening entertainment is for men only. Don't bring your spouse unless specifically invited.

Thais eat Continental style—almost. They use a fork and spoon instead of a fork and knife. Cut with the spoon. It is an honor to be offered the last bit of food on a serving dish. Refuse several times before accepting.

Dress well as a sign of status, but avoid wearing a black suit, which is reserved for funerals.

A smile could mean yes, hello, thank you, never mind, or excuse me.

The first meeting is to get acquainted, but you should eventually restate your business so that Thais can determine who should be at the next meeting, if there is a next meeting.

Eye contact is desirable.

Thais hesitate to ask questions. It implies that someone is a poor presenter. Public criticism is a form of violence.

If you are selling in Thailand, build in a "brokerage cost" of between 5 and 20 percent. If you are buying, you can expect to negotiate the price down by about 25 percent.

Government is almost always involved in business transactions, and public officials expect fees even for a small service.

Malaysia

According to the Malaysian constitution, a Malay is someone who speaks the Malay language, professes Islam, and practices Malay customs. Eighty percent of the inhabitants speak Bahasa Malaysia, and many speak English.

Islam was brought to the region by Arab traders. Remember that the holy days of rest are Thursday and Friday (this varies in different parts of Malaysia). The overlay of Islam and Arab culture onto a previously collective culture is demonstrated in the necessity for praise and self-esteem rather than not wanting to stand out. Credit is lavished on the smallest successes. Status and power are not just organizing principles; they must be demonstrated.

Do not invite a Moslem to lunch during the month of Ramadan (about September). He will be fasting.

Malays greet Westerners by a very light hand clasp, which may be held for 10 seconds. Don't rush the greeting. Ethnic Malays used to have no family name. Use the first name. This is also used for ethnic Chinese. It is all right to ask for the proper form of address. When you explain how you should be addressed, match their level of formality.

There is a significant Indian population in Malaysia.

Reciprocity and public recognition facilitate decision making. Cash is not commonly used to speed up decisions.

Economic control lies with the Chinese minority.

Representation in Malaysia is essential. Large trading companies usually control the importing of goods. Personal contacts are important.

The term *manager* does not denote someone very senior in the organization.

Gifts should not be given on the first meeting. Never give trivial or token gifts, such as corporate mementos.

The visitor should never shout, show emotion, or curse.

Never challenge the status, power, or prestige of a Malay.

Early presentations should include a history of your company, some remarks about the leading executives, description of special awards, and mention of important customers.

Malay executives value problem avoidance and will not easily agree to anything new.

Status is important and is indicated on the business card by titles and degrees.

Dress for hot weather, but note that white long-sleeve shirts are a mark of prestige. A "lounge suit" refers to a dark business suit.

Do not blow your nose in public. Spitting is forbidden.

Do not host a social event until you have been invited as a guest. Let your host make the first invitation.

Avoid giving any gift that might be construed as a bribe.

Although the weather is hot, dress formally until you determine what degree of informality is accepted by the people you are meeting.

Singapore

Capitalism reigns in Singapore, and the Chinese are in control, representing 76 percent of the population. Singapore is the closest thing to a meritocracy in the Far East. Few people get ahead without long hours and hard work.

Even though they appear Western in their work ethic and meritocracy, Singaporeans conduct all other protocol generally along the Chinese model. Communication and feedback are not direct; saving face is important; relationships are a must.

Foreigners should use local advisers to understand how to get things done in Singapore.

Sending low-level representatives is a waste of time.

Be punctual.

Singaporeans laugh as a sign of anxiety or embarrassment, not levity.

Use a limp hand clasp as a greeting. Use the person's title and first name, which is usually the family name, or use the appropriate given name if the person is a Moslem Malay.

Singapore prides itself on being the least corrupt state in Asia. Gifts are given only to friends. Decline a gift three times, and do not open it in the presence of the giver.

Business moves fairly quickly—by Asian standards. Communication channels are usually clear.

After an initial meeting of about 45 minutes, the visitor should initiate leaving.

An invitation to one of Singapore's private clubs confers prestige.

Refusing hospitality indicates bad manners.

Indonesia

Indonesia has the largest Moslem population in the world. See the Arab world game for much of the protocol that is appropriate in Indonesia. However, Indonesia is naturally a collective culture base with Islamic culture overlaid. Hierarchies tend to be more authoritarian.

A majority of Indonesian businesspeople are ethnic Chinese, so it is important to know the Pacific Rim game as well.

In the Bahasa Indonesian language, it is difficult to converse with a person until you know his status relative to yours. Pronouns depend on relative status.

At social gatherings, those of lesser status should arrive first. An invitation may tell you when to arrive. If you are asked to arrive early, you can be sure you are not the most important guest.

Indonesians follow the Arab concept of time. It is called rubber time. Chinese expect punctuality.

The response "yes, but . . ." means no.

Facts are "degrees of probability." Compromise and accommodation are always in order.

Decisions require consensus.

Agents' fees and such may crop up. Foreigners should stay out of this type of negotiation and allow Indonesians to attack the issue.

Although Moslem, Indonesians do not like to be singled out in a group, as is true of their collective nature. Do not compliment an individual, but compliment the group.

Like Arabs, Indonesians are accustomed to physical touching between members of the same sex. This is often part of a close relationship, unlike in other parts of Asia.

Shake hands only upon initial introduction and before and after a long separation. Use a weak hand clasp. Do not rush the greeting.

Naming conventions are not standardized. Some people have one name; some have several. Ask how to address the person. If he is Chinese, use the first name.

Gifts are given often. Any small occasion is appropriate, even when someone comes to tour the factory. Gifts need not be expensive. Do not open gifts in the presence of the giver. Refuse the gift three times before accepting.

A dinner guest should wait to begin eating or drinking until asked to do so. If you are the guest of honor, refuse the honor several times before accepting.

Be careful not to invite a Moslem to lunch during the month of Ramadan. He will be fasting.

The Philippines

The Philippines form a country that is a predominantly Catholic. The Christian culture overlies an inherent collective base. The result is an emphasis on power. The public sector is important to all private business transactions. The country operates under a system of guided free enterprise. Power is ultimately held in the government. Entrée into the Philippine market requires a local agent, one who knows the fine line between legal and illegal. Selecting the right agent is important. He must have the proper social connections.

Business is a process, and decisions are not made on factual input. People factors are most important.

Greet the Filipino with a firm handshake, but not with much pumping. Titles should be used along with the surname. Many names are Spanish, for the Philippines were colonized by Spain. Therefore the proper surname would be the next to the last name—the name of the father's family.

The culture exhibits its tribal behavior by encouraging praise and building self-esteem through compliments, unlike in most of Asia. This is a country that learned machismo from its Spanish ancestors.

Business is not discussed at the first meeting. If the host casually says he would like to hear your proposal sometime, that is a sign to leave and schedule another appointment with the secretary. The second meeting should include a luncheon invitation from you.

A confrontational style is not appropriate in negotiations. Harmony should prevail. The visitor should plan a multimedia presentation. Local representatives should be present at all negotiations.

Those in upper management do not respond to detail. Rather, they prefer to see the big picture. Control on all issues rests with the CEO, who is a member of the landed oligarchy.

Filipinos run on Latin time. Unlike the collective cultures of their region, they are not punctual. They do expect you to be on time though. Waiting is often a status game.

If decisions are delayed, negotiators may require a commission, or rebate, or bonus. This is a complex issue for Americans, who cannot, by law, provide kickbacks. All the more reason to have a local agent to counsel you on tactics.

Dinner invitations are the sign of a good relationship. Entertainment will be lavish. Dinners are social affairs and may include wives. Reciprocate invitations.

The visitor should project an air of importance and subtle power. Wealth and social status are important.

Business relationships do not extend to the company. If you are replaced, the new person will have to start all over, unless he is a blood relative.

Filipinos are more relaxed about business cards. You should offer yours first. They may or may not give you theirs.

At the end of a business deal, invite your counterpart and associates to dinner. You may have to ask several times whenever issuing an invitation, because an invitation may be offered casually only as a polite gesture.

Social events may end with dancing and singing. Be prepared to sing if asked. Public drunkenness is not acceptable.

At Christmastime, give gifts to everyone you know, in business or socially, especially secretaries of important clients.

Dress conservatively until you know how casually the people you are meeting with will be dressed.

Vietnam

One of the misconceptions about the Vietnamese is that they hate Americans. This is not so. They are now eager to become players in the international marketplace. They encourage American partnerships.

The typical collective pattern is followed: group meetings, greeting every person at the meeting, accepting hospitality, discussing business only when the host is ready, and establishing trust and friendship before business is conducted.

Unlike those in other parts of the world, Vietnamese should be addressed by a given name, which happens to come last in order of appearance. In other words, use the last name, which to us would be the first name.

Establishment of doing business in Vietnam requires knowledge of the local ways of doing things. A local representative is very important. It is important to make the right contacts at the beginning. Your agent can help with this.

Make your business very clear. Start with basics. Do not assume that your counterpart will fill in the blanks.

The government is socialist and very directly involved in private business. Find out who the real decision makers are. The government frequently changes policies, and what you once thought was a deal might now have to be renegotiated.

THE CENTRAL AND EAST EUROPEAN GAME

The field of play in Central and Eastern Europe is dominated by Russia with respect to its great size and by its legacy of communism. The new Russia, with its movement toward a free market economy, certainly represents one of the great opportunities for global business players. Other nations within the region are aggressively reforming their socialist systems to gain entrée to Western markets. Along with Russia, other countries including Poland, Czech Republic, Hungary, Ukraine, and the Baltic countries have been able to make substantial gains into the free market economies of the West.

Central and East European countries share not only a common recent history of communist domination but also a common past in their Slavic heritage. This fundamental unifying factor is important to an understanding of how the East European culture was affected by communism, how they behave in business today, and how East Europeans will change in the future.

The governing principles are founded in the basic perception of the divine in nature. East Europeans personify this divinity as someone who benevolently provides for them through the power of nature. Mother Nature or Mother Earth rewards their work. They are separate from God. There is a client-provider relationship. They work, and they are provided for. Their society is a blend of hierarchy and common equality, but not in the sense of the collective society. This group of people personifies God and are separate from the deity. There is a sense of conformity within a hierarchical structure, but their ultimate focus is outward. Their clan, or family work group, is very important. They derive their identity from the family group, but there is an external consciousness that gives them direction.

This culture should be classified as tribal, but it varies from the tribal forms seen in Latin America, the Mediterranean, and the Middle East. It is what we shall call *progressive tribal*. This means that the family tribe is not the entire reason, or justification, or validation for existence. The tribe has an outward responsibility. The major manifestation of this difference is in the work ethic. The productivity of progressive tribal cultures is, in the Western sense, greater than that of purely tribal cultures.

As in all tribal societies, one's identity is relative to one's family group. Self-esteem is derived from the respect that others show for one's achievements. Achievements are measured relative to the group. Honor and pride are motivating factors, because validation does not come from within. The identity group is one's focus in life. It is the foundation from which people draw their identity and their protection. Communism shattered that cultural foundation.

Communism forced collective cultural behavior onto tribal people. The extended family group was no longer the building block of society. A person's identity had to now lie with the state. Family identities were lost. Persons became nonpersons. There came a crisis of identity.

Communism is a religion in the same sense that Confucianism is a religion. Neither is so much a religion as it is a way of life. In the case of Confucianism, it mirrored the people's perception of reality. Communism did not reflect the fundamental beliefs of the people. It imposed nameless, faceless conformity onto its members. The security of the commune was substituted for the security of the family. The tribal personality could not feel secure in the new culture, for the family was divided.

The effects of communism were this fundamental: Personal responsibility, self-worth, motivation, and personal security were the greatest casualties of the communist system. Communism held control through fear, punishment, and absolute power. For fear of punishment, no one took risks, and no one claimed responsibility. The best one could hope for was to become invisible, yet this was against the fundamental nature of the people.

In tribal societies, elevating the person is important, for a person derives self-worth from others in the group. Without a system of rewards, without positive feedback and praise, the self-worth and motivation of the individual suffer. The equality that communism promoted was an equality of conformity. It became an equality of suspicion and an equality of disdain. "No one treats me nicely, so I'll do the same."

What is happening now is the reemergence of the tribe. The family is the only unit of security. No one else is trusted. People now are motivated to support their families as they were never motivated to support the collective. For the same reason that the Reformation had to happen in northern Europe, so communism had to fail in Central and Eastern Europe. When one cultural type overlays a different indigenous culture, the indigenous culture eventually surfaces. This is not to say that the imposing culture does not leave a mark. Roman Catholicism was not merely ejected; it was transformed into an acceptable form for the native culture. In the same way, communism's demise did not return Eastern Europe to monarchies, but gave way to free market democracies.

Be aware, however, that the style of democracy and capitalism that is evolving will reflect the inherent progressive tribal type and will not eventually become just like the style in the United States. The exceptions to this are Estonia, Latvia, and the former East Germany. These are all pluralist cultures. Estonia and Latvia have had a strong bond with Denmark, Germany, and Sweden over the centuries. The Western Germans are finding out the effects of communism on their strongly pluralistic culture. It is taking much longer to reunite the two Germanies than had originally been imagined. Even with communism gone, the eastern German people are not nearly as productive or motivated as their western brethren. An entire generation has been trained in the communist way, and it will take more than a few years to return them to their natural behavior.

The subject of age must be stressed. In all of the countries that were under communist domination, for more than 40 years, there is a huge generation gap. The older generation has been well-trained in the communist ways and has been conditioned to secrecy, distrust, and fear. It is not the driving force behind the new economy. The younger generation is able and eager to make the transition from a closed society to a free one. The behavior of the younger businessperson will be very different from the older worker or manager. The younger will be more open and relaxed in dealing with Westerners. But do not make the mistake of presuming too much. Attitude is one thing, and performance is another.

The communist system of education stressed the concrete. Technological education often stressed applied knowledge rather than the theoretical or philosophical approach. Training programs were utilitarian rather than inventive. Central and East Europeans are very good at working with what they have in front of them. If they have a computer with no manual, they will go into the machine language and decipher the program. However, their management skills have been seriously neglected. Only those at the very top did the planning, budgeting, and scheduling. Management training will be a high priority for these nations.

Management implies hierarchy. Although communism espoused equality, there was actually a strong system of rank, if not class. With the political changes taking place, leaders in the region are more leaders from within. The tribe always had leadership, usually based on age, but there was more of a family consensus approach also. There was no dictator. The leaders today rule on behalf of the group. The external directing force is nationalism, and the individual sees rewards for his family in the future. Hopefully the future will not take long to arrive.

The concept of a consensus versus absolute leadership is an interesting differentiator between Central and Eastern Europe. The argument finds a perfect analogy, or reflection, in the religions of the area. Figure 4.5 shows the division between predominantly Roman Catholic areas and Eastern Orthodox regions. There are two major philosophical dividing points between the two Christian religions. One regards the nature of the Trinity, which we won't get into here, although it does have some bearing on the perception of hierarchy. The other major contentious issue is in the organizational structure of the church.

The Roman Catholic Church has a strong vertical power hierarchy. It is patristic in nature, with power concentrated at the top. The East Orthodox church has a less vertical hierarchy, with power distributed horizontally throughout a group of archbishops. They, along with the Holy Synod, constitute the decision-making body of the Orthodox religion. Decision making is by consensus. This model of power accurately reflects the perception of divine/human reality of native East European culture.

Central Europe, which was under the domination of the Hapsburg dynasty and the Austro-Hungarian empire for many centuries, held strictly to Roman Catholicism by the Hapsburg monarchy. One can expect Central European business institutions to exhibit a more patristic, vertical structure. It will be interesting to see whether these cultures will gravitate back to original perceptions or whether the influence from the West will now tend to shape their institutional behavior.

Noting this one obvious difference between Central and Eastern Europe, we can reasonably construct a player portrait for a representative Central or East European player. The game plan will follow.

CENTRAL OR EAST EUROPEAN PLAYER PORTRAIT

What does he believe is a person's responsibility?

To take care of and contribute to his family group. To contribute beyond his group to the good of the country.

Figure 4.5
Religious Orientation of Central and East Europe

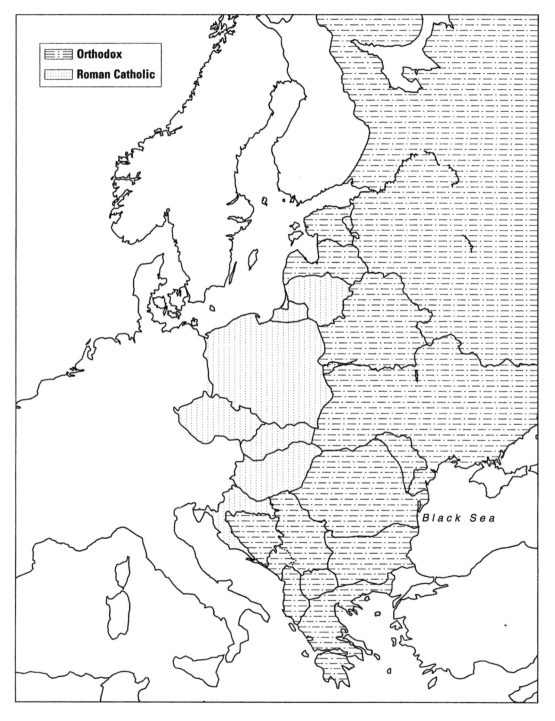

What does he expect of others?

Mutual support, sharing, family loyalty, honesty.

How does he interact with others?

He assumes equality of all players. He does not show deference, but is modest in his interactions at first. He must build a relationship before he trusts enough to interact openly.

What impresses him? What does he respect in another?

Competence, loyalty, honesty.

What is his attitude toward foreigners?

His first responsibility is to the family clan, so he is averse to strangers. Once it is perceived that there is no threat to the group and that the foreigner will benefit the group, the foreigner is welcomed and treated with warm hospitality.

Why is he in the game?

This player works to live and lives to work.

What is his main objective?

His main objective in completing his business is to achieve a minimum of disruption to life. His work should not cause stress in his family life. He is beginning to look for achievement in his work.

How does he define winning?

Win-win.

What is his business environment (physical and hierarchical)?

There is a loose hierarchical structure, with authority accepted at the top. Requests for decisions flow up the ladder, and causal goal setting flows down. Middle management is gaining more power. The physical space should be open, but close-knit. People are not likely to be singled out for prime office space. Functionality should direct the physical plant. Aesthetics might be important, as might light and windows.

How does he conduct business?

He prefers to conduct business by partnerships and teamwork. Communication is restricted and indirect. Only those who need to know will get information, in order to limit the possibility of negative feedback. In general, criticism is not given. There are no performance reviews.

How does he learn?

He tends to work from the general to the specific and relates abstract concepts to concrete knowledge. Use of physical analogies and visual description is recommended.

How does he give feedback?

So as not to be disruptive or held accountable, he gives only sparse and vague
feedback. This is changing as fear of reprisal diminishes.

How does he make decisions?

He is not accustomed to being responsible. Action items are bumped upstairs to the
person accepting ultimate authority for the business unit's work. Decisions are
difficult because issues are not well-defined. In Eastern Europe, decisions are likely
to be made by way of a consensus of experts.

What is his attitude toward time, schedules, plans, and change?

Time is not linear. There is not much regard for keeping to schedules. There is no
association between time and money. He is process oriented and may become
absorbed in the process at the expense of the schedule. Change is accepted if it is
not disruptive. New information can be absorbed into the process.

How does he approach problem solving?

There are no problems. Whatever happens is absorbed into the process. The entire
project may simply downgrade, because a problem must be assimilated into the
project. Problems are simply thought of as change orders. All this is because no
one wants to give bad news, so bad news is changed to neutral news. He is
reactive by nature. He does what he can do. Those in authority may never even be
informed of a change.

Central and East European Game Plan

This culture forms closed groups for mutual support and security. The members will
definitely feel more comfortable remaining on their own turf. They are wary of
strangers, especially foreigners that appear more powerful than they. If they discern
clear benefits to working with you, they will welcome you but keep dealings strictly
business. Your goal is to communicate that you seek mutual benefits in approaching
this culture to do business.

Relationships are exceedingly important in business. In order to minimize their perceived threat from you and to open the way for relationship building, you must approach with an introduction. A professional, yet impersonal introduction will be accepted because they highly regard competence, which is attested to by a professional
reference. A personal introduction is especially useful, as it will break down barriers
and open doors more quickly. These businesspeople are not so suspicious of strangers
that they will let their fears get in the way of a clear benefit, yet the form of a congenial business relationship is necessary before substantive talks can begin.

It is important for you to recognize and respect their brand of conformity and modesty. You should not exceed their culture's ability to provide material goods. This

means one should not dress in an ostentatious or expensive manner. One should not entertain lavishly. One should not assert American values of personal gain in order to motivate them. Accept their modest and moderate ways. Accept their way of doing things and their group accomplishments. Don't try to mend them. Show that you respectfully propose business that will benefit the group on their terms. This means for the good of the group. For a progressive tribal culture, this group is both family and state.

All tribal players feel an obligation to better the position of their group. All need to demonstrate their competence by receiving value from the outsider. However, this culture believes in the value of mutual support and sharing. They are win-win players, as are most Americans, and they will negotiate for the good of both parties once their group is taken care of. Be prepared to give them a guaranteed gain in exchange for equal value. Minimize risk to them in what they are to receive and in what they are to give.

To value the person is to value the relationship. Focus on the shared respect you have for each other and on your enthusiasm for the new relationship that is being forged. Your host's primary identity is through his family group. Ultimately, a display of respect and concern for his family is a great compliment. Always be sincere, for honesty is highly valued.

Don't entice the person with personal material wealth unless it will benefit his entire clan. This player's welfare in business is most commonly defined as the path of least resistance. Show him how to do his job more easily, more harmoniously, and with less risk of failure. This is his immediate objective.

In all former Soviet and Soviet satellite countries, law is an important subject. The commercial codes of each country are currently in a state of flux. Most contracts provide for third-party arbitration. Ownership is also an issue. Be sure to look into the local laws pertaining to your business and be aware that they may change during the term of your contract.

The application of this game plan to an actual game has largely been done in Chapter 3—the hypothetical case that was actually Russia without the influence of communism. Some things change due to the communist legacy, but in general, the protocol of that game will hold, and so it will not be repeated here. To fine-tune protocol for each country, the following supplemental notes are offered.

Supplemental Notes

Russia

Russians have an affinity for Americans. This may be because both are used to life on a broad canvas. Their nations' territories are extensive, and their political power has been broad ranging. Although they stood at opposite ideological poles, there is much the two peoples have in common.

Don't hire an expatriate Russian to represent you in Russia.

Russians believe, and those who know Russia agree, that Russia has a soul. Russians feel that they must take their own path, and not copy the West.

Russians see themselves as rational and conscious realists. They are also romantic and sentimental.

Private business is done on trust. This makes relationships very important to doing business. Initial contacts should be made through a trusted third party.

European manners are used. Keep your hands out of your pockets, use good posture, don't cross your ankle over your knee, and remember that whistling indoors brings bad financial luck.

Be punctual. They may not be.

Shake hands coming and going and when introduced. Use a firm handshake.

Never shake hands with gloves on, and do not shake hands across a threshold.

Address your host by last name. Do not use the term *comrade*. When you become friendly, he may suggest any variety of nicknames to call him by. A respectful way to refer to someone with whom you are on familiar terms is by using the first name and the second name, which is a patronymic (indicating "son of so-and-so").

Observe age and rank, and adjust your protocol to honor them.

Dress is conservative, and fashions tend to lag behind the West by about 20 years. Try not to appear too affluent. From a safety standpoint, it would be wise to buy a pair of Russian shoes. Thieves can easily spot a Westerner by their good-quality shoes. Save your good shoes for business meetings.

You will probably need an interpreter. But the presence of an interpreter doesn't mean Russians do not understand English. Avoid making off-the-record comments in English. Translate written materials into Russian, especially sample contracts, to save time in translation.

Bring many business cards. There are few telephone books, so people collect cards. They may not have a goodly supply of their own cards. Write down a list of meeting participants and their phone numbers. Business cards should be printed in English and Russian.

Token gifts are often exchanged at the first meeting. Go to Russia prepared to give a lot of gifts, and bring an extra bag for the ones they will give to you. Reciprocity in gift giving is very important. Gift giving indicates sharing, respect, interest in the person, and generosity—all the values one would want in a friend.

Business will begin soon after a bit of conversation. They may ask you to sign an agreement of cooperation, which is not a contract to work together, but to express mutual interest. It is all right to sign it.

Be clear about your intentions for this first meeting. If it is merely exploratory, say so. They may have expectations of you as their savior.

Government permits are not necessary to open an office. If you are hoping for a long-term relationship, establishment of a local office demonstrates commitment. Local employment agencies can assist you in staffing the office.

You may save some money and find other advantages to renting an apartment by the week instead of staying in a hotel room. Russians love to talk around a table. After the first meeting, invite the Russians to your apartment for further discussions. Serve them tea, and sit around the table.

The Russian negotiating team will usually have specialists with different interests, such as price or quality. The head of the team will do the most talking, and you should direct most of your remarks to him.

Keep your pricing consistent with other European nations. The Russians will have done research. Prepare to make a small price concession.

If you want to make a big impression on them, invite them to come visit you in America. You will be responsible for their expenses in the United States, but they will pay the airfare.

Negotiations may take time. Time is not money. Time is wisdom.

Management skills are often lacking. Don't leave anything unsaid. Don't assume they will fill in the blanks properly.

Presentations should be concrete, visual, and factual, with detailed specifications.

Decisions are often made subjectively, based on emotion. Logic is considered second.

They are not afraid to express emotion, and they use it as a tool. Sometimes they will storm out of a meeting, only to return later. Don't lose your temper, but it is wise to meet emotion with emotion. It is often necessary to play hardball.

Be creative in offering partnerships, coproduction, training, office equipment, and service.

End all meetings with a summary of the meeting and action items for the next meeting.

Very few people stop for lunch. Lunch is taken more often in Moscow than elsewhere. There are only a few decent restaurants anyway. At the end of talks, host a dinner at a hotel restaurant. Wives are generally not included.

The Continental style of eating is used.

There will be much toasting, usually with wine or vodka. When a bottle of vodka is opened, it must be finished, not saved. The host starts the toast with a little speech, and the guest replies. Alcohol is served during a meal, not before.

If you are invited to someone's home, which is rare, bring an odd number of flowers. Even numbers are for funerals.

Businesswomen are respected in Russia. There is no risk of harassment.

Belarus

Tribal affiliation is especially important in Belarus because of the country's weak national identity. Belarus has been dominated by Poland, Lithuania, and Russia throughout much of its history.

A good local representative is important. He should understand your business and be able to discuss details when asked. He should not only make introductions but also attend meetings and follow up afterward. He can arrange translation services.

Send your proposal to your targeted company before your visit. The company will be interested in whether you have proposed it elsewhere in their country and the response it received.

Western business practices are not generally understood. Explain everything.

Documents from your company should bear the corporate seal.

Negotiations and presentations are similar to those in Russia.

Shake hands with a firm grip while stating your last name. Men and women shake hands with each other.

Small gifts are appreciated.

Dress conservatively.

Use European manners, as noted in the section on Russia.

Accept hospitality, whether you are invited to a restaurant or a home. Expect substantial drinking, but if business is discussed, you will be held to what you say.

Ukraine

Russia finds it hard to accept losing Ukraine. The region had been controlled by Russia for centuries, and Russians feel it is truly part of Russia. Ukrainians do not.

Until the Mongol invasion in the 13th century, Kiev was the center of the Russian empire. Thereafter, Moscow became the capital.

The Cossacks originated in Ukraine. These peasants banded together to fight the Polish Jesuits who were trying to make Ukraine a Roman Catholic country. Even today there is animosity toward Jesuits. They asked Moscow for protection in 1654, and Russia responded by making Ukraine a serfdom.

Ukrainians are independent thinkers who are capable of both objective analysis and subjective decision making. Their emotions often take precedence over logic.

They do not have a strong central government at this time, and the Eastern Orthodox Church is providing a focal point for the progressive tribal culture.

Beware of both of the words yes and no during decision making. Both are used tactically—either to stall talks until more information has arrived or to keep you talking when you seem to be losing interest. Nothing is certain until the contract is signed.

Negotiations may become emotional. Play hardball.

Avoid compromises. They make you appear weak. Ukrainians are schooled in business the same as Russians. See the previous notes on Russia.

European manners are used.

Ukrainians are generally more easygoing than Russians. Otherwise, many of the business and social customs are similar.

Romania

Early in its history, Romania was dominated by the Roman empire, of which Romania was a province. The Romanian language is based on Latin. However, Romania's proximity to the subsequent Byzantine empire along with its progressive tribal nature resulted in a predominantly Orthodox Christian state. After World War II, Romania came under the influence of the USSR. In 1965, Romanians declared themselves an independent communist state. Human rights violations and corruption ensued. Today Romania is a democratic republic and one of the poorest countries in Europe.

The people distrust authority and are reverting to an insular tribal structure.

They have very weak business management skills.

The more educated a person is, the more objective he is in decision making. Subjective emotions do play a part.

The current priority among all Romanians is to feed and house their families.

Opinions and emotions are freely expressed.

Send letters in English. Romanians give higher priority to English-language documents. A letter that must be translated is more respected.

Distrust makes it difficult to make contacts. Use local representatives. Once you are accepted, the relationship will have a strong bond.

Romanians are status conscious. Stay in the best hotel. Have your title and degrees printed on business cards.

Small gifts are appreciated at the first meeting.

Shake hands often: each time you see someone in a day, as well as when you are introduced. Use a firm grip. Use last names and professional titles.

Romanians gesture a lot with their hands. You should not, for many of the American gestures can be seriously misunderstood.

Eat Continental style.

Use European manners.

Bulgaria

Bulgaria was dominated by the Ottoman Turks until World War I. It fought with Germany during World War II and then came under Soviet influence. Currently, it is reversing the communist hold, privatizing industry, and returning collective farmland.

Bulgarians admire the United States and Western Europe. They admire the entrepreneurial spirit and apply it in a tribal sense.

The family is taken into consideration during any decision making.

Bulgarians have a strong work ethic.

They respect openness, strength, competence, honesty, and loyalty.

Management skills are lacking.

European manners are used. Respectful behavior toward others is important.

The head-nodding gestures Americans use to mean yes and no are reversed in Bulgaria.

Croatia

Croatia was ruled by the Hapsburg dynasty for centuries. After the fall of the Austro-Hungarian empire after World War I, Croatia, Slovenia, Bosnia, and Serbia were held together in a federation known as Yugoslavia. After the dictator Tito's death and the fall of the USSR, it was nationalism and ethnicity that separated these countries. Strong tribal identity now operates.

Croatians are primarily Roman Catholic. Expect a stronger power hierarchy and centralized decision making.

Croats value kinship bonds, education, and a good career.

European manners are used.

It is acceptable to express emotion and opinions.

Hungary

Hungary developed a high level of culture during the Renaissance. The country came under the influence of the Hapsburg dynasty in the 16th century, and in 1867 a dual monarchy was declared, beginning the Austro-Hungarian empire. This was a union of Germanic and Slavic peoples that lasted until the end of World War I. In 1949, Hungary became a communist socialist state. It is now a democracy and one of the most prosperous East European nations.

The country is two-thirds Roman Catholic—a result of the Austrian association—and one-quarter Protestant. Religion is not a big part of Hungarian life.

Vertical hierarchy is preferred, but consensus decision making may prevail until greater confidence in business is achieved.

Hungarians value family, education, job security, private property, and travel.

They admire professionals and intellectuals over the merely wealthy.

Intentions, feelings, and opinions may be directly expressed. Deviousness is not respected.

Once you have a local representative, do not change to another or you may have to start over in your agreements.

Your host will probably entertain you. Hospitality is important to Hungarians. At the end of negotiations, you should host a cocktail party or dinner at a good hotel.

A firm handshake is used when meeting and leaving. Use family names until invited to use first names. In Hungary, the family name precedes the given name.

When visiting a company, bring many small gifts for distribution to everyone you meet.

Hungarians love horses. You may be invited to go riding. If you know how to ride, this is a good topic of conversation.

Slovakia

Until World War I, Slovakia had been under Hungarian rule for about a thousand years. After World War II it was united with the Czech Republic as Czechoslovakia, a democratic republic. In 1948, the country came under communist domination. In 1989, Czechoslovakia became an independent democracy, but nationalism surfaced. In 1992, the Czech Republic and Slovakia became separate nations.

Slovakians are proud of their peasant roots and peasant values, which include hard work, generosity, honesty, and modesty.

They view entrepreneurs as greedy.

They do not value aggressiveness and individualistic self-confidence.

Education is valued above wealth.

Use titles when greeting someone.

Print your titles and degrees on your business card.

Many hand gestures are used. Avoid using American gestures, as some of them are offensive to Slovaks.

European manners are appropriate.

The Czech Republic

During the 15th century, Prague was a center of the Protestant Reformation. In the 16th century, the Czech Republic (the former Bohemian empire), came under the rule of the Austrian empire, which reasserted Roman Catholicism. Today, 40 percent are Roman Catholic, and the majority of the rest are unaffiliated Christians. They believe in a personal relationship with a universal being.

After World War I, Czechoslovakia was a stable and affluent democracy. It was unable to repel Hitler during World War II, however, and in 1948 came under Soviet control. It has always held an independent line against the Soviet Union and openly rebelled against the latter several times. In 1989, after the collapse of the USSR, and the separation from Slovakia in 1992, the country became the Czech Republic.

Independent thought has always been encouraged, but Czechs are truly tribal people. Cooperation and contribution are valued over individual accomplishments. The family unit is considered in all decision making.

Hierarchies tend to be formed. Leadership is valued.

The most important values are education, social standing, modesty, and cleverness. European manners are followed.

Translation of material into Czech will impress your host, but English is acceptable.

Czechs are detail oriented and will study all aspects of an agreement. Expect negotiations to move slowly.

Present information clearly, highlighting major points and using visual aids when possible.

Don't get down to business too abruptly. Relationship is important and slow to form.

Dinner entertainment is more common than lunches. Do not discuss business during a meal.

Greet a person by using a firm but brief handshake. Use the last name, which is the family name. Use professional titles when they are known. Wait to be introduced if there are more than two people present.

Avoid using your index finger, waving, or beckoning.

Keep your feet on the floor.

Business gifts should be inexpensive but of good quality.

Dress conservatively.

Be aware that the Czech word for yes is *ano*, which Czechs often shorten to no. They shake their head up and down in agreement. This can be very confusing for people who speak English.

Poland

Poland has been a Roman Catholic country for over a thousand years.

In 1791, Poland adopted a constitution modeled after that of the United States, but it retained its monarchy and nobility. In 1795, Poland was partitioned by Prussia, Austria, and Russia and no longer existed as a nation. The Polish identity was maintained through the Roman Catholic Church in Poland. In 1948, Poland came under Soviet control. It is now democratic and has a free market economy.

Poles value punctuality, skill and intelligence, privacy, family, and loyalty to the Polish nation.

They have a strong work ethic.

They are critical of themselves and their institutions.

Direct communication is preferred.

Facts are more important than emotions in decision making, but relationships are more important than laws.

Poland has strong power hierarchies and is a male-dominated society.

Translate materials into Polish.

A local representative will make the handling of business and social arrangements much easier.

Business lunches and dinners are popular. Expect to stay out late, or you may insult your host.

Shake hands to meet, greet, and say good-bye. Use last names.

Avoid loud behavior in public.

Polish men have more traditional views of women. A woman should not talk to a strange man, or it will be considered flirting.

A gift is appropriate at the first meeting.

Dress conservatively.

Lithuania

Lithuania and Poland have had close ties for centuries, including their Roman Catholic faith. They developed along the same lines until they were partitioned in 1775. Lithuania then came under Russian rule until 1920, when it regained independence briefly. In 1940, it was again annexed by Russia and in 1990 declared independence.

Customs and protocol are similar to Poland's.

Lithuania's democratic institutions are not as well developed as Poland's, and much of the focus is on strengthening the country's internal institutions.

Estonia and Latvia

These countries are unusual among the Slavic nations in that they were more dominantly influenced in their early history by the Scandinavian nations and Germany. Estonia and Latvia are small countries that tend to be more pluralistic and exhibit stronger need for self-expression and personal achievement. Their values and protocol follow the Swedish and Danish models.

5

Other Important Games

Additional countries that are of interest have not been included within the major regional games covered in Chapter 4. The reason is that certain countries are significantly different from those around them because of religion or ethnic background. In all cases, the governing principles are different from those of nearby cultures. This is most easily illustrated in the Pacific Rim game. Technically, Australia is located in the Pacific Rim. Yet to discuss its culture at the same time as discussion of those of China and Japan and every collective society of the Far East would not be logical. The primary inhabitants of Australia are of British descent, making their cultural background unique in Asia.

Similarly, Israel has been extracted from the Arab world playing field because it is not an Arab culture, yet it is a significant global player. Religion in Israel is not the only factor distinguishing it from its neighbors. Its unique culture is a mixture of northern European and Mediterranean cultures. The large immigrant population gives the Israeli game its own set of rules.

India is a huge nation that does significant international business both as a member of the Commonwealth of Nations and as an independent democracy. India stands in close proximity to two strong cultural systems: Islam to the west and east, and Confucianism/Buddhism to the north. Yet it maintains its own religious beliefs and mode of operation as representative of those perceptions.

Canada is a tremendous region on its own. It houses two distinct cultures that must be addressed separately. It is very important for Americans to make the distinction between doing business in Canada and doing business in the United States.

THE AUSTRALIAN GAME

Australia is an independent member of the British Commonwealth, and as such one would expect the Australians to be similar to the English in many ways. England is a tribal culture, as discussed in the West European game, but Australia is not. Australia is pluralist. It is easy to see the evolution from tribal ancestry to pluralist culture after an examination of the founding of Australia.

Capt. James Cook claimed possession of the eastern coast of Australia for the British in 1770. Shortly afterward, the British arrived and founded penal colonies in the area. The original inhabitants of Australia, therefore, were convicts and soldiers. The transport of convicts to Australia stopped in 1868. Free settlements were established with the discovery of gold in the mid 1800s. The free population largely comprised adventurous men seeking their fortune.

What is clear from that background is that the family was not the organizing unit of Australian society. The country was born of the disenfranchised. The English nobility and related class structure were not transported to Australia. The population consisted mostly of those who had gone outside the system, those who did not accept lower-class status and acted out, and those who were not obedient to the laws of society. Even the free men who came made a statement by their presence that they were not satisfied with what they had and were willing to take great risks to improve their material situation. The convicts and the free men did not fit into the tribal culture of England. Their inner beliefs—or inner corruption—drove them out.

The other notable aspect of the early inhabitants of Australia was that they were almost entirely male. The family was not the group from which identity was derived, but from the male "club." Men formed strong bonds, which continues as a major social institution in Australia even today. Men feel that their friendships with other men are more important than their relationships with their wives. The man has very little to do with household affairs, yet he is the symbolic head of the family. Australian society fosters a very strong masculine stereotype. Part of that stereotype is portrayed by the strong, independent, tough individual. It is an identity of strong individualism, but at the same time it is an identity of conformity. The concept of *masculine* is well-defined, and the group is easily threatened by any deviance by a member, such as homosexuality, oversensitivity to the needs of others, growing long hair, and wearing jewelry. (Of course, some of those standards change with time, but only by group consensus.)

These traits make the Australian businessman very difficult to classify. He behaves as a strong individualist who is self-directed and equal to any man, yet he is defined by the identity of the group. His group identity appears to be tribal because of the element of self-awareness, unlike that of the the collective member, who seems to have no identity apart from the group. Yet the Australian is not truly tribal because his sense of identity is not related to a family or hierarchical structure. One who is a member of the identity group "male" is equal to every member. So we have an independent individual who is defined by his conformity with the collective group but who is self-aware within the group. Such conflicting cultural identities are evident to those who study the country. The inhabitants of Australia are, by international survey, the happiest people on earth. At the same time, they have one of the highest suicide rates in the world. They are easy to get to know, they're friendly and generous—and just below the surface—they're aggressive and violent. Much of that aggression is expressed relatively harmlessly through the attention they give to sports, especially contact sports, which is a major aspect of life in Australia. There seems to be a general crisis of identity.

The Australian wholeheartedly believes that one man is as good as another. Until recently, tipping in restaurants was unheard-of, because it suggested a servile relationship between guest and waiter. Bus drivers are considered every bit as valuable as those who ride on the bus. The original self-concept of Australians was that of a nation of the working class. Now, with greater affluence and education, it is a nation of the middle class. There is a strong desire for competition and there is a drive for material wealth, but there is also the attitude that if one exceeds the level of success of the group or if one sticks his neck up above the crowd, he should be cut down to size. Everyone is an equal, and that's how everyone should remain.

This may be a paranoid reaction to the looming prospects of an elite upper class that might result in a class-based British-type society: an idea abhorrent to almost every Australian (royalists though they may be). Any hint of supercilious behavior is scoffed at. The behavior of acting out against anyone who puts himself above the group serves as a mechanism for cultural stability. Thus the protocol of the society supports the cultural objective of equality.

This is not to suggest that there is no upper class in Australia. The upper class is small and made up of a few landowning families and those with great industrial wealth. It is less an upper class after the British model than it is after the American model. There is mobility among classes, for one does not accept one's station in life. There is the possibility of entry—mostly through acquisition of wealth. One can gain access to the upper crust through self-improvement—and not only through heredity. The existence of the upper class is not supported by cultural behavior. Those in the upper class may have more, but they are not due more respect. To an Australian, no man is his master and no man is his servant. Arrogance is the worst sin, and deference, the next. There is no strong inner drive to make one's way up the ladder, as there is in the United States.

Because of the belief that one makes one's own station in life and because of social and occupational mobility, this culture should be classified primarily pluralist. Keep in mind the strong equalizing forces of conformity, however. With this background in mind, we can develop a player portrait and game plan for Australia.

AUSTRALIAN PLAYER PORTRAIT

What does he believe is a person's responsibility?

Personal satisfaction and enjoyment of life; independence.

What does he expect of others?

Equal treatment.

How does he interact with others?

Open and friendly. Very informal. First names are used almost immediately.

What impresses him? What does he respect in another?

Accomplishments through use of masculine traits.

What is his attitude toward foreigners?

Friendly and not defensive. Foreigners are held separate from the group if their culture is very different. Australians are intolerant of different behavior.

Why is he in the game?

He works to live.

What is his main objective?

To maintain his individual independence and enjoy life. Purposeful hedonism.

How does he define winning?

Win-win.

What is his business environment (physical and hierarchical)?

Separate but equal. Privacy is important. Power hierarchy based on achievement, but the Australian is strongly antiauthoritarian.

How does he conduct business?

Communication is not held in strict secrecy, and there are no rigid lines of communication. He is direct and not subtle with communication. Interaction is not formal, but pragmatic.

How does he learn?

Detailed data, facts, and concepts, empirical and theoretical knowledge.

How does he give feedback?

Directly, specifically, and objectively. He is not afraid to say no. Does not account for another person's feelings.

How does he make decisions?

Individuals have power to make decisions, but must be consistent with company policy. Decisions are based on objective facts and policy, not on emotions and friendship bonds.

What is his attitude toward time, schedules, plans, and change?

Punctuality is important in business interactions. However, workers are very
independent when it comes to the use of their time. They must be shown a
personal benefit to being on time. Schedules and plans are precise and important to
those responsible for them. They are moderately adaptable to change.

How does he approach problem solving?

Problems are assessed objectively, but a bit casually. There is a slightly carefree
approach to work.

The Australian Game Plan

Australians suffer from a sense of isolation from the rest of the world. It is important
to show interest in them and their country by physically going there. Follow-up can
be done by phone, but visits should take place at least twice a year.

Because of the distance involved, it would be wise to keep a local representative on
staff who can stay up-to-date on local developments and keep your name prominent.
Initiating a business contact can be done by phone, but it is always better to have a
letter of introduction. Government is not so important in Australian business, so
having a high-placed government contact is not as important as having an important
bank reference or referral by a notable businessperson.

Australians do not suffer from an inferiority complex among nations, but they do
demand respect and recognition. They are very proud of their country and their
unique culture. They do not want to be thought of as a little America. Any display of
superiority will turn them away. Equality and antiauthoritarianism are their strongest
values. Treat them as equals. Likewise, do not defer to them. No man is a servant, and
no man is a master. Be sure to structure your presentation to emphasize the equality
of the two participants.

Part of Australians' of equality is their informality. Accept this and do not make
your manner of behavior overly formal compared with theirs. They appreciate consideration, but dislike stuffy, stiff formality. Do not be offended if they use your first
name. Also, do not assume that if they do, it indicates friendship. Use of first names
is a way to mutually disarm and equalize opponents.

Australians do not react kindly when insulted by an inflated price. Bargaining as an
art is a waste of time. However, they do have a competitive spirit and want the best
deal they can make. Be ready to give up something, if needed. But the competition for
price should take place within your own company while deciding on pricing to be presented. In other words, take your best shot and live with it.

The Australian's self-worth is based on his feelings of equality and masculinity.
Deference and compliments will not have the desired effect. Behaving in a way that
acknowledges an Australian's ability and independent reasoning is the best tactic. Val-

idate his importance to you in what you are hoping to achieve for your mutual benefit.

An Australian's motivations in decision making are based on company policy and national interest, but there is also strong personal interest in his own performance. Help to identify and offer solutions to his problems. Your proposal may require interaction with unions that are contentious with management. Find out the obstacles in the way of the Australian's decision in your favor. He is usually straightforward and will appreciate your partnership in addressing solutions.

Supplemental Data: Australia

Greet an Australian with a firm handshake and a hello. Australians tire of hearing non-Australians say "g'day." Begin with last names, but first-name usage will follow almost immediately. Don't wait to be asked, but if he uses your first name, respond in kind.

Give your business card at the introduction. Expect that your counterpart may not give you one. Cards are not very important in Australia.

Titles and degrees do not impress an Australian. He will make his own judgment as to the quality of the person with whom he is dealing.

Business dress is conservative and not overly elegant. Leave the gold chain and other ostentatious jewelry at home. They are too showy and considered not masculine.

Be friendly, relaxed, modest, and unpretentious. Don't try to impress your host.

Gifts are not given unless you are invited to someone's home.

Don't fill your presentation with hype or glitz. A simple, direct presentation is more effective. Get to the point.

Decision making can occur at lower levels, but things still take longer than in the United States.

You may be invited out for a drink after work. Don't bring up business unless your host does. Australians make a clear distinction between work and play. Each person pays for a round of drinks. Don't miss your turn. Sports is an excellent topic of conversation. Find out something about Australian Rules football and rugby. When discussing sports, do not use the term *root* as in "root for the home team." It means something obscene.

There is a difference between afternoon tea and tea. Tea is actually the dinnertime meal served between 6 and 8 P.M.

Until recently, women were not permitted in bars. Bars were for men only. Women are legally equal, but socially an underclass, although men may not admit it.

Although New Zealand will not be covered separately in this book, it is important not to overlook it as a separate nation. The European development of New Zealand came from colonization by Australia. The prison colony in Sydney spawned a group of fortune-hunting men who colonized New Zealand for their own profits by using prison labor. In the early 1800s, New Zealand was a frontier of Australia. The local residents, the Maoris, were pressed into service on land, on trading ships, and on whaling vessels.

To colonize the new land, the English later sent settlers. who were mostly cultivated representatives of English county families and their retinue. New Zealanders are therefore more British in behavior than Australians, yet they remain more like Australians than like their English ancestors.

THE CANADIAN GAME

Americans often ignore the importance of learning the customs of our northern English-speaking neighbors, because most of us think Canadians are just like us. Don't let the language fool you. They are not Americans and do not wish to be thought of as Americans. In fact, many Canadians fear U.S. dominance and believe that, given the chance, the United States would annex their country.

Canada is the second-largest country in the world. With such an extensive land mass, it isn't surprising to expect that there would be a variety of cultural influences represented. Canada grew in much the same way that the United States did in that immigrants from all over the world have come to settle there. Canada was a North American colony of the British at one time and is today an independent member of the British commonwealth. The Queen of England is the head of state. A prime minister leads the country with no interference from England.

Although the nation used to be entirely under British rule, such was not always the case. The province of Quebec Province was a colony of France for two centuries. A westward expansion, similar to the western expansion in the United States, extended Canada to the Pacific. The frontiersmen endured many of the same challenges and conditions as did the early settlers of the American West. Therefore, for a cultural understanding of Canada, one should really think of it as three countries.

Let's divide Canada as follows: French-speaking Quebec Province, English-speaking Ontario, and the western provinces. In fact, the concept of division, of separating cultural groups, is relevant to Canada. The major difference between America and Canada is that America tends to assimilate diverse cultures into one system. Canada holds ethnic groups separate. This is because most of Canada is tribal.

The French Canadians in Quebec are fiercely battling against being assimilated into one country and one culture. Their language is the most obvious differentiating factor, and it actually stands as a symbol of their culture. When they are forced to speak English, they feel they are losing their identity. French Canadians are perhaps more tribal than the French in France. France, as we discussed earlier, exhibits a combination of pluralist and tribal tendencies, with the tribal influence stronger in the south. French Canadians exhibit more of the tribal culture, especially with respect to their exclusion of outside cultures and their need for identity as members of a group.

Ontario is also tribal. It is the most British part of North America. During the American Revolutionary War, a large number of people loyal to the English king fled to Canada. They were the people of America who did not fit the pluralist mode of behavior, and they continued a more tribal existence in Ontario. Ontarians are respectful of authority, function best in a strong cultural hierarchy, and believe in the need for state control. Compared with U.S. culture, they are more elitist, less achievement oriented, and more socialistic. Power is centralized and tightly held. Although they have an exclusionary society, there is social mobility—although not as much as in the United States—and social status is not offered to immigrants. They are ethnocentric.

The upward mobility of the ethnic cultures that have come to reside in the western provinces owes its progress largely to American businesses that came into the area and had no restrictions against hiring into management positions people of diverse cultures. Some say that if Americans had not come to Canada, the oil in the provinces would still be in the ground. The limitations imposed by the "British" Canadians caused their development to be different from that of the United States.

This brings us to the western provinces. Due to the greater American influence and the pioneering psychology of the western inhabitants, this region tends to be more pluralist. So, if you want to do business in Canada the way you would in the United States, your best bet is the western provinces.

The tribal aspects of eastern Canada are also reflected in religion. The two dominant religions are Roman Catholicism and Anglicanism. Both support the culture with strong internal hierarchy. The American Protestant work ethic is not a subconscious driving force.

The attempt to construct one player portrait for all of Canada raises some problems. The tribal French Canadians are not the same as the tribal English-speaking Canadians, and they all differ from Canadians of the provinces. The approaches to be taken are to construct a modified French player portrait in Quebec, a modified English player portrait in Ontario, and a general pluralist player portrait for the provinces.

The French player portrait is modified to reflect a more relaxed and pragmatic approach to business. Emigration to a new nation requires sacrifices and causes challenges that become a part of the new culture. This is reflected in the way Quebecers do business. They are somewhat less cynical, but are focused on their fight to preserve their culture in the English world that surrounds them. Here are a few additional notes on Quebec:

- All presentation materials should be printed in both French and English. Assume that you will be conducting business in French.
- French Canadians are less reserved than English-speaking Canadians, and they tend to use more gesturing.
- Physical space is closer. They may touch you while conversing.
- Use a reasonably firm handshake, and shake upon first meeting, greeting, and departure.
- Use last names until your host switches to first. He may go back and forth.
- Eat Continental style.

Modifications to the English player portrait generally remove the strictness of the social hierarchy. It is definitely there in Canada, but it is a bit more relaxed. There is mobility within Canadian society. Canadians are less formal than Britons, but not as casual as Americans. More emphasis is placed on one's ability and education. There is a greater sense of equality, but this is limited to the English-speaking majority. Canadians have more motivation to produce than do Britons, but they do not, in general, show an entrepreneurial spirit.

The Canadian Game Plan

A tribal game plan should be followed for eastern Canada, and a more pluralist approach should be taken in the west. The game plan should be made specific to the person with whom you will be meeting and the area where he works. Refer to the English and French game plans for the approach. Alter your tactics slightly to reflect a more egalitarian social structure. In the west, self-interest will be more of a factor, as opposed to the group mentality. Be aware that many other ethnic groups have recently arrived in Canada. In Vancouver, there is a large group of Chinese from Hong Kong. Certainly, you should use the game plan that most suits the person with whom you will be meeting.

Supplemental Data: Canada

Handshakes are firm. Shake upon introduction and greeting, but not upon leaving.

Use last names when introduced. First names will be used very soon thereafter. Wait for your host to initiate this.

English Canadians are not comfortable with speaking or touching at close range.

Privacy is important.

Business meals are common. At dinner, wait for your host to bring up business.

In business situations, maintain good posture. You can be more relaxed in social settings.

Business gifts should be modest. Gifts are opened immediately. An invitation to a
restaurant is considered a gift.

Eat Continental style.

THE GREEK GAME

Greece is considered separately because it does not fit exclusively in either the game
of Western Europe or the game of Central and Eastern Europe. The major difference
between Greek tribal culture and other tribal cultures of the northern Mediterranean
is the Greek rejection of Rome as the seat of religious allegiance.

The factors that make Greece different from other Central European cultures is that
it is not Slavic and has not been dominated by communism. Where there are differences there are also similarities. Greece has a traditional tribal culture with a basic belief in the separation and personification of God. It is a predominantly Christian
country, supporting the Greek Orthodox Church and not Roman Catholicism. But it
stands somewhere between the more abstract Latin interpretations of the relationship
of man to God and the more concrete and personalized expression of that relationship
found in Orthodox Christianity.

Greeks tend to share behavioral traits with their Mediterranean neighbors, such as
in the tendency to act from emotion and subjectivity, greater use of nonverbal language as in hand gestures, self-praise, emphasis on hospitality, and a lax notion of
time. Greeks are more closely related to their northern, progressive tribal neighbors in
their preference for a consensus power hierarchy, as opposed to the strong authori-
tarianism of the patristic Latin model. They value education and work. They are hard
working, yet are not pressured by time.

As a tribal culture, Greece shares its basic social requirements with all tribal cultures: obligation to family, loyalty to friends and family, and traditions that reinforce the social framework. Although throughout history Greece has been besieged
by foreign invaders—from the Romans and Ottomans to Hitler and the threat of
communism—it has always maintained its unique cultural identity and has always returned to the guiding principle of democracy, which was first espoused by their ancient ancestors.

Supplemental Data: Greece

It is wise to use a local intermediary to establish contacts.

Relationship building is important, and friendship comes with obligation.

Be punctual, even though your Greek counterpart will not be.

Shake hands with a firm grip, and don't break away too quickly.

Use last names and titles when introduced, showing special respect for older
people.

Business cards should be printed in both Greek and English. Hand the card Greek side up, being sure that the writing is right side up.

Dress conservatively.

Presentations should include a variety of presentation techniques, many of them visual.

Treat the senior member in a group with special respect. Authority usually rests with him, although there is a need for consensus in decision-making groups.

Expect to bargain and make quick decisions.

Patience is important in negotiations, but be prepared to move quickly on a moment's notice.

Language is often exaggerated and emotional.

Business is frequently conducted over a cup of coffee. Informal meetings may be held in a coffeehouse.

Lunch is the main meal of the day. Dinner is small and is served late.

The communal approach is followed in some restaurants, where diners share several dishes.

The head-nodding gestures indicating yes and no can be confusing because they are traditionally reversed in Greece. Unfortunately, many Greeks have taken to the American method, and so it is hard to know what is meant. Don't assume that you do.

A smile can mean anger as well as pleasure.

Don't give business gifts at the first meeting. Don't give token gifts merely to display your company logo.

THE INDIAN GAME

India is home to a very ancient civilization. Much like China, it has had a rich culture founded on an inherent system of beliefs. There are some similarities between the ancient Chinese and Indian cultures, but there are also important differences. Present-day India must be understood in context with its religious beliefs. Hinduism, followed by 88 percent of the population, is central to 800 million Hindu lives. Let's look at the governing principles for India by summarizing Indian religious beliefs.

The Indian perception of reality is quite mystical. Spirit is the true nature of reality. Matter exists as a result of spirit; it has no absolute existence on its own. The physical world exists solely as a medium in which the soul can improve itself and attain higher levels, eventually attaining oneness with God through absorption into God. The use of the term *God* may be too strong a suggestion of a separate God, as in the Jewish or Moslem sense of the word. Indians do believe that the essence of a God-reality is personified in Lord Krishna, but he is an emanation of the divine nature in the same way that our souls take on human form to become part of the physical world.

The goal of human existence is liberation from suffering on earth. Suffering is caused by metaphysical ignorance or by not understanding the true spiritual nature of one's existence. Through an extensive series of reincarnated lives, the soul gains greater knowledge until finally it achieves the necessary knowledge of selflessness and is absorbed into the primordial oneness. The law of Karma directs each successive life on earth. What you do, or do not do, in one life is accounted for in the next. One can progress as a result of actions, but one can also regress. The outward, physical evidence of a soul's level of advancement is the caste into which it is born.

Castes represent a hierarchical arrangement of society, very similar to the rigid class systems of tribal and collective societies. Originally there were four castes, and those who are below them are the outcasts, or untouchables. Through the centuries, many subcastes were recognized. The original four castes are interesting in that they parallel the Confucian system of a four-class society. Indians assumed that those who were the wealthiest and most powerful had more highly developed souls and that their good Karma caused their exalted status. People did not question their place in society. It was determined by the law of Karma.

Liberation from suffering is possible at any level through the practice of yoga, in which the spirit learns its true nature. Lord Krishna guides and intercedes, allowing release by his grace. There is a belief in perfectibility, but its focus is on improvement of the soul and not improvement of one's physical condition. This is why Indian culture devalues physical life. One cannot change one's physical condition—only one's spiritual condition. Spiritual concerns are more important than one's daily work. People—in terms of their souls—are more important than money. Power and authority are accepted as a privileged person's right.

The caste system has been legally abolished, but it is so much a part of the Indian belief system that inequality is rarely challenged. Women, except in the highest caste, have had no power. They are legally equal, and if they choose to enter business, they are allowed to compete. Yet many women do not choose to work in business.

Indian culture is a blend of tribal and collective influences. The extended family is the most important unit of survival. This can be a very large group, bordering on a collective. A strong sense of separateness in the tribal cultures, resulting in a strong power hierarchy, is somewhat muted in India. There is a sense of oneness and long-term perspective that is more a part of the holistic, collective communities. In either case, one's identity is formed relative to the group. An appropriate term for a unit of the social structure is *tribal collective*. Relative status is important, especially with regard to age. Indians defer to elders. The oldest member of the extended family is its head.

Family structure figures prominently in Indian business. There are four types of private businesses: affiliates of multinational companies; so-called large houses, which are major companies each controlled by a family; smaller family-run businesses; and companies set up by a partnership of technical professionals. In the family-owned and family-operated companies, the head of the family is usually the head of the company. Decisions are made at this level.

The British dominated India for 200 years. During that time, they transferred their system of etiquette to the upper castes. Therefore, in dealings with top-ranking and professional Indians, English standards are appropriate (refer to the West European Game). One element—the use of time—raises some problems for Indians. Their perceptions result in a nonlinear, or cyclical, comprehension of time. The British system stresses punctuality, and this is right for business appointments. However, do not assume that this sense of punctuality extends to the maintenance of schedules or the development of plans. Long-term planning is difficult, resulting in much crisis management. Adherence to deadlines can be improved if the reason for the deadline is explained. Hands-on management is the best approach.

With this background, we can now develop the player portrait and the game plan for India.

INDIAN PLAYER PORTRAIT

What does he believe is a person's responsibility?
Contribution to the family group. Spiritual awareness.

What does he expect of others?
Mutual support from the group.

How does he interact with others?
Formal interaction is along British model. He tends to be more friendly and more interested in people.

What impresses him? What does he respect in another?
Knowledge and experience.

What is his attitude toward foreigners?
He needs to know where the foreigner fits into the social fabric. Once the person is identified relative to the group, he is not considered a threat.

Why is he in the game?
He works to live.

What is his main objective?
To do his work to benefit his family. He is passive to the law of Karma.

How does he define winning?
Win-win.

What is his business environment (physical and hierarchical)?
Space is at a premium. Status is conferred both by the staff you have working for you and by a private office. Business is hierarchical.

How does he conduct business?

He can be either direct or indirect. He wants information, but does not like to say no. Harmony between individuals is valued, but being emotional is acceptable. Communication is directed along hierarchical lines.

How does he learn?

Presentations should be visual as well as verbal. Content should be more concrete than abstract. Better-educated professionals are excellent analytical thinkers.

How does he give feedback?

Negative feedback is indirect. He does not like to say no, and will say, "I'll try," instead.

How does he make decisions?

Decisions are made at the top. Subjective feelings are more important than objective data.

What is his attitude toward time, schedules, plans, and change?

Time is nonlinear. Schedules are not always followed because planning may be lax. He appears adaptable to change because it happens so often. Plans must be adjusted to account for present conditions.

How does he approach problem solving?

Problems are embarrassing, negatives are minimized, and blame is not sought. Solutions are developed by a group approach.

The Indian Game Plan

The Indian attitude favors the personal over the commercial. It is always important in tribal and collective societies to be present, to meet face-to-face. This lessens an Indian's resistance to you and shows that you value the interaction. It is important to maintain contact with your Indian counterpart after you return home. Although Hindi is an official language, English is used in business. You need not translate your materials.

High-level businesspeople require some sort of reference before granting an appointment. It is important that an Indian know your status and the status of your company. The best references come from banks, embassies, or professionals with whom he is acquainted: the more personal the introduction, the better. Local representatives are very useful in scheduling appointments, but there is some hesitancy from public employees in working with agents. Corruption is often visible, and even the hint of corrupt activity should be avoided.

Choose your agent carefully. The agent can be useful in researching which government permits are necessary for you to do business in India. He can help maintain the complicated links between the public and private sectors. An agent is never a principal to a contract; he should be used primarily for marketing support and the services required in contract preparation and afterward. He should not be present at presentations or during negotiations.

Indians are by nature modest and humble. Matching that demeanor is the best tactic. Respect is shown by the use of good manners, as defined by the British model. Formality of dress is also an indication of respect. Don't be ostentatious in dress or accessories. Indians are not excessively materialistic and may be turned off if you appear so.

Submit to the Indian system of business. Do not try to speed things up by hint of a bribe or by demands and threats. If the deal involves a significant amount of money, the government may be involved, and dealing with the government takes time. Family-owned businesses move faster, but not as fast as American businesses. Don't expect results from the first meeting. The meeting is intended to open discussions. Additional meetings will be necessary.

Even though you have hired a local representative to keep contacts alive, you should visit occasionally to show personal interest in your Indian counterpart. Also keep in touch by fax; the mail system is not reliable.

Bargaining is not common in India. The price offered should be close to that of the final deal. There should be some room for movement, but don't expect extended price negotiations. Other issues may require negotiation. Be prepared to respond to requests for secondary concessions.

An Indian's pride usually derives from his education and occupation, which should be the focus for complimentary observations. Use academic titles when appropriate. Because Indians are not materialistic, the benefits of making the deal should appeal to a sense of group involvement. An Indian will be looking for business that benefits his company, especially if the company is one of the private, family-run businesses. Ultimately, this benefits your counterpart's tribal collective.

The issues of concern that should be addressed first are initial investment capital, overall price, reliability, service, and prompt delivery. Keep in mind that Indian companies are probably not looking for labor-saving devices, for their workforce is enormous. The government will not think highly of proposals that take away jobs.

Supplemental Data: India

A medium-firm handshake is the proper greeting for business. You may see people greeting each other with the *namaste* (\nah-mah-STAY\), which one does by placing the hands together as if in prayer, fingers pointing up, and bowing the head slightly.

Use the last name, along with *Mr.* It is not appropriate for a foreigner to use the term *sahib.*

Do not shake a woman's hand unless she offers it; men generally do not touch women in public. It is polite to refer to women as ladies.

A business card printed in English should be provided. It should include your title, academic degrees, and professional affiliations. This will help the Indian to position you in his universe.

Be punctual. Your host may not be.

Relationship is important, but the Indian will get down to business fairly quickly.

Accept any hospitality offered.

Social distance may be close, but touching is not common in conversation.

British manners prevail. Be subdued. Self-control is favored over impulsiveness. A quietly self-confident aura breeds trust and respect. However, one should be friendly and communicative.

Indians are tolerant of others. Be cautious in giving criticism. Indians take offense easily.

Use the right hand when passing papers and objects and when eating.

Keep shoes and feet on the floor.

Whistling is considered rude.

The mail is unreliable. Request meetings via fax or telex. Use a courier service if necessary.

Your first meeting should include the head of the company, who will probably make the final decision on your proposal. Always try to match the status of meeting participants. If you send your chief technical person, make your appointment with a technical person. Speak to the secretary of your targeted person to be sure you are contacting the right person at the appropriate level.

A business lunch is appropriate after an interest in your business has been established. It is acceptable to talk business over the meal.

Dinner invitations should be offered only after some sort of relationship has been established.

Entertaining is usually done in private clubs or in restaurants.

The guest of honor should be seated to the right of the host. There are no other seating formalities.

There is no toasting ritual. Your host may offer a toast in the British manner if he has spent time in England.

The Continental style of eating is used in most Westernized restaurants. The traditional manner of eating is by using the right hand and no utensils.

Hindus do not eat beef.

Gifts are a sign of friendship. They should be modest and reserved for later meetings.

There is a significant Moslem population, especially in the northern section of the country. Study the Arab world game for proper interaction with a Moslem. Be sure to use only your right hand; be considerate of Moslems who fast during the month of Ramadan; and remember that Moslems do not eat pork or drink alcohol.

THE ISRAELI GAME

Israel is perfectly suited as a model for our methodology of determining protocol. In 1890 an Austrian began the Zionist movement, encouraging Jews to return to their spiritual homeland in Palestine. Modern Israel was created in 1948, when the country claimed itself independent from British control. The nation is made up of immigrants from around the world. Although held together by a shared religion, Israel's inhabitants came from many cultural backgrounds. Only 60 percent of the population is native to Israel. Business practices may emulate the North American, Russian, European, or Mediterranean type. To play the game, you must keep in mind exactly who the other players are.

Jews are usually divided into two ethnic heritages. Sephardic Jews come from the western Mediterranean area, North Africa, and the Middle East. Ashkenazic Jews come from eastern Europe. Ashkenazic Jews are dominant in politics and religion; Sephardic Jews are dominant in government and business.

In terms of global protocol, Ashkenazic Jews tend to show strong pluralist tendencies; Sephardic Jews are tribal. The Jewish religion promotes, or rather, reflects, a tribal perception. Even though some Ashkenazic Jews come from strong pluralist countries such as Germany and the Netherlands, their culture has always maintained the tribal hierarchy. Protocol and etiquette support the needs of the family over the needs of the individual.

About 50 percent of the Jews in Israel are Orthodox Jews. It is interesting to note that they share many customs with Moslems. Many strict laws adhere about eating, general behavior, interaction between men and women, and the details of appearance.

It is difficult to develop a player portrait that applies in general to an Israeli businessperson. The approach in Israel would be to study general tribal culture, the Arab world game, the Central and East European game, and the West European game. Such study will cover the range of cultural diversity in Israel.

The game plan for a Sephardic contact is similar to that of the Arab world game plan: Things happen slowly. There is not much regard for time. People and their problems and concerns are more important than striking a deal. It will take many meetings to complete a deal. Spatial attitude in Israel is also similar to that in the Arab world: People stand close together and touch to emphasize a point. Israelis put a high regard on hosting, as do Arabs. Coffee is served at the end of a business meeting, as in Moslem countries. In Israel, control of the body in posture and gestures is similar to that in the Arab world.

The game plan for Ashkenazic contacts is more European in style. Punctuality is important. Formality and reserve are noted. People tend to get down to business faster. But don't disregard the tribal tendencies of Ashkenazim. They still maintain strong hierarchical structure and must come to trust a person before doing business.

The major differences in business customs between Israel and other Middle Eastern countries are the following.

- Israel has a democratic and egalitarian culture that values competition.
- The Israeli negotiating style is much more confrontational. Israelis love to argue and debate.
- Women are legally equal in status and even serve in the military. However, men still dominate, as in all tribal societies.
- The security of the state is taken into consideration when Israelis make major decisions.
- The holy days are Friday and Saturday each week. Judaism and Islam both use a lunar calendar. Israelis are used to thinking in 28-day months.
- Use engraved business cards. Print them in both English and Hebrew (Arabic, if you are visiting an Israeli Arab).
- Businesswomen should not extend their hand to greet an Orthodox Jewish male. The latter's religion has laws against touching women. A woman should also never hand something directly to an Orthodox male, but should put it next to him so he can pick it up. Orthodox Jews can usually be identified by their yarmulke, or skullcap. Half of Israel's Jews are considered secular and do not observe these rituals.
- The common greeting is to shake hands and address the person using *Mr.* plus the surname. *Shalom*, which means *peace*, is said both when greeting and when leaving.
- Conservative business suits are appropriate, and in general, modest dress is required.
- The Continental style of eating is most widely used.
- Pointing at someone with the index finger is rude, as in most of the world beyond America.

THE AFRICAN GAME

The African continent is amazingly diverse. One can choose to play the game on a microethnic scale, which means selecting one of hundreds of unique cultures, or one can play the game on a macroethnic scale. In both cases the dominant cultural type is tribal. The original black African cultures are all strongly tribal. Cultural influences from Arab invasions in the north and European colonization everywhere else have modified African religious beliefs and customs somewhat, but the governing principle is still tribal.

Generally speaking, the African continent can be divided in half, with Moslem influences in the northern part and Christianity prevalent in the south. In the center, there is a more or less equal representation of Islam, Christianity, and animism. Whites in Africa tend to follow ethnic patterns. The Dutch, Germans, and British who colonized South Africa are largely pluralist, whereas the Portuguese are more tribal.

The extended family is the root of society. Individuals' needs are secondary to the needs of the group. Sharing and cooperation are necessary to survival. Group harmony and avoidance of criticism are important. These are all strong tribal traits.

Because there is such variety of local customs among the historically isolated tribes of Africa, the methodology outlined in this book is useful for devising strategy for the particular location you may be visiting. Some background research will be necessary to determine local influences. It is safe to say that if you observe tribal protocol in the general sense, you should do fine. Always know the ethnic background of the individual with whom you will be meeting in order to prepare properly.

6

Bending the Rules: Women as Players

Throughout the previous chapters one message has been clear: business is a man's game in most of the world. But that doesn't mean that the game excludes women. It just means that the game is more challenging for a businesswoman because there are more obstacles to overcome. This chapter examines those obstacles and develops an alternative game plan. Please note that the chapter should be read not only by women but also by men who may be deciding whether to send a woman to a foreign country as the company's representative and by men who may be traveling with female team members.

THE THIRD SEX

In the previous chapters very little was mentioned about protocol concerning women in other countries, although the point was made that interaction between men and women, especially in tribal and collective cultures, is strictly regulated by society. The reason for the lack of attention to businesswomen is as follows: When an American businessman prepares to play the game on someone else's turf and humbles himself by accepting the rules of protocol that apply to that person's turf, this is good strategy. When a businesswoman does the same, she is making a grave tactical error, for the rules are different for women.

Most women in positions of responsibility are found in pluralist cultures. Most businesswomen who travel abroad representing their companies are from pluralist cultures. Most are from the United States. Why? Because pluralist cultures do not assign individuals rigid functional roles within society. Pluralist women are not bound by roles. There are traditional stereotypes, but there are no cultural rules that if broken will threaten the smallest unit of survival, because the smallest unit of survival in a pluralist culture is the individual. We are not talking about threatening a man's ego; we are talking about a threat to the structure of society.

In pluralist culture, identity is formed from within. One does not find identity relative to the tribe or the collective, in which family and functional roles are so important to the social fabric. The pluralist abides by social conventions by consensus. When a consensus decision changes, the rules change. This is what happened with the women's movement in the 1960s and 1970s, during which time the rules of tribal and collective cultures did not change. The cultures may have gained more awareness of the abilities of women—or at least Western women—but the modification of the roles of women in those cultures would have completely altered the way those entire cultures are organized. Because social organization is a reflection of fundamental beliefs, such alteration would have seriously threatened the existence of those cultures. It was not an issue of women's working, but an issue of power.

Power hierarchies are clearly defined and necessary in tribal and collective cultures. Their structure is important to the protection and welfare of the group. Those in power are not likely to relinquish power, turning the social structure upside down to see if that way works just as well. There is too much at risk.

Far more significantly, the power structure is usually maintained by religious institutions. In the case of Islam, the male power structure is the rule of religious law. Religious laws concerning women may be interpreted less harshly in some Arab countries, but religious doctrine clearly states both that men and women are different and that God has given men the power of leadership.

In all of the collective societies that are founded on the teachings of Confucius, the argument is similar. By doctrine, women are to be kept separate from men. They are not equal and they cannot share power in the social hierarchy.

The Roman Catholic Church, with its own internal hierarchical order, acts as a model for social and tribal hierarchy. The church clearly supports the male-dominant, patristic model, in which men make rules that directly affect women's actions and decisions. By contrast, the Druids—the Celtic religious leaders who were precursors of pluralistic culture—did not exclude women from power. Women had equal rights and equal opportunity to hold power in the form of property ownership and direct leadership.

The women who have risen to positions of power in tribal and collective societies, such as Indira Gandhi, Benazir Bhutto, and Isabela Perón, have generally done so as symbolic representatives of their family. In strongly class conscious and tribal cultures, the power of the family is what is important—not the power of the individual. When the husband or father is assassinated, power can still be associated with a close female relative, such as a wife or daughter. It is far more difficult, if not impossible, for a woman with no powerful family name to rise to a level of great power in these cultures.

Only in a secular, pluralist society is there no foundation to support separate and unequal roles—and especially power sharing—between male and female. Male-dominant power structures are merely traditional—and usually borrowed from ancestral tribal structures. Immigrants from tribal cultures to pluralist cultures, such as the United States, tend to bring their tribal power structure with them. But the society at large does not have a motive to support that power structure. Women from tribal or collective ancestry find accepting power or gaining power within their families more difficult than do women from purely pluralist backgrounds.

A tribal woman who enters business on a management level would have to step outside the rules of her culture. She would have to behave differently from the behavior assigned to her culturally defined role. When she does so, her identity relative to the group is changed. She no longer acts like a woman in that society, yet she is not a man. She is something else: a third sex.

In the same way, Western businesswomen are perceived to be a third sex. They are not held to the strict limits that the foreign culture imposes on its own women. Foreign men are not so threatened by doing business with a Western businesswoman because the latter's nonadherence to his culture's rules does not destabilize the structure of his society. She will simply go home once the business is done. He is far more threatened to see the women of his own country demanding entry into positions of power.

A Western businesswoman must, in fact, *accentuate the differences* between herself and women of the foreign culture. If she is perceived to be similar, she will be treated like women within the culture are treated. She will not be taken seriously, and the man will take offense from the company's choice of representative. She must also take care not to behave as a man does. There is a cultural identity for men as well as women. A woman acting like a man will be considered a phony.

Thus foreign businesswomen must hurdle a tremendous obstacle: not only does the culture gap have to be bridged, but the relative gender association must be defined. A clear definition of one's gender and its associated protocol is necessary to success. You will recall that, especially in collective societies, a person's status or position in the social structure dictates protocol. Relative status must be defined even before introductions can take place. Relative rank must be understood so that the proper deferential behavior can be determined.

It is a woman's responsibility to define herself in a way that will result in the treatment she requires in order to accomplish her objectives. She is playing a game with a common objective, but the game cards are stacked against her. What is required for her to have an equal chance of winning is to *bend the rules*. These are the new rules that a woman will play by and from which she will develop her own game plan. What is the purpose of these rules? To give the game a structure that enables one to win.

BENDING THE RULES

Always remember that the definitive rules of the game, that is, the rules that define the game of global business, never change. They are as follows:
- Never try to become like them.
- Never judge another culture as being better or worse than your own.
- Never forget the human element in business.

The rules should not be changed, but enhanced.
- Never try to become like them: Separate yourself from the cultural stereotype in operation; become the third sex.
- Never judge a culture: Recognize that all people have a culture-based need that must be satisfied, such as individual expression and survival or tribal or collective security.
- Never forget the human element in business: Opponents or teammates will respond to one another personally; therefore, project self-confidence.

The strategic rules are the ones we can bend without changing the nature of the game. The original strategic rules—along with their modification—are the following.

Old rule: Go to their office first.
New rule: Stake out neutral ground.

Going to their office meant operating by their rules, speaking their language, and, in general, making them comfortable. A woman's mere presence makes these impossible. The best a woman can hope for is to meet on neutral ground by defining the rules that will make both participants comfortable.

Old rule: Approach as a friend, not as a stranger.
New rule: Define a friendship of the third kind.

This rule minimizes distrust and establishes a woman's credibility. The man will naturally distrust the businesswoman's intentions, sincerity, authority, and capabilities. A third-party referral can help to overcome all these obstacles before an appointment will be made.

Old rule: Humble yourself.
New rule: Lay down your arms, but hold your shield.

To show humility is to accept the protocol of the opponent's culture. Unfortunately, this usually works against a woman, who must show respect for the culture but submit only to power protocol—not to social protocol.

Old rule: Concede turf.

New rule: Define and control the turf; set limits.

A businesswoman must be prepared to give up something. She must be very certain that she is not assumed to be synonymous with the assets of her company.

Old rule: Show your counterpart that you are at the same level of self-worth.

New rule: Show your counterpart that you share the same degree of self-worth.

A foreign businessman will feel slighted if he does not meet a person of authority, someone of equal standing to himself. A woman must show she is the man's equal.

Old rule: Make his welfare your purpose.

New rule: Give him a reason to play the game your way.

Show him how he will gain personally in a way that is important in his culture. Overcome his objections to dealing with a female before he objects.

We will apply these rules for all cultures when we develop a game plan. Before we do so, it is necessary to develop an extended player portrait for each culture. Let's expand the player portraits to include two more items of interest: How does the player perceive women in his own culture? and How does he perceive Western businesswomen?

TRIBAL PLAYER PORTRAIT—SUPPLEMENTAL

How does he perceive women in his own culture?

The woman has a specific purpose within the tribe. The strong male power hierarchy protects the women of the tribe, but by doing so, requires the women to take subservient and domestic roles.

How does he perceive Western businesswomen?

A U.S. businesswoman is outside the tribe. She is not protected, nor is she bound by the rules of the tribe. She is fair game, until she takes control and sets limits.

COLLECTIVE PLAYER PORTRAIT—SUPPLEMENTAL

How does he perceive women in his own culture?

Each person, including a woman, has a specific function within the collective. Historical doctrines have taught that men and women are different and must be separated. Men are dominant, and women are subservient.

How does he perceive Western businesswomen?

U.S. businesswomen are outside the collective. They are unknown. They do not meet the definition of women in his culture. He does not know where to position her in social rank and role, and therefore he does not know how to behave in her presence. He is confused and uncomfortable in her presence.

PLURALIST PLAYER PORTRAIT—SUPPLEMENTAL

How does he perceive women in his own culture?

Women are equal, but they are very different from men. Therefore, he is skeptical of her abilities.

How does he perceive Western businesswomen?

The United States is a pluralist culture. Men in other pluralist cultures, as well as in the United States, accept her but perceive her to be more aggressive than other women in their society. If she does not show great self-confidence, they will be confused and tend to associate her with the stereotypical role of a female in their society.

With this information, we are now ready to develop a game plan for female players in global business.

The Game Plan for Western Businesswomen

Stake out neutral ground. Even though you are in his territory, he will not feel comfortable with you because the territory no longer defines the rules of encounter. For instance, normally, two people who are in Spain will observe the protocol of Spain. But his protocol does not account for your being a woman. Thus, the first order of business is to put your male counterpart at ease. You do this by the following tactics.

- Speak his language.
- Define the appropriate protocol.
- Dress appropriately.

Speak his language means two things. First, it means literally to speak his language if at all possible. You may have to put more effort into the relationship than your male colleagues would. Speaking the language will make personal interaction more comfortable and will remove a barrier that surely exists. Second, it means to discuss subjects in which men of his culture are likely to be interested. Relationship building is important in almost all cultures. It is especially awkward between men and women of different cultures. Getting to know someone requires conversation. What you discuss can brand you as someone men enjoy being with or someone with whom they have nothing in common. The most universal language among men is sports. Learn about the country's most popular sports and the local teams, and become able to discuss them in detail, giving informed opinions as well as asking intelligent questions.

You define the appropriate protocol by using it. You are quick to offer your hand and give a *firm* handshake. You introduce yourself by your title, whether professional or corporate, not using *Miss* or *Ms.* You speak confidently as you introduce the members of your team, if you are the team leader, or you defer to the leader if you are not. You allow senior participants to go through doors ahead of you, and you explain to those of another culture, such as the Japanese, why you would like them to go ahead of you. Your reason should always be to show respect or to defer to power. You should know the difference between social protocol and power protocol and use social protocol sparingly on social business occasions. When confusion occurs, you should be the one to put others at ease by graciously explaining to them the way businessmen and businesswomen interact in America.

Dressing appropriately as a representative of your company should show power, achievement, and sensitivity to local laws, customs, and styles. Be sure not to dress the way the women who work in the company you are visiting. Do some research. Foreign women in business often have uniform-type restrictions on clothing. Dress conservatively, yet elegantly. Avoid feminine details, for it causes distraction and confusion. *Simplicity* should be the key word. Check local colors to be sure you are not dressing in a color designated for only the queen to wear, and so on. Do not dress like a man, but do not emphasize your female body.

The greatest visible detractor from a woman's professional appearance is her handbag. Men do not understand why women need them, and so handbags become points of male/female miscommunication. A woman should carry a briefcase or portfolio. It is preferable to use a flat clutch bag that can be slipped into the briefcase and taken out to go to lunch when the briefcase may be left behind. Bring only essentials. If a handbag is carried, never place it on a conference table, desk, or dining table. Place it under your chair.

Define a friendship of the "third kind." A third-party introduction is important, but even more so when a woman is the sole representative or the leader of a team. An agent will first represent the company to the targeted organization. Once those two agree to a meeting, the agent will pave the way for the initial contact by the female businessperson. Preparation is important to lessen the men's sense of insecurity and overcome initial objections. Your agent or your communications must accomplish the following.

- Communicate the purpose, nature, and benefit of your proposal.
- Inform the targeted company of the identity of the person who will represent the American company, along with that person's position and qualifications. This will make it clear that the person will be a woman.
- Detail what her responsibilities are; emphasize her relative power in the company.
- Clearly define her authority in negotiations. Represent that authority as given her by a male superior or a board of directors.

The presence of a woman on the negotiating team might actually be a plus for your company. Some cultures are fascinated by this unusual life form and look forward to the novelty of actually meeting a member of the third sex.

Relationship building is very important in tribal and collective cultures. In these more diffuse cultures, your company may benefit from sending a woman because women are sometimes more tolerant of, and better at having to take the time to get to know someone. However, the route to friendship will not be the same as that taken by two men. Businesswomen should avoid the standard get-together at a bar after work or club-hopping after dinner. They probably won't be invited anyway, but they should not offer such invitations, knowing that they are standard custom. She will have to find other means, such as dinner invitations that involve other women or dignitaries from her embassy. Women should look for alternatives, but not neglect this aspect of business just because of the inherent limitations.

When discussions do not involve business, a woman should not discuss family or domestic issues that the tribal or collective man might not feel proper discussing with a woman of another culture. To avoid possible stereotyping, a woman can turn to subjects that *he* finds interesting, such as history, culture, and sports. A woman should show her intellect and knowledge of his culture, and not her expected knowledge of domestic affairs. She should accentuate the differences between herself and the women that he commonly encounters. This is a woman's only chance to establish a working relationship with him, one in which he will treat her with respect.

Lay down your arms, but hold your shield. A Western man must learn to humble himself, but a woman is assumed to be humble. Do not defer to your host in any way that shows subservience. At the same time, do not appear too aloof or superior. Treat your host as an equal, or else he will not respect you. Show respect and humility verbally, but never through body language.

In previous chapters, the use of time has been shown to have a humbling effect on Americans who are eager to accomplish business. The less your counterpart thinks of you, the longer he will make you wait. He may have made the appointment grudgingly, or you may have been passed off to a lower-level manager who does not want the interview. In any case, you will be kept waiting. Be persistent. Persistence is not expected of a woman. Do not accept it as an insult. Minimize its importance by expecting it. Most important, always be precisely on time yourself.

Do not confuse humility and weakness. Always appear self-confident through use of:
- good posture.
- a powerful visual image (conservative, elegant styling with subdued color and accessories).
- a strong and well-modulated voice (not loud, yet confident and unemotional).
- formal language appropriate to the culture (e.g., symbolic visual associations for collective listeners, precise technical communication for pluralist audiences, and concrete or flowery speech, depending on the tribal culture).

Define and control the turf; set limits. You must be prepared to make concessions, but you also must bargain with more intensity than a man. Do not give in easily or you will lose respect.

Defining the turf means keeping the focus of conversation on the business topic at hand. This is especially important in Latin American societies. You are not a negotiable asset of your company. All negotiations should take place separate from entertainment or relationship building. Negotiate only at an office. Stay focused and keep your counterpart focused.

Show your counterpart that you are at the same level of self-worth. All business cultures use some form of hierarchy, and it is important to acknowledge a man's position within his hierarchy because he derives considerable self-esteem from his position. When a meeting is being planned between companies, it is good practice to match the authority level of the people who will be meeting. Senior executive should meet senior executive, technical chief should meet technical chief, and so forth. When a woman is sent, sometimes a man who is not accustomed to dealing with Western businesswomen will feel slighted, for he assumes that she is a low-ranking employee. You must communicate both before the meeting and during the meeting that you are his equal. This can be done by:

- communicating rank and level of authority.
- detailing your technical capabilities and experience.
- showing detailed knowledge of the other company.
- demonstrating knowledge of the culture.
- remaining focused while appearing personable.
- maintaining an aura of self-confidence.
- putting others at ease.

Give him a reason to play the game your way. In order for him to accept the game on your terms,

- he must respect your intelligence and capabilities.
- he must believe you have authority.
- he must be impressed immediately by your presentation.
- you must not present a problem to him by virtue of being female. (This includes not being a distraction for him, not provoking peer or family pressure, and not being concerned about possible illegal behavior on your part.)

THE POWER OF THE THIRD SEX

Knowledge is power. It also can be stated that confusion is power, that is, when your opponent is the one who is confused. When a foreign businessman encounters a Western businesswoman, there is usually an initial period of confusion and uncertainty on the part of the man. He is searching his memory banks for clues as to how to behave with this female person. He may be trying to assign you to a social stratum that does not exist. During his brief period of confusion, the woman, who is not confused, has the upper hand. In that moment of time, she has the power to define the terms of their future business relationship.

Depending on the situation, a woman may be able to establish rules of interaction that the man previously would not have known to use. She may be able to put the German engineer at ease and discuss technology as though they were sharing a joke. She might enable a Japanese to put aside his formality and use her as a sounding board for problems he is having in the assembly of a new product. French draftsmen may confide in her regarding middle-level managers who are alienating the labor force. All these feats have come to pass.

It is quite possible that a woman might be the best industrial spy there is—and perhaps the best negotiator. Because she is an unknown, her allegiances are also not well understood. Men tend to confide in women before they confide in men, especially if feelings are involved. They may simply be underestimating her importance. Therefore, assuming that the information may be of no consequence to her, a man may answer her questions truthfully; the truth might have been withheld from a male employee of a competing company.

Women tend to have the ability to perceive beyond the spoken word. They are more likely to pick up on the body language, voice inflections, and overall attitudes of other meeting participants. We have learned that this can be very valuable information in many cross-cultural meetings.

Creating entirely new rules of conduct for a man in another culture can be done slowly as a process of education. For instance, the Japanese will never ask a potentially embarrassing question. The businesswoman must ask the unasked questions for them: "You might be wondering whether it is unusual for a woman to be given so much authority to act for her company in America." Then she must answer the question for them. This is a way for the businesswoman to tell them what she wants them to know and what her expectations are.

She also has the power to help them see her in terms they can understand. In a collective culture, a businesswoman may take on the identity of her company. This is to her benefit when entertaining. It depersonalizes the invitation, which might have made the men uncomfortable coming directly from her. She might say, "My company would like you to be its guest for dinner tonight." She settles the bill offstage and plays the part of "her company."

There is power in being able to define oneself for someone else. It is the advantage one gains not by mere acceptance of the existing rules but by the creation of entirely new rules that govern the game.

KEY POINTS

- Men in other cultures view American businesswomen as being very different from the women in their own culture. They consider American businesswomen a third sex.
- It is to a woman's advantage to accentuate the differences between herself and the women of the culture.
  - She should separate herself from cultural stereotypes of women.
  - She should define herself through her personal image.
  - She should use business protocol, not social protocol.
  - She should define a strict business relationship and set limits.
  - She should speak his language and talk about what is important to him.
  - She should dress for business.
- Western businesswomen can gain an advantage over Western businessmen when doing business in cultures that require relationship building, but only if they define themselves as members of the third sex.

7

Conflicting Rules: Ethics and Integrity

Our fundamental beliefs shape our values. What we value is what is important for us to maintain and protect. Anything else is negotiable. Outside our value system, we can let things slide. As we have seen, beliefs and values are not the same for all cultures. Each culture develops a value system that helps to uphold fundamental beliefs. Each person's behavior is measured by that value system. Anyone acting against that value system is a threat to the culture and may be branded as a criminal.

In the previous chapters, we discovered cultural behavior that is very different from our own in America. Some rules of protocol actually contradict the protocol that Western culture considers appropriate to the needs of society and human interaction. For instance, the concept of saving face can lead one to choose lying over telling the truth. It is a fundamental value of American culture that one should not lie. For Americans, that value—truth—takes precedence over offending someone. Yet in other cultures, saving face is so critical to the stability and functioning of the culture that it takes precedence over telling the truth. This raises an interesting question for American courts of law when witnesses from such a culture are asked to testify under oath. What techniques must an attorney use to elicit a truthful response without compromising the witness's values?

When basic value systems come into conflict, the businessperson sees that something is "wrong." The opponent's behavior is perceived to be unfair, dishonest, or even illegal. These are all value judgments that are made with respect to the businessperson's culture. Whether or not the person is aware of it, those judgments are not universal.

Americans value the notion of fair play. It implies that everyone has equal opportunity to compete and to win. The Chinese, as an example, do not highly value the notion of fair play. They value advantage, deception, and cunning. Putting an opponent at a disadvantage is commendable. The Chinese player gains an advantage over the American player by some trickery or manipulation, and the American cries, "Unfair!" The Chinese reply, "So what?"

WHEN IS A GIFT NOT A GIFT?

You now know that the first rule of global business is never to judge another culture, but this presents a dilemma: Must we sacrifice our values to play by others' rules? What effect will this have on us and on our culture if we do? The U.S. government has said that we shall play by *our* rules no matter what. This is eloquently stated in the Foreign Corrupt Business Practices Act of 1977, a law that was enacted subsequent to a bribery scandal involving a major U.S. aircraft manufacturer. The U.S. government now requires Americans and American companies doing business outside the United States to refrain from paying bribes to any foreign government, company, or individual. This makes sense when U.S. companies are competing for the same markets abroad, virtually extending the American playing field beyond its natural borders. But when an American company must compete with companies from other countries and cultures, the American company becomes a player with serious limitations on the ability to compete.

Recently, there has been much debate in an attempt to clarify what constitutes a gift and what makes a gift a bribe. The government and individual companies have established policies concerning the monetary value of gifts and appropriate forms of entertainment proper for ethical business purposes. The U.S. businessperson is advised to check company policy before developing a game plan related to gifts and entertainment.

So, when is a gift not a gift? The answer: When it is a bribe. In our culture, a bribe is a gift given with strings attached. When you give someone an expensive gold watch in appreciation for some great kindness, this is a gift. When you give someone an expensive watch with the expectation that he will make your company his primary supplier, this is a bribe. These definitions are based on the idea that a gift is something freely given to express appreciation of another person. It carries no burden of obligation.

By this definition of a bribe, all gifts are bribes in tribal and collective cultures. Reciprocity and obligation are operating principles in these societies. Giving and receiving must go both ways, or else their values will be out of balance and harmony will be broken. Sharing and mutual respect are fundamental values. To give someone a gift or to extend hospitality *requires* something in return. Gifts are exchanged among friends. Business is done among friends. Friends take care of each other. This is why a friendly relationship is so important to doing business in these cultures. With friendship comes obligation.

Westerners are quick to vilify businessmen of other cultures who exclude them from competition and give contracts to their less competent friends. But foreign businessmen are equally incensed by the American who accepts lavish hospitality and gifts, who socializes easily with them and calls them by their first name, and who then rewards a major contract to someone else. This leaves many non-Western businessmen asking what they have to do to get through to these people. The reply is that we are open to the best product at the best price as soon as possible—friend or no friend. These are the values we use to award contracts; we do not use friendship and obligation. Who is right?

FRIENDS, FAMILY, AND EVERYBODY ELSE

Tribal culture is dedicated to the survival and welfare of the extended family. The strength of this type of culture derives from the motivating force of family cohesion, status, and prosperity. It is the individual's purpose in life to protect and contribute to the strength of his family. Similarly, collective cultures must at all costs perpetuate the collective unit. Each member of the group is devoted to the well-being, security, and harmony of the collective group. Whatever strengthens the tribe or collective is good. Whatever methods secure the future of the tribe or collective are good. Doing business with family and friends is the best way to ensure that all are motivated by the good of the tribe or collective. If one can control business in such a way that guarantees that a company will do business only with friends and relatives, all the better.

Because monopolies and cartels are consistent with the tribal and collective social structures, monopolies and cartels are considered to be useful, beneficial, and secure business structures. To Americans, they are restrictive and exclusive and therefore unfair. Group cultures disagree, and they don't care about your opinion either. If you are outside the group, you will not be motivated by their objective of group security. If you are outside the group, either you are of no consequence to tribal societies or you simply don't exist in the minds of collective peoples.

When people from these cultures do find it necessary to go outside the group for whatever reason, but have not taken you in as a friend, anything can happen. Outside the group they are not constrained by the morality required by the group. This is a danger zone, where the cultural boundaries of ethical behavior can become blurred.

To your counterpart, cultural ethics do not apply. Is he operating according to the ethics of his culture, which are different from yours, or is he acting outside the boundaries of his culture's value system?

When an American bank sent former beauty queens as its representatives to a Latin American country and paid them to invite prospective clients to their hotel rooms for the night, it did so hoping that the clients would later take out loans with the bank. Did the bank act unethically, or did it use cultural knowledge strategically? Even though that type of behavior is recognized and accepted in Latin culture, it does not mean that it meets the Latin criteria for ethical behavior. It is simply going on "outside the tribe." Americans should not assume that encouraging or participating in such behavior is in any way morally ethical within either culture.

The best approach for staying on track is to understand the values of the country in which you will find yourself, so that you can determine when your counterpart is aware that he is acting unethically, when he believes he is not, and when it doesn't matter to him. Then, if you find yourself outside the tribe and approaching the danger zone, you will be better prepared to judge when prospective business should be abandoned.

IF IT LOOKS FISHY, CHECK FOR AN ODOR

American companies have a great deal of expertise in writing contracts. U.S. corporate legal staffs are legend in most of the world for writing exhaustive and precise contract language. We have developed standard methods for achieving complex goals, and we have developed complex agreements for achieving standard goals. American business lawyers by now should have seen it all. That is why many financial and other business institutions have corporate antennae that go up when unusual language or mechanics are written in to what should be a straightforward agreement.

What most financial institutions are trying to guard against are money-laundering schemes, especially those involving drug money. The U.S. government is constantly on the lookout for such involvement. Counter trade agreements also get a great deal of attention, with corporate attorneys making certain that no laws are being compromised. Western businesspeople must be attuned to the possibility of their dealings being used for unethical and hidden purposes.

However, with the opening of the Central and East European nations to free market economies, a new problem exists for America's corporate lawyers. Many proposed contracts come back with wording and procedures that are unfamiliar or unintelligible. Is something shady afoot, or do these people simply not know what they are doing? Sometimes it is the former, but most often it is the latter. Management skills in the former Soviet bloc countries are seriously lacking. Standard business procedures are unknown. Legal standards are even more obscure, for the commercial codes of most of these countries are still evolving. There is the potential for corruption in such a climate. Usually, however, the new businesspeople know what they want to accomplish; they just don't know the mechanism or procedure for accomplishing it. They may know just enough legal or financial lingo to make others think they know what they are talking about. Western professionals must take extra time to identify true intent, and not assume that the contract was intended verbatim.

Sometimes an apparently shady business transaction can be used to quietly right a wrong. One U.S. bank finally untangled a web of legal language to reveal that an East European entity that had years before hidden a large sum of money outside the country was trying to bring the money back into the country for investment in the national economy. There was no law against bringing money into the country, so the bank wondered why the terms made the matter so difficult and complex. The party was merely trying to avoid being questioned as to where the money came from originally. In effect, the intent was to right a wrong—quietly.

THE PRICE OF INTEGRITY: WHO PAYS?

There are many cultures, especially those that promote lineage as a prerequisite for power and prestige, in which racial discrimination is as natural as the social order. Such nations have historically excluded outsiders. Racial purity meant tribal and national strength and stability. Those of outsider races were generally given status at the bottom of the social ladder.

In the United States, racial integration is a complex problem. However, our pluralist culture generally promotes the equality of the individual, regardless of race, and this is the law under which we operate in the United States.

One important rule of protocol in all cultures is to match levels of power, or status, among individuals who are establishing a business relationship. Top executives meet with top executives. Middle managers meet with middle managers. In some cultures, not only rank must be matched but social status as well.

In many Asian and Latin American countries, color and race denote social status. In those countries, an executive may enjoy high corporate standing but have low social standing. This presents confusion for the foreign executive.

Top U.S. managers must be well educated about the cultural behavior and attitudes of prospective business clients or partners. They should use this strategic information to develop the best presentation, negotiating strategy, and team. They may feel compelled to select team members based not on the latters' expertise but on their cultural or racial compatibility. Within their own culture such managers would never make such a decision based on race, but they are unclear with respect to the effect that the presence of a minority will have on the success of any proposed business.

When making a biased decision, a manager not only sacrifices his own integrity but also restricts an employee's ability to do the job. In many multinational corporations, advancement is contingent on overseas experience. Restricting minority employees from gaining such experience limits their ability to advance within the company, for their potential success within the company—and in their career in general—is no longer dependent on their capabilities but on their racial compatibility. This chain of events applies not only to, say, African-Americans but also to Jews, Arabs, Hispanics, and any other national, religious, or racial affiliation that is deemed culturally inferior and therefore incompatible.

A significantly large group of individuals that biased behavior adversely affects is businesswomen. American management may deny a female executive or professional a position on a cross-cultural negotiating team for fear that the other team will take offense or feel awkward by the presence of a woman. We have seen in Chapter 6 that such need not be the case and that a woman can actually be an advantage on a negotiating team.

When a manager neglects to act with integrity in the decision-making process, then that manager's conscience may suffer, but the person who pays the price is the player who's been benched. It is not easy to choose between one's conscience and the bottom line. However, there are ways to minimize misunderstandings between cultures in these cases. There are ways to ease incompatibilities, but the manager is faced with a choice between the more difficult path and the easy way out.

While you are preparing your game plan, decide not only what points of your proposal you are willing to compromise but also, which of your own values are open to compromise. At what point do you abandon a deal? Make sure that your judgments are always culturally based, and act from knowledge.

KEY POINTS

- Definitions of right and wrong behavior are not the same for all cultures.
- Fair play is not valued by all cultures.
- In tribal and collective cultures, friendship and gifts come with obligations.
- Tribal and collective cultures do not value equal opportunity; instead, they promote friends and family.
- Tribal and collective people may abandon cultural moral values outside the tribe or collective.

8

Bringing the Playing Field Home: Hosting International Visitors

To some people of the world, such as the Chinese and the Russians, a business trip to the United States constitutes a prestigious event. To others, it is an ordeal. Business travelers around the world vary in their acceptance of novelty. Even tourists require some familiarity after an extended stay. For the traveler who is not the adventurous sort and in addition does not speak English, a trip to the United States can be very tiring. Working in another culture causes stress and distractions. If you hope that your visitor will conduct productive business while in America, it is to your benefit to see that the person is well taken care of and that difficulties are minimized.

WHAT GAME ARE WE PLAYING?

So now you are playing on familiar territory. Now you have the advantage—or do you? Often when we are taken out of our element, our antennae go up. We must be more attuned to the situation. The very facts that the surroundings are unusual and that another language is being spoken prompt us to pay attention to small details that we might never notice at home. How often do you walk into work and think about how you will greet your secretary? When someone walks into your office, do you offer the person a chair? You probably just expect that the person will sit down. How many people do you refer to by nickname? We don't pay much attention to the customs of our own culture until we are asked to look at them through the eyes of a foreigner.

When that foreigner is someone who is important to your company, it would be wise to take a look at your place of work and your everyday behavior in light of the visitor's expectations and cultural needs. Each major culture type presents a list of basic needs. The Asian must never be criticized and always save face. The Arab must feel safe and in control and be able to fulfill certain religious requirements. The northern European must be able to accomplish goals without distraction or interference. Even when traveling, we each take with us our minimum cultural requirements. Are your visitor's needs likely to be met in your daily environment? Or is the routine at your office so different from his that he will feel his basic needs at risk?

What game are we playing? It's the same game—global business—but with one critical difference: *We are playing the game of global business while looking through a mirror.* Everything else is the same. You have an objective; the players are defined; you will need a game plan; and of course there are rules.

WHOSE RULES DO WE PLAY BY?

Whose rules do you want to play by? Yours, of course. It's much less work. But are you likely to win if you insist your rules be used? Let's assume you've already visited your host's country, you've studied his culture and protocol, and you've behaved according to his expectations to show respect and lower the barriers between your two cultures. The two of you have established some kind of relationship, or business would not have advanced this far. That relationship has been based on his comfort level of working with you within his culture. If he arrives at your offices to continue play and you change the rules, do you think he might reconsider whether he wants to play the game this way? How will you tell him that the rules have changed?

Once the rules of behavior change, the game has changed. You may have to start things all over again to establish trust, respect, and communication if you change the game. If your behavior changes, you have changed something about yourself that is important to your counterpart. Just because the playing field has changed, know that the players have not. This leads to an important rule of global business: If you have already started a game on one playing field, do not change the rules when moving to a new playing field with the same players.

OBJECTIVES OF THE GAME

As in any variation on the game, it is your objective that will dictate your actions. Whether you are continuing negotiation on a major contract or simply reciprocating hospitality, the reason for a visit by your counterpart will dictate your agenda and what kind of events you will need to plan. Objectives may be as follows.

- Your foreign counterpart may be visiting your plant before agreeing to a joint-venture agreement.

- Your counterpart may be coming to observe procedures at your plant to plan a training program.
- Your counterpart may wish to see how your product is made before placing a major purchase order.

Of course, the list can go on. The point here is to define the actual reason your playing partner is coming to your U.S. offices so that you can:

- Plan an agenda to accomplish your goals.
- Determine who will be on the home team.
- Revise your game plan for play on your playing field. The rules may not change, but their strategic application does.

The agenda is the path your game will take. This path could include a brief reception at your office followed by a plant tour. After the tour, you may meet with technical, sales, management, or legal staff—or all of these. Lunch will follow, then more meetings before dinner. Or maybe your guest will be making a technical presentation to a group of interested American businesspeople. Maybe the visitor wants to tour your area. Is his wife accompanying him? Does she need to be entertained while he is in meetings?

Even if your guest is very much like yourself—from another pluralist country—a certain amount of basic planning must take place that should include not only business but business entertainment also. In planning events, you should consider not only the obvious objective of the activity but also the underlying message that the form of the activity suggests. Will the event be casual or formal? Will you invite the guest to dinner at your home or at an expensive restaurant? What message do you want to communicate? Will you meet in your office? Or should you meet in a formal conference room? Is the meeting room at your office sufficient? Or should you arrange for an elegant meeting room at a hotel? Review the game plan you have been using to determine which kind of event will help you accomplish *your* goals.

THE HOME TEAM

You may have been on your own when first meeting your counterpart abroad, or you may have been accompanied by your technical staff. When you bring the game home, there are more players on your side. These include the receptionist, various secretaries, technical and lower-level management staff, production line supervisors, production workers, and perhaps legal and accounting staff. Consider these players rookies. They were not with you when you began the game. They did not prepare as you did. They do not know the game or the game plan, much less the opponent.

Your foreign visitor will, without a doubt, come into contact with more than a few of these people. They can either help you achieve your goal, or they can hinder or reverse your progress. The team you coach is a reflection of you and your abilities. The respect the team shows you will not be lost on the visitor. And remember, that visitor will be evaluating that respect relative to the norms of his own culture. If your guest is Asian and your secretary either constantly interrupts you with requests, or calls you by your first name or a nickname, or makes a joke about your choice of tie, your guest will not be impressed by the lack of respect therefrom.

Similarly, the guest must be treated with the same respect that you have taken such pains to establish on your trip abroad. If you show your counterpart respect but those beneath you do not, the message he receives will be mixed. Every person with whom he is likely to come in contact should be educated as to the proper behavior to accomplish your team goals.

Notify *all* employees whenever a foreign visitor is arriving. Do not tell them merely *how* to act, but tell them why. Once you yourself had developed an understanding of the reasons behind cultural behavior, it made sense to make accommodations. Provide the members of your team with the same information so that their actions toward your guest will be sincere.

One player who is not normally on the team—an interpreter—must also be educated. An interpreter may not always be necessary, but don't overlook the benefits of having one nearby. When people come to America, we often assume they already speak English. This is a burden to most visitors, especially older people who have not necessarily studied English in school. An interpreter can also serve as a liaison.

Some member of your team should be designated as the liaison who will see to all arrangements for the visitor before he travels and will escort and support the guest while he is in the United States. If your guest does not speak English, it would be wise to hire your interpreter to perform this crucial role. If language is not a problem, then assign a person from your office to take care of all details during your visitor's stay. It would be wise to choose a male if your visitor is Asian, Latin American, or Arab. It will save both people from the obvious potential for miscommunication of intent. It will also make the foreign visitor's conduct toward the person less confusing, for American businesswomen will not (and should not) behave the same way that a woman in his culture would behave toward him.

It is important to have a liaison person assigned not only for the duration of the visit. The liaison should also work with the visitor's support staff in making arrangements prior to travel. Ask your counterpart to designate one liaison person on his side whom your person can contact with all questions.

THE GAME PLAN FOR HOSTING VISITORS

They will be coming to your *turf*. They may bring their turf with them—in terms of cultural expectations—or they might leave it far behind. Most likely, they will bring their cultural judgments with them. These include their definition of correct table manners, their understanding of hospitality, their status-conscious protocol, and their expectations of Americans. Even though they are here, their cultural baggage will not be left at home (unless they have become as educated as you have in the game of global business).

Just as easily, certain people may take the opportunity to cut loose. Tribal players, when away from the tribe, may feel they are no longer constrained by expected behavior and therefore may do things they would never do at home. You should allow them their behavior and never refer to it when once again you visit them in their tribal surroundings.

Approach as a friend. He may no longer be a stranger, but is he a friend? If the business relationship is still in the early stages, you will probably not yet qualify as a friend by his standards. Be aware that in America we tend to treat everyone as a friend. In your own country you may naturally want to act more familiar. But it is important to maintain the level of formality you arrived at in his country. Let him continue to set the terms of the relationship and therefore not misinterpret your informality, or that of your staff, as pressure toward unwanted friendship.

You can show him that he is accepted in your hometown by surrounding him with friendly faces. Mutual friends or acquaintances, especially those from his home country, could be invited to nonbusiness functions, if appropriate. Notify his local consulate of his visit. The office may extend a special welcome. Provide both an interpreter with whom he can speak easily and a liaison person upon whom he can depend.

Humble yourself. Maintain the protocol regarding relative status that you observed when in his country. Thank him for visiting you. The guest always does the host an honor by a visit. The host humbles himself by providing hospitality for the guest. Refer to the previous chapters to be sure you use *his* definition of hospitality. To an Arab, this may mean that if you do not offer him three different meat entrées, you are stingy. Reciprocate the hospitality that you would receive in his country.

Concede turf. Continue negotiations as you would in either country. Bargain by his standards. To gain concessions from him may offset an act of giving on your part, which may consist of extended entertainment, travel within your country, or an appreciative gift. Your company will usually have a policy regarding gift giving as it pertains to negotiations. See Chapter 7 for more information.

Elevate your counterpart's sense of self-worth. This is easy. Make your guest feel important. It's done by paying attention to detail. Consider doing the following.

- Make hotel reservations for your guest in advance. Preregister him if possible. Make it clear before the trip who will be paying.
- Meet with the hotel staff to alert them to your visitor's special needs and the ways you would like them to treat him. Stay at the hotel yourself, if possible, before your guest arrives so that you can anticipate any problem that might arise.
- Have flowers (appropriate number and color), a fruit basket, or candy in the room before his arrival.
- Have the liaison person meet him at the airport and handle the baggage and transportation. Do not leave this to a limousine driver.
- Have the hotel provide him with either his local newspaper or one in his language each morning, if possible.
- At your office, fly the flag of his country (correct side up!).
- Always use china coffee cups and saucers, never plastic. Do not use tea bags. Find his usual green tea, British tea, Turkish coffee—whatever he is likely to want. (Wouldn't you have appreciated a cup of American coffee at his office?)
- Have a photographer take commemorative photos of the visit. Check with his liaison person in advance to be sure this is acceptable. In turn, if there are places in your factory where picture taking is not permitted, be sure to tell your visitor in advance.
- During meetings and when entertaining, be sure to pay attention to the seating arrangement. Most cultures have a prescribed seat for the guest of honor. Plan ahead your seating arrangements for meetings and restaurants and entertaining in your home.
- The greatest honor you can give a person from most tribal or collective cultures is to invite him to your home. Most foreigners would love to see how Americans live. It also shows the desire for friendship, gives an indication of trust, and further lowers cultural barriers. Brief your family on appropriate cross-cultural expectations as you would your staff at the office. (One tip: household pets should not be invited to meet the guest, unless your visitor has expressed interest in your pet.)

Make his welfare your purpose. Think of his needs when making plans. Consider his dietary restrictions and normal diet. Don't serve heavy sauces if his diet is simple. Don't serve pork if he is an Arab or an Orthodox Jew. Don't serve beef if he is Hindu. Check with his liaison to be sure you learn of any allergies before inviting him to your home. Does he have any medical needs while he is away from home? Is smoking an issue? Consider how you will handle his smoking if you live and work in a smoke-free environment. Offer him access to your office communications equipment so that he can stay in touch with his office.

In general, minimize his sense of insecurity in your culture. Take care of him personally. Don't assume he wants to be on his own to explore. Some will, but not all do. Ask what he would like to do while in the United States. Accommodate him whenever possible.

Here are a few supplemental notes for three specific cultures, each of which represents a major culture type.

Germany

Be punctual at all times.

Provide an agenda, and start and end your meetings at the stated time.

Have cold German beer available in the hotel room, and serve it at lunch.

Prepare your secretary, receptionist, and others he will meet. Have them stand for the guest when introduced and then greet him with a firm handshake each day on his arriving and leaving.

Gift giving is not necessary.

Offer an architectural tour of your city.

Allow him sufficient time to explore on his own.

At home, the guest of honor should be seated to the right of the hostess.

Saudi Arabia

Make sure no food or sauces are prepared with pork.

Provide a place where a Moslem may pray five times a day. Be mindful of his prayer schedule when planning meetings. Check with his liaison.

Do not rush meetings, and do not be upset if he is late. Notify drivers not to expect him to be on time.

If he greatly admires a possession of yours, you are expected, in terms of his culture, to give it to him. It will not likely come up, but be aware of the custom and plan a response. He will be obligated to reciprocate.

Provide bottled water, fruit, and olives in his hotel room.

Tell stories, legends, or fables that are germane to your region.

Instruct your staff, especially your female staff, in what to expect on introduction to an Arab. Equip your team with the knowledge that he may stand close to them when speaking and that they should not back away. Women should not get physically close. They will have to extend their hand first to shake hands when introduced.

Provide him a place to smoke.

When dinner is over, end the evening soon thereafter.

If dining at home, be sure to offer food three times or your guest may starve, for he will refuse twice before accepting.

Neither offer alcohol, nor prepare any sauces with alcohol or pork.

Do not give him an expensive gift that could be considered a bribe.

Japan

Do not serve cream sauces. Japanese have a low tolerance for lactose.

Suggest he send you menus and recipes he would like your chef to prepare.

Serve good-quality beef and a melon when entertaining. These are very expensive in Japan.

Take him to the best restaurant or club in your town, not one with "character."

Inform him of the appropriate dress code by being specific. *Casual* has different meanings around the world.

Have a photo taken of the entire delegation in front of your company, with the company logo and yourself visible. Offer it as a memento.

When you entertain in your home, he will want to meet your family and have photos taken with you and your family. Do not show him your kitchen or bedrooms. These rooms are considered private to the Japanese.

A *warning regarding colors*. Many Americans underestimate the psychological power of color. Many of the more symbolic cultures associate clear meanings with certain colors. One American company literally killed a deal with an Asian company by decorating a ballroom in black and white. Here are a few pointers.

- Black and white represent death in Asian countries.
- Purple symbolizes death in Mexico and Brazil.
- Blue, representing heaven, is the color associated with death in Syria.

If you hire an event planner or hotel designer to decorate for a function, have the planner do research with respect to color and other symbolism. It could be very important to your business deal.

KEY POINTS

- What game are we playing? It's the same game—global business—but with one critical difference: We are playing the game of global business while looking through a mirror.
- If you have already started a game on one playing field, do not change the rules when moving to a new playing field with the same players.
- Plan an agenda to accomplish your goals.
- Determine who will be on the home team.

- Revise your game plan for play on your playing field. The rules may not change, but their strategic application does.
- Notify *all* employees whenever a foreign visitor is expected. Do not tell them merely *how* to act, but tell them *why* they should.
- One member of your team should be designated as the liaison person who will see to all arrangements for the visitor before he travels and who will escort and support the guest while he is in the United States.
- Take care of all arrangements and every detail at the airport, hotel, and office.

9

The Exciting Game of International Dining

The objective of dining with business associates is not merely to eat. If it were, we would all simply fill our stomachs and leave the table without a word to anyone. No, dining is definitely a game. The greater the differences are between your culture and that of your dining partner, the more exciting and challenging the game will be.

Even among people of the same culture, it is a *game of position*, a *game of skill*, and a *game of honor*. Those three elements are evident in every group dining experience. Position refers to where one sits and the importance derived from that location; most cultures have some sort of seating hierarchy that places the most important person in the seat of honor relative to the host or hostess. Skill comes into play in the method of eating: the utensils used and the use of the hands and body; it is important to be skillful so as not to be perceived as an inexperienced player and an unworthy participant. Honor between host and guest has to do with the interplay of giving and receiving hospitality; some cultures require much gamesmanship in the interaction of host and guest.

The purpose of dining protocol is the same as the purpose of any culture-based protocol, as discussed in Chapter 2: the purpose of protocol is to promote and protect the basic beliefs of a culture. Dining protocol in each of the three major cultures—tribal, collective, and pluralist—reflects the culture's underlying value system. The tribal dining method reflects the communal aspects of the culture. The collective approach stresses symbolism and ritual. The pluralist method is more pragmatic and egalitarian.

Business protocol also has purposes, which are to communicate information about the people who are involved in the business interaction and to show respect and define limits within the relationship. Business dining also promotes these goals. So we are back to the original three definitive rules of global business:

- Never judge. (Show respect.)
- Never try to become like someone else. (Define limits.) Never try to make someone become like you. (Trust.)
- Never forget that business is about people. (Communicate.)

The purpose of business associates' eating together is not to extend the business meeting through mealtime, as most Americans tend to believe. It is an opportunity for opponents to become noncontentious. Two (or more) people who are negotiating to satisfy different needs come together during a meal with a common goal and common interest. They share a common behavior in the utensils they use. And they give and take freely among themselves in the giving and receiving of hospitality or the passing of bread and salt. Conversation is no longer at cross-purposes, but is an enjoyable interchange in association with the pleasure of eating. Even when business is not being discussed, a great deal of business can be done by the extending of the depth of a relationship, by the communicating of equality and respect, and by the repairing of any overt hostility that may have come out during a meeting. However, if the dining game is not played according to the rules, more harm may be done than good. Dining protocol is important to your business success.

THE GAME OF POSITION

The most commonly used seating arrangements in Western society are the French and the British methods. Both arrangements assume that the normal dining table will be rectangular or oblong, creating two long sides with a head at one end and a foot at the other. Both methods came about through social dining, when spouses were also invited. Social seating protocol and business seating protocol are different. Let's look at the social arrangement first.

In the French method, the most important people—the host and hostess—sit at the center of each long side, facing each other. The most important male guest sits to the right of the hostess, the most important female guest sits to the right of the host, the next most important male guest sits to the hostess's left, and the next most important female guest sits to the left of the host. Men and women alternate in this way, with the least important guests seated farthest from the hosts. No one sits at the ends of the table.

In the British method, the host and hostess sit one at the foot and one at the head of the table. The most important male guest sits to the right of the hostess, the next most important male guest to her left. The most important female guest sits to the right of the host, the next most important female guest to his left. Men and women alternate in this way, with the least important guests seated at the center of each side. One wonders whether there was a miscommunication between French and British dinner guests one evening that might have led to the Hundred Years' War.

In social settings, note how important it is to be paired off into couples. A single male or female guest will throw off the whole arrangement. The American objection to the use of such strict arrangements is that inequality of importance is highlighted. When one entertains one's boss or wants to show additional respect to an exceptional guest or client, the hierarchical seating arrangement offers the opportunity to communicate respect. But among friends, most Americans drop strict seating rules. Pragmatism rules. For instance, an honored guest may be seated so that he or she has the best view of the garden. Seating relative to another's importance is not what's kept in mind.

In business dining, the operative principle is to achieve your goal: honor your important business guest with a seat next to you or as close as possible so that you can influence and enter into the conversation. In the French method, the hostess would be replaced by a cohost or second in command. The side-central seating is maintained, with the most important guest to the right of the primary host. The next most important guest is seated to the right of the cohost. If all goes well, these two pairs will be of similar rank. In the British method, the highest-ranking guest sits to the right of the host, the next highest-ranking guest to the right of the cohost. If the group is small and there is no cohost, the next most-important guest should be seated to the host's left in either method.

In Asia, tables are usually either circular or square. The honored guest is seated facing the door. In China, the host sits opposite the honoree, with his back to the door. In ancient times, this symbolically indicated that the host knew of no planned attack and therefore was not afraid to have his back to the entrance. The guest, on the other hand, could see an attack coming. The next most important guest sits to the left of the most important guest; the next most important guest, to the primary guest's right; and so on, so that the host is seated—humbly—between the two least important guests. The Japanese arrangement is the same, with the host in the least desirable location. At a long banquet table, the host would sit in the middle of the side, with the honored guest to his right, the next important to his left, and so on. Women do not figure into the arrangement, because at important dinners, women often eat separately.

In Middle Eastern cultures, seating is usually circular, but not necessarily around a table. Guests might sit on the floor. Communal bowls are usually placed at the center, equidistant from the diners. In Middle Eastern cultures, someone's right-hand side is the preferred side, for the left hand is considered unclean. Therefore, it is easy to remember to seat the most important guest to the right of the host. Women usually eat separately.

THE GAME OF SKILL

There are basically three games of skill: eating with cutlery, eating with chopsticks, and eating with the hands. Yes, even eating with the hands is not random and does require skill, especially when one is permitted to use the right hand only. Eating with cutlery implies cutting, which is the distinguishing mark of this method. Continental style is the most dominant form of this type of eating. The entire Western world uses this method with the one exception being the United States, where we eat zigzag. Your refined American table manners that your mother took great pains to teach you will make you look like a back-woodsman in any country that uses the Continental style. Eating with chopsticks precludes the need to cut food. All cutting is done in the kitchen, and only bite-size pieces are served.

Each major form is be discussed here. Whichever method you use, commit to it. For example, don't switch between American and Continental style during a meal.

To develop any skill, you must practice. Before traveling overseas, practice the dining method you will be using so that you will appear polished and confident. Before we take the skills you may not have, let's review the skills that you should have:

American Style

To cut, the fork is held in the left hand, tines down. The knife is held in the right hand and used only to cut. Both index fingers point down the utensils.

After a piece is cut, the knife is rested across the side of the plate with the blade toward the center of the plate. The fork is switched to the right hand to eat the piece of food, tines up.

The fork remains in the right hand unless it is necessary to cut a piece of food.

The resting position is with knife along the edge of the plate as usual and the fork in a 10 to 4 position on the plate.

The signal that you are finished is to place both knife and fork together pointing toward the left side of the plate.

Napkins are kept in the lap.

When only the fork is being used, the left hand should be placed in the lap.

Continental Style

There are four methods of serving the meal:

1. Service à la française requires you to serve yourself from a platter held to your left by a servant. Use the serving fork and spoon together, and replace them on the tray next to each other when finished. This is the highest form of service and the least economical.
2. Service à l'anglaise has a servant serve you from a platter on your left.
3. Service à la russe presents the main course in one piece on a platter, usually on a cart beside the table. The meat is carved in front of the guests, and a waiter places a plate in front of each guest. Often the cooking is completed at the table in this way, perhaps with a flaming sauce.
4. American service places a complete serving on individual plates and comes straight from the restaurant kitchen to the guest.

The fork and knife are held in the left and right hands, respectively. The forefinger of each hand points down the utensil. The tines of the fork always face down. One does not cut and then put the knife down. The two utensils are used for items that do not need cutting as well as those that do.

Hold the food with the fork, and cut with the knife.

Eat the food off the back of the fork. Don't twist the fork in your hands so that the tines face up as they enter your mouth.

The utensils for the fish course, which precedes the meat course, are handled a bit differently. The fish knife, which is broad and flat, is held like a pencil is held, not with the index finger in a position to push down for cutting. This is because the fish knife does more scooping than cutting if the fish is cooked properly. The fork is held in the left hand, tines down, with a gentler grip; the thumb and index finger extend to the same point, forming an O.

Salad is eaten with a knife and fork, using the knife to fold the lettuce onto the fork tines. Do not cut the lettuce.

The resting position is placing the knife and fork with the tines of the fork pointing down on top of the knife. They form an angle of 90 degrees at the bottom of your plate. Don't leave your utensils like this at the end of the meal, because it signals the waiter that you are not done. Bring them together when you are finished.

While in the rest position, keep your hands visible by resting your wrists on the edge of the table. Never rest your hands in your lap.

Do not use your personal butter knife for yourself serving butter onto your bread plate. Use the knife that is placed at the butter. Use your butter knife to butter one bite-size piece of bread at a time. Your bread plate is to your left.

For a meal consisting of several courses, your place setting will have more than one fork, spoon, and knife. They are usually arranged with the utensils for the first course at the outer edges. Work your way in toward the plate.

Photo 1
The Plate, Napkin, and
Beverage Glass

Photo 2
The American
Place Setting

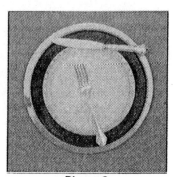

Photo 3
The American
Resting Position

Photo 4
The American
Finished Position

Photo 5
The Continental
Place Setting

Photo 6
The Continental
Resting Position

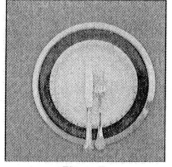

Photo 7
The Continental
Finished Position

Photo 8
Soup Bowl
and Spoon

Photo 9
Soup Plate
and Spoon

NOTES
Photo 2—*Right of the plate, outside in:* soup spoon, dinner knife. *Left of the plate, outside in:* salad fork, dinner fork. *Top of the plate:* dessert fork, handle to the left; dessert spoon, handle to the right. *Right of the plate, goblet nearest soup spoon:* white wine, red wine water (always the goblet at the tip of the knife that is closest to plate). *Left of plate:* napkin. *Above the forks on the left side:* bread and butter plate with butter knife.

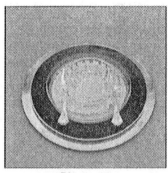

Photo 10
Finger Bowl
Presentation

Photo 11
Where to Place
the Finger Bowl

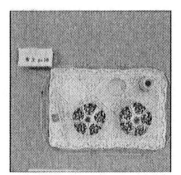

Photo 12
The Japanese
Place Setting Presentation

Photo 13
The Japanese Place
Setting without the Tray

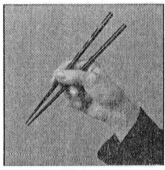

Photo 14
Holding the
Chopsticks

Photo 15
Thai
Place Setting

Photo 16
Formal Thai
Place Setting

Photo 17
Holding the Arab
Coffee Cup

NOTES

Photo 5—*Right of the plate:* oyster fork (tines resting in the soup spoon), soup or broth spoon, fish knife, dinner knife, salad knife. *Left of the plate:* fish fork, dinner fork, salad fork. *Top of the plate:* dessert fork (handle to the left), dessert spoon (handle to the right). Napkin is left of forks (can be placed in the center of the plate). Bread and butter plate and knife is above the forks. *Stemware arrangement to right of plate:* sherry, white wine, red wine, water, champagne.

Soup is eaten by spooning away from you toward the center of the bowl. Eat the soup by sipping it from the side of the spoon. If you are served soup in a soup bowl (Photo 8, page 244), place the spoon on the right side of the service plate. If you are served soup in a soup plate (Photo 9, page 244), place the spoon in the soup plate. Do not place your other hand in your lap. Rest your wrists on the edge of the table.

Note that in Europe, the salad is served *after* the main course, and so the salad fork and knife are placed closest to the plate.

The dessert fork and spoon are placed at the top of your place setting. In very formal service, the dessert spoon and fork arrive on a plate with a doily and a small bowl of water: your finger bowl. Remove the fork to the left and the spoon to the right. Place the doily and the bowl to your upper left.

When dessert is served, use only the fork if it is cake or pie and use only the spoon for ice cream or pudding. For anything else, use the spoon in your right hand and the fork in your left hand.

Once your dessert dish has been removed, place the finger bowl and doily in front of you. Dip the fingertips of one hand at a time, drying one hand before dipping the other and patting the fingertips on your napkin. (In Europe the term for napkin is *serviette*.)

Wait until everyone is finished and until the host and hostess make the suggestion, before leaving the table.

Place your napkin to the left side of your plate before leaving the table.

Chinese Style

Tables are round or square, and guests sit equidistant from the serving dishes, which are placed on a lazy Susan in the middle of the table.

Communal dishes of meat, fish, and vegetables are placed in the center. These are considered merely condiments. The real dinner is the rice.

Each person is given a small bowl of rice. The rice bowl is always accepted with two hands, not just one. Never eat the other foods before the rice is served, or you will be thought greedy.

When the host gives a signal, the guests may take food from the central serving dishes. There may be special serving chopsticks in some countries. Usually, you just use your own chopsticks to take food. Use the larger end for dipping into serving dishes.

Chopsticks are never used to pierce food. If cutting is necessary, prod the food until its natural fissures are exposed and it falls apart.

Chopsticks are held between the first three fingers. The bottom stick is held still while the top stick is maneuvered against it.

Never leave chopsticks sticking into your rice. When you are resting, place chopsticks against the chopstick rest or across the top of the bowl. Never lick or bite chopsticks to remove food stuck to them. Do not search through the serving dish with your chopsticks. Eat the piece in front of you. Do not grip single pieces of rice between chopsticks. The rice is sticky and is lifted to your mouth by way of the sticks.

Hold the rice bowl in your left hand throughout the meal. When every last grain of rice has been consumed, this indicates that you are done. Leaving rice in the bowl is disgusting behavior and shows a lack of appreciation for the effort that people have made in producing the rice.

Don't pour sauces into your rice bowl. Use sauces for dipping.

All the common dishes should be shared equally. It is bad manners to look as though you favor one food over another. Try everything.

At the end of the meal, place your chopsticks side by side on the rest or the side of the bowl, not on the table.

At a Chinese banquet, the distinction between a lavish banquet and a normal meal is made by minimizing the importance of the rice. Meat, fish, and vegetables are now the important foods. Rice may not be served at all until the end of the meal. If you ask for rice, it means that you are through eating. Banquets could consist of 12–20 courses. Don't eat very much at the beginning.

The host should be praised excessively during the banquet.

Japanese variations:

Napkins are not used during meals. Hot towels are passed to the guests to wipe their hands. Some men wipe their faces. Women do not.

Sake, a potent rice wine, is served hot before the meal. It is poured into a tiny ceramic cup held with the right hand and supported by the left hand. It is polite to fill one another's cups.

Each diner receives a tray with a rice bowl on the left, a soup bowl on the right (both of these bowls are covered), and an entrée dish at the top. Remove the bowl covers to the left and right of the tray. Dishes remain on the tray unless you pick one up to eat from.

Start with the soup, lifting it to your mouth to drink a portion, then picking out a morsel from the broth with your chopsticks. Soup spoons are not provided.

Next, pick up the rice bowl and eat a small amount. The rice bowl will remain in your hand throughout the meal; set it down only to pick up the soup bowl. The rice and the soup should last through the meal. All food should be paced to be finished at the same time.

Leave a little rice in your bowl to receive more. You should eat at least two bowls of rice during a meal.

In the eating of noodles, it is good to slurp them in while sucking air.

If the host passes you a tray, put your rice bowl onto it to be refilled.

Save the pickles for the end of the meal.

Replace the covers on your rice bowl and soup bowl when you are done.

Korean variations:

When eating, don't raise the rice bowl or any other bowl to your mouth.

Soup spoons are provided. Place the soup spoon in your soup bowl or over your rice bowl, not on the table.

People never pour their own drinks. Watch your neighbor's glass, and refill it when it is empty. If there is some beverage left, do not refill the glass. Always lift your glass while someone pours for you.

Don't completely clean your plate. This implies that your host did not provide enough food.

If you want seconds, refuse twice and accept the third time. If you are hosting, always offer food three times.

Middle Eastern Style

Traditional Middle Eastern seating is on the floor with communal dishes at the center of the circle of diners. Individual dishes are not always provided. Be sure the soles of your shoes do not face anyone.

Before the meal, a servant may bring a pitcher and a bowl. This is for washing your hands in full view of everyone, so everyone can know your hands are clean.

Eat with your right hand, keeping your left hand behind you.

Sauces are often provided for dipping bread.

The quantity of food will be huge. This is to show the guest that the host is not skimpy. Sometimes the tablecloth is removed after each course. To get an idea of how much food to expect, count the tablecloths.

Take food from the edge of the plate, rather than the center, or you might burn your hand.

Someone may put a choice piece of food on your plate (if there are plates). If you don't want it, you don't have to eat it.

Never reach beyond your space of the communal dish.

If you are not given a spoon to eat couscous, take a small handful and form it into a ball, then pop it into your mouth without touching your lips. Your hand will be returning to the communal dish!

Wipe your fingers on a piece of bread between bites. Lick your fingers only at the end of a meal to indicate you are done.

Don't clean your plate, or you will insult your host. Leave a small amount.

Refuse second helpings several times before accepting.

THE GAME OF HONOR

The social function of dining is not only for the purpose of honoring a guest. Sharing a meal requires sharing the honors. Giving does not flow in one direction. The host not only gives food and honor to the guest; the host also receives in return praise and obligation from the guest. The host in a tribal or collective culture will entertain lavishly—providing more food than anyone needs—in order to show he is not stingy and that the guest is important. In so doing, he elevates both himself and the guest. He expects to receive the same degree of hospitality in return. If he does not, it is considered a serious offense. The guest who does not reciprocate is viewed as greedy, selfish, and thoughtless of others. It is cause for excommunication from the tribe or collective, as it goes against the most basic values of the culture.

The pluralist cultures outwardly maintain the equality of the individual host and guest. They are equally important. The host and hostess sit in the most prominent locations, able to control the event from their "thrones." They surround themselves with the most interesting and honored guests. The hostess is served first, and all wait until she begins. The host and hostess do not humble themselves to their guests. It is quite the opposite. They maintain their position of honor and invite their guests to join them in that honor. Praise is not necessary. In fact, to some, praise would be a backhanded insult, implying that guests are surprised to be served such a good meal and that the host does not usually dine so well. Thanks is required, but praise is not. As a compliment to the chef, a diner should finish all of the food on the plate.

In tribal and collective cultures, there is an elaborate and symbolic "dance" of humility. The host offers, the guest declines, the host offers again, the guest refuses again, the host insists, the guest accepts. Never for a minute did anyone doubt that the guest would accept in the end, but to accept right away would appear greedy and self-centered. The dance applies to such issues as who walks through the dining room door first, who sits in the seat of honor, who takes the first serving from the common bowl, and who takes the last serving from the bowl. The guest of honor does. Once he eventually gives way and accepts these honors, he must praise the host effusively for the hospitality and insist upon his own unworthiness. It is not enough to behave correctly and thank the host. The guest must *convince* everyone that he is truly impressed.

Following are a few more dining tips that will prevent you from offending any tribal or collective host and being branded as an unappreciative guest.

- Accept the food as presented. Do not add salt or other seasoning, except for sauces. (In some pluralist cultures, salt is acceptable because individual tastes are valid.)
- Try everything. Never decline what is offered to you unless it is so unusual that it might make you ill. In that case, make up a medical reason for declining.

- The locals in many cultures may not believe that eating quietly is necessarily bad manners. Slurping, smacking, and belching are all compliments to the host, indicating that the meal is being enjoyed. You, however, should not join in too exuberantly.
- Finishing everything on your plate implies that you have room for more and that your host did not feed you enough.
- Business discussions have no place during a display of hospitality. Your host may bring up business after dessert, but you should never initiate a business discussion over a meal.

PLAYING WITH FOOD

There are two categories of foods that should be avoided when hosting and should be prepared for when visiting: foods that are hard to eat and foods that are hard to swallow. There is a difference. Foods that are hard to eat include artichokes, clams, corn on the cob, and spaghetti. Foods that are hard to swallow include monkey's brains, sheep's eyeballs, and stir-fried bees. It gets worse. One American traveler was entertained in Vietnam at a restaurant where the menu was kept in cages outside. The choices included cats, turtles, snakes, dogs, and other small creatures. The blood sauce was not euphemistically referred to as au jus. This experience can only reinforce one's appreciation for refrigeration, not always available in the Third World.

The first rule of the game of global business is not to judge another culture as being better or worse than your own. This rule applies to food as well. The best strategy is not to ask what it is. Take small bites, pretend it's your favorite meat, and swallow quickly. Otherwise, pretend to eat by pushing the food around on your plate. In Asian cultures you could try declining certain foods on the grounds that you are not worthy to eat whatever it is.

Consider that in turn other cultures find some of our foods repulsive. The list includes corn (which other cultures feed to animals only), grits, marshmallows, peanut butter, pecan and pumpkin pie, and commercially preserved white bread. When hosting, consider the guest's normal diet. Avoid serving foods that are so traditionally American that they border on disgusting.

When hosting or ordering in a restaurant, avoid hard-to-handle foods. If you are served difficult foods, here is a selected short list of what to do.

Artichokes: Whole artichokes are eaten with the fingers. Each leaf is pulled off one at a time; the soft part is dipped in sauce, then scraped off with the teeth. Place the remainder of the leaf on the side of the plate. Do not eat the leaf. When the leaves have been pulled off, the center thistle is removed by fork and knife. The heart, at the very bottom, is cut and eaten with a fork.

Celery and radishes: These can be taken from the serving dish with your hands and eaten with the fingers.

Caviar: Spread it on toast, along with crumbled egg and other condiments, if you like. Eat the caviar on toast held in your hand.

Oysters, mussels, and clams: On the half shell, they are held by the shell in one hand and removed from the shell with the small oyster fork. Dip into sauce and eat in one bite.

Soft-boiled eggs: Served in an egg cup, they are eaten out of the shell. Slice the top off with a knife.

Fruit with seeds or pits: These can be eaten with the hands, removing the pits from your mouth by placing your hand over your mouth, dropping the pits into your cupped hand, and placing them on the side of your plate. In Continental dining, most fruit is eaten with fork and knife. Follow the lead of your host or hostess.

Pâté de foie gras: Place on a piece of toast or bread with your knife, and eat with your hands.

Spaghetti: Use a fork to pull out a few strands at a time. Twirl them around your fork against the rim of the plate or bowl.

Baked potatoes: Eat them from the skin with a fork. Do not mash them first. Place butter on the potato by taking butter *from your own bread plate* with your dinner knife. Do not use your dinner knife to take butter directly from the butter serving dish.

Shrimp cocktail with the tails on: Hold by the tail with your fingers, dip into sauce, bite off the shrimp, and discard the tail on your plate.

Snails: If tongs are provided, hold the shell with the tongs. Otherwise, use your hand. Pull the snail out with the oyster fork. Eat it in one bite. The extra garlic butter sauce may be soaked up by a piece of bread.

KEY POINTS

- Dining is a game of position, skill, and honor.
- Most cultures have some type of seating hierarchy that places the most important guest in a seat of honor relative to the host.
- There are three types of skills: eating with cutlery, eating with chopsticks, and eating with the hands.
- The game of honor is played between the host and the guest, with the interplay of giving and receiving. Some cultures raise this to a ritual.
- Avoid serving or ordering foods that are difficult to eat and foods that are difficult to stomach.

10

Cut to the Chase

The following pages serve as a quick reference guide to many individual nations. If the nation you are interested in is not listed, refer to the culture map in Figure 10.1. Determine which major culture type the country falls under, and follow the methodology presented in Chapters 1 and 2.

The listings in this chapter are arranged alphabetically. For each listing, there will be important information regarding culture, such as major culture group, local factors that may modify the culture as categorized, and primary motivations. This brief information will give you a cultural orientation so that you will have the essential knowledge you need to be effective in business. I strongly recommend that you refer to the background information for the culture group listed before arriving at your destination. You will find this in Chapters 1 and 2. The playing field is listed, referring to the game in Chapters 4 and 5 in which the country and its regional orientation are explored. Chapters 4 and 5 also offer in-depth player analysis and game plans.

The culture information is followed by points that should be addressed in your business game plan. This includes suggestions for strategic use of business protocol. Following this information, local customs are listed that may be important for your business dealings.

ARGENTINA

Cultural Data

Culture type: Tribal
Playing field: Latin America

Figure 10.1
World Culture Map

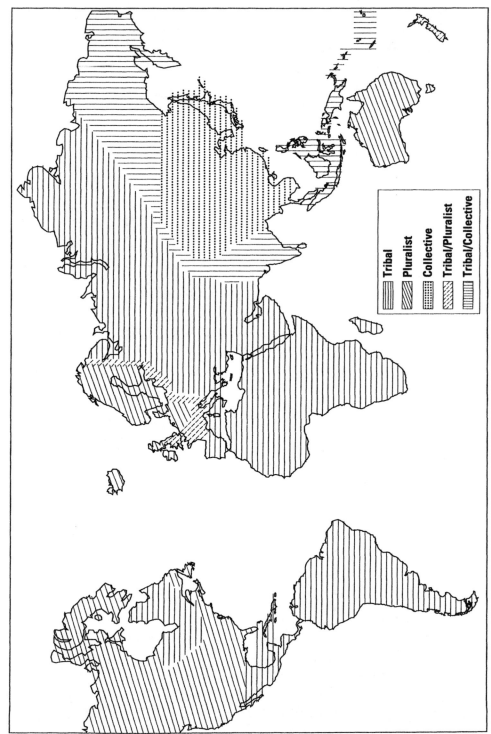

Local influences: Eighty-five percent of the population is of European descent, including Italian, Spanish, German, English, French, and Russian. Be cognizant of the person's background, even if he speaks Spanish as his first language. There is likely to be a cross-cultural influence. Buenos Aires is a very cosmopolitan city with European sophistication.

Primary motivations: The family's status, power, and welfare come first.

Game Plan

Establish contact through a well-regarded local agent.

The first meeting should be on your host's turf.

Send the seniormost person from your company, along with one or two subordinates.

Plan on using an interpreter. Translate materials into Latin American Spanish.

Always address a Latino formally, using his title and family name (next-to-last name).

Expect to spend time establishing a relationship. Don't press toward a business discussion until your counterpart offers an opening.

Maintain formality in dress, posture, and speech until he relaxes the interaction.

Your image is important in communicating your own status.

Don't back away if your counterpart chooses to stand close during conversation.

Be prepared to make concessions, but only after appropriate resistance. Do not appear to negotiate these concessions. Latinos like zero-sum games.

Minimize risks in any proposal.

As an American, humble yourself. Do not assume you hold the most power because you are from the United States.

Entertain at the best restaurants.

Eat Continental style.

Once a relationship has been established, your company should not change the U.S. contact person, or else the process will have to begin again. Latinos trust people, not companies.

Local Rules

Use a firm grip when shaking hands. Maintain good eye contact.

Learn to keep your hands still. There are many gestures that we use that are offensive or have different meanings in parts of Latin America.

Argentines might make personal observations about you. This just means that the person is comfortable with you.

Opera is a good topic of conversation in Argentina, as is sports. Learn about soccer (*futbol*) and the status of local teams.

AUSTRALIA

Cultural Data

Culture type: Pluralist

Playing field: Australia

Local influences: The country was born of the disenfranchised. English class structure was not transported to Australia. The society fosters a strong masculine stereotype. Identity is not derived from the family, but through the individual.

Primary motivations: Equality and antiauthoritarianism are their strongest values. No man is a servant and no man is a master. Personal welfare is primary.

Game Plan

Decrease your Australian host's sense of isolation by holding the first meeting at his offices.

A local agent is not necessary, but a third-party introduction always makes contact easier.

Keep a local representative on staff to keep up on local developments and give you a local presence.

Keep equality in mind at all times—from the structure of your business proposal to opportunities for socializing.

Return your host's informality, but don't initiate it.

Bargaining is considered to be a waste of time. Take your best shot.

Be sure to communicate the importance to you of your mutual business objectives. Do not defer to him, yet do not project superiority.

Be straightforward.

Local Rules

Greet an Australian with a firm handshake and a hello. Australians tire of hearing non-Australians say "g'day." Begin with last names, but first-name usage will follow almost immediately. Don't wait to be asked, but if he uses your first name, respond in kind.

Give your business card at the introduction; your counterpart may not give you one. Cards are not very important in Australia.

Titles and degrees are not impressive. He will make his own judgment as to the quality of the person with whom he is speaking.

Business dress is conservative and not overly elegant. Leave the gold chain and other ostentatious jewelry at home. It is not only too showy, but is is not considered masculine.

Be friendly, relaxed, modest, and unpretentious. Don't try to impress your host.

Gifts are not given unless you are invited to someone's home.

Don't fill your presentation with hype or glitz. A simple, direct presentation is more effective. Get to the point.

Decision making can occur at lower levels, but things still take longer than in the United States.

You may be invited out for a drink after work. Don't bring up business unless your host does; Australians make a clear distinction between work and play. Each person pays for a round of drinks. Don't miss your turn. Sports is an excellent topic of conversation. Find out something about Australian Rules football and rugby. When discussing sports, do not use the term *root* as in "root for the home team." It means something obscene.

There is a difference between afternoon tea and tea. *Tea* is the dinnertime meal served between 6 and 8 P.M.

Until recently, women were not permitted in bars. Bars were for men only. Women are legally equal, but socially an underclass, although men may not admit it.

BELARUS

Cultural Data

Culture type: Progressive tribal

Playing field: Central and Eastern Europe

Local influences: Belarus has been dominated by Poland, Lithuania, and Russia throughout much of its history. The country is strongly seeking a national identity.

Primary motivations: Tribal affiliation is especially important in Belarus because of the citizens' weak national identity. Tribal welfare is their primary focus.

Game Plan

Approach with a personal reference or through a local agent.

First meeting should be at your host's offices.

Trust must be established before you will be accepted.

Participate in Belarus's brand of conformity and modesty. Do not flaunt affluence.

Do not entertain lavishly.

Negotiate a win-win outcome.

Sharing is important. Gift giving is common and should be reciprocated.

Presentations should stress minimizing risks.

Respect age. Seniority comes with age. However, be aware that the younger generation has become more entrepreneurial since the demise of the communist system.

Local Rules

A good local representative is important. He should understand your business and be able to discuss details when asked. He should not only make introductions but also attend meetings and follow up afterward. He can also arrange translation services.

Send your proposal to your targeted company before your visit. The company will be interested whether or not you have sent your proposal elsewhere in their country and whether or not it received a favorable response.

Western business practices are not generally understood. Explain everything.

Documents from your company should bear a corporate seal.

Negotiations and presentations are similar to those in Russia.

Shake hands with a firm grip while stating your last name. Men and women shake hands with each other.

Small gifts are appreciated.

Dress conservatively.

Use European manners, as noted in the section on Russia.

Accept hospitality, whether invited to a restaurant or to a home. Expect substantial drinking, but if business is discussed you will be held to what you say.

BELGIUM

Cultural Data

Culture type: Pluralist/tribal

Playing field: Western Europe

Local influences: Belgium is a transition country between the strong pluralism of the Netherlands and the more tribal French to the south. Ethnic identity is an issue and can become contentious. Brussels is predominantly French in its culture. Most likely you will be doing business here and should, therefore, study the French game plan as well.

Primary motivations: Self-interest and tribal welfare.

Game Plan

Know who the primary person is that you will be meeting. Does he speak French or Dutch? Prepare to use an interpreter.

Go to your host's office. Leave your American superiority complex at home. It will not be appreciated here.

Use a prestigious third-party introduction.

You should project a sophisticated image, but not a supercilious one. The best way is by use of good, formal manners and by display of a knowledge of world affairs.

Do not try to find common cultural ground, but show knowledge of Belgian culture.

Presentations should be logical and linear. Appeal to Belgian self-interest. Solve your host's problems.

Local Rules

Shake hands on meeting and leaving. Shake quickly with a light pressure. When being introduced, repeat your name.

Be sure to shake hands with secretaries when arriving and leaving.

At a large party, let your host introduce you. You don't have to shake hands with everyone.

Belgians value tact and diplomacy over blunt honesty.

Don't discuss language differences in Belgium.

Don't use the same business contact in both French and Flemish Belgium.

If you translate your materials, provide both French and Dutch versions.

The first meeting is usually for getting acquainted. Belgians lean to the tribal side on this point. In the Flemish north, this will not always be the case.

Schedule business entertaining over lunch. Belgians like to spend the evening with their families.

A businesswoman who wants to entertain a Belgian businessman arranges payment in advance or says that the company is paying. He won't allow her to pay otherwise.

BOLIVIA

Cultural Data

Culture type: Tribal

Playing field: Latin America

Local influences: This is an isolated, landlocked country that still maintains a navy just in case it ever gets its coastline back from Chile. The population is 50 percent Indian, 30 percent mestizo, and 15 percent European.

Primary motivations: Family status, power, and welfare come first.

Game Plan

Establish contact through a well-regarded local agent.

The first meeting should be on your host's turf.

Send the seniormost person from your company, along with one or two subordinates.

Plan on using an interpreter. Translate materials into Latin American Spanish.

Always address a Latino formally, using his title and family name (next-to-last name).

Expect to spend time establishing a relationship. Don't press toward a business discussion until your counterpart offers an opening.

Maintain formality in dress, posture, and speech until he relaxes the interaction.

Your image is important in communicating your own status.

Don't back away if your counterpart chooses to stand close during conversation.

Be prepared to make concessions, but only after appropriate resistance. Do not appear to negotiate these concessions. Latinos like zero-sum games.

Minimize risks in any proposal.

As an American, humble yourself. Do not assume you hold the most power because you are from the United States.

Entertain at the best restaurants.

Eat Continental style.

Once a relationship has been established, your company should not change the U.S. contact person, or else the process will have to begin again. Latinos trust people, not companies.

Local Rules

Machismo is very strong in Bolivia.

Bolivians believe that seeing a black person is good luck.

It is OK to talk business over lunch, but not over dinner.

Our hand gesture that means *so-so*—palm down, rocking the hand back and forth—means *no*.

BRAZIL

Cultural Data

Culture type: Tribal

Playing field: Latin America

Local influences: Brazil is the only Portuguese country in South America. The population contains a larger number of Africans than the neighboring Hispanic countries. African-Brazilians are descendants of slaves imported by the Portuguese. They have been assimilated into the population, predominantly in the north. In the south, there is a substantial Japanese community. Germans are also represented in São Paulo, the largest city.

Primary motivations: Family status and welfare, and the enjoyment of life are strong motivators.

Game Plan

Establish contact through a well-regarded local agent.

The first meeting should be on your host's turf.

Send the seniormost person from your company, along with one or two subordinates.

Plan on using an interpreter. Translate materials into Portuguese.

Always address a Brazilian formally, using his title and family name (next-to-last name).

Expect to spend time establishing a relationship. Don't press toward a business discussion until your counterpart offers an opening.

Maintain formality in dress, posture, and speech until he relaxes the interaction.

Your image is important in communicating your own status.

Don't back away if your counterpart chooses to stand close during conversation.

Be prepared to make concessions, but only after appropriate resistance. Do not appear to negotiate these concessions. Brazilians like zero-sum games.

Minimize risks in any proposal.

As an American, humble yourself. Do not assume you hold the most power because you are from the United States.

Entertain at the best restaurants.

Eat Continental style.

Once a relationship has been established, your company should not change the U.S. contact person, or else the process will have to begin again. Latinos trust people, not companies.

Local Rules

Brazilians are better than most Latinos at abstract thinking, but they still make decisions based on feelings and personal interests.

Look for German and Japanese influence in São Paulo. This city operates more like northern cities. Expect a faster pace.

The Brazilians seem very different from their Hispanic neighbors. Their attitude is very light and optimistic. They have good expectations for the future. One does not sense this optimism in the other countries of Latin America.

When thinking, don't absentmindedly rub your fingers under your chin, as some men with beards do. It means you don't know the answer to a question.

BULGARIA

Cultural Data

Culture type: Progressive tribal

Playing field: Central and Eastern Europe

Local influences: Bulgaria was dominated by the Ottoman Turks until World War I. Bulgaria fought with Germany during World War II and then came under Soviet influence. Currently, the country is reversing the communist hold, is privatizing industry, and is returning collective farmland.

Primary motivations: The welfare of the family group and the security of the nation.

Game Plan

Approach with a personal reference or through a local agent.

First meeting should be at your host's offices.

Trust must be established before you will be accepted.

Participate in the Bulgarian brand of conformity and modesty. Do not flaunt affluence.

Do not entertain lavishly.

Negotiate a win-win outcome.

Sharing is important. Gift giving is common and should be reciprocated.

Presentations should stress minimizing risks.

Respect age. Seniority comes with age. However, be aware that the younger generation has become more entrepreneurial since the demise of the communist system.

Local Rules

Bulgarians admire the United States and Western Europe. They admire the entrepreneurial spirit and apply it in a tribal sense.

The family is taken into consideration during any decision making.

Bulgarians have a strong work ethic.

They respect openness, strength, competence, honesty, and loyalty.

Management skills are lacking.

European manners are used. Respectful behavior toward others is important.

The head-nodding gesture Americans use for *yes* and *no* are reversed in Bulgaria.

CANADA

Cultural Data

Culture type: Tribal/pluralist

Playing field: Canada

Local influences: Canada can be divided as follows: French-speaking Quebec Province, English-speaking Ontario, and the western provinces. The major difference between America and Canada is that America tends to assimilate diverse cultures into one system. Canada holds ethnic groups separate. This is due to the fact that most of Canada is tribal.

Primary motivations: Self-interest of the ethnic group in the east, and individual progress in the west.

Game Plan

Identify the part of Canada that you will be visiting. Your game plan will vary depending on which ethnic group you are to address. Use a collective game plan when meeting with a member of the large community from Hong Kong in Vancouver.

Do not pretend that a Canadian is an American.

Do not project superiority because you are an American, and do not assume Canadians wish they were Americans.

In Quebec, cater to the French culture. Try to speak French. This will greatly enhance your image.

Local Rules

Quebec Province:

All presentation materials should be printed in both French and English. Assume that you will be conducting business in French.

French Canadians are less reserved than English-speaking Canadians. They tend to use more gesturing.

Physical space is closer. Your French Canadian host may touch you while conversing.

Use a reasonably firm handshake, and shake upon first meeting, greetings, and departures.

Use last names until your host switches to first. He may go back and forth.

Eat Continental style.

English-speaking Canada:

Handshakes are firm. Shake upon greeting and introduction, but not upon leaving.

Use last names when introduced. First names will be used very soon thereafter. Wait for your host to initiate this.

English Canadians are not comfortable touching or speaking at close range.

Privacy is important.

Business meals are common. At dinner, wait for your host to bring up business.

In business situations, maintain good posture. One can be more relaxed in social settings.

Business gifts should be modest. Gifts are opened immediately. An invitation to a restaurant is considered a gift.

Eat Continental style.

CHILE

Cultural Data

Culture type: Tribal

Playing field: Latin America
Local influences: Chile's population is 95 percent European—primarily Spanish, German, and Italian. Use global protocol when meeting someone from Chile.
Primary motivations: Family status, power, and welfare.

Game Plan

Establish contact through a well-regarded local agent.

The first meeting should be on your host's turf.

Send the seniormost person from your company, along with one or two subordinates.

Plan on using an interpreter. Translate materials into Latin American Spanish.

Always address a Latino formally, using his title and family name (next-to-last name).

Expect to spend time establishing a relationship. Don't press toward a business discussion until your counterpart offers an opening.

Maintain formality in dress, posture, and speech until he relaxes the interaction.

Your image is important in communicating your own status.

Don't back away if your counterpart chooses to stand close during conversation.

Be prepared to make concessions, but only after appropriate resistance. Do not appear to negotiate these concessions. Latinos like zero-sum games.

Minimize risks in any proposal.

As an American, humble yourself. Do not assume you hold the most power because you are from the United States.

Entertain at the best restaurants.

Eat Continental style.

Once a relationship has been established, your company should not change the U.S. contact person, or else the process will have to begin again. Latinos trust people, not companies.

Local Rules

There are more professional women here than in any other Latin American country. This is the best place for a businesswoman to work, but it is still very difficult.

The northern European influence results in a strong desire for progress and advancement through education. There is a significant middle class.

Avoid aggressive behavior.

Don't raise your right fist to head level. This is a communist gesture.

For best results in Chile, try to overcome Chileans' sense of physical isolation by making frequent trips and keeping in contact.

Business gifts are not customary. If someone gives you a gift, open it immediately.

CHINA

Cultural Data

Culture type: Collective

Playing field: Pacific Rim

Local influences: Chinese culture dominates the Far East. It is based on Confucian philosophy, which dictates rules of behavior. Today, the Republic of China is governed by communist politics, but enterprise is allowed and China is open to global players.

Primary motivations: The welfare of the collective group is paramount. People work to benefit the group and to uphold its honor.

Game Plan

Approach through a local representative.

Personal relationships must be established before business is done. Do not assume this means you are a personal friend.

Top management should be present at the first meeting. Your company should be represented by a group of specialists at the first meeting. Do not include a lawyer.

Negotiations will be time-consuming. Expect to make many trips. Be patient.

Study *Bing Fa* strategy.

One who is powerful and successful shows his humility.

Harmony must be maintained. Do not confront or question anyone in a negative way. Never say no. Expect Chinese to always say yes, which might mean no.

Allow your host to win something in negotiations.

Recognize and respect the social position of all you encounter. Do not expect them to require equality.

Never compliment a person directly. Never praise a person in front of his superiors. Praise the group.

Negotiations may appear cyclical rather than linear. Be prepared to discuss any subject out of sequence at any time.

Local Rules

Establish contacts before you go. The U.S. Department of Commerce can help.

Everything shuts down between noon and 2 P.M.

In your presentation, avoid using colors. Colors have symbolic meanings.

Bring at least 20 copies of your proposal. You will meet with many groups.

Relationships are important before a deal is closed.

At the end of a meeting, leave before the Chinese.

Reciprocate banquets, but never outdo your host in lavishness.

Spouses may be invited to banquets.

Guests arrive on time for banquets.

Refuse hospitality three times before accepting, so you don't look greedy.

Wait for the host to eat or drink.

The host offers the first toast.

If you are greeted by applause, applaud back.

Never put your hands in your mouth.

Gift giving is technically illegal. Don't give anything expensive in front of others. A gift from your company to the Chinese organization is acceptable. When giving or receiving a gift, use both hands. The gift is not opened in the presence of the giver. Chinese will decline a gift three times to not appear greedy. Keep insisting. Never give a clock. It is associated with death. Do not give gifts until all business is concluded.

Everyone belongs to a work unit, which becomes each one's collective. The work unit takes care of housing, medical needs, and vacation plans, as well as employment. The smallest unit of survival is the collective.

COLOMBIA

Cultural Data

Culture type: Tribal

Playing field: Latin America

Local influences: The population is 58 percent mestizo, and 20 percent European. The business elite is primarily European.

Primary motivations: The welfare, status, and power of the tribal family group is most important.

Game Plan

Establish contact through a well-regarded local agent.

The first meeting should be on your host's turf.

Send the seniormost person from your company, along with one or two subordinates.

Plan on using an interpreter. Translate materials into Latin American Spanish.

Always address a Latino formally, using his title and family name (next-to-last name).

Expect to spend time establishing a relationship. Don't press toward a business discussion until your counterpart offers an opening.

Maintain formality in dress, posture, and speech until he relaxes the interaction.

Your image is important in communicating your own status.

Don't back away if your counterpart chooses to stand close during conversation.

Be prepared to make concessions, but only after appropriate resistance. Do not appear to negotiate these concessions. Latinos like zero-sum games.

Minimize risks in any proposal.

As an American, humble yourself. Do not assume you hold the most power because you are from the United States.

Entertain at the best restaurants.

Eat Continental style.

Once a relationship has been established, your company should not change the U.S. contact person, or else the process will have to begin again. Latinos trust people, not companies.

Local Rules

The only professional title that is used is *doctor.*

Be sure when meeting someone that you drag out the greeting. Don't be in a rush. Chat for a minute.

Gifts are not opened in front of the giver.

Women are restricted in some aspects of business.

Leave small amounts of food on your plate to indicate that you are done and don't want more.

COSTA RICA

Cultural Data

Culture type: Tribal

Playing field: Latin America

Local influences: The population is 95 percent European, which is unusual for a Central American country. Costa Rica has maintained a fairly stable government and a dynamic capitalism.

Primary motivations: This is a tribal culture with strong tendencies toward equality. Costa Ricans work for the benefit of their tribe, but also value personal achievement. There is a strong work ethic, but they are not completely goal oriented.

Game Plan

Establish contact through a well-regarded local agent.

The first meeting should be on your host's turf.

Send the seniormost person from your company, along with one or two subordinates.

Plan on using an interpreter. Translate materials into Latin American Spanish.

Always address a Latino formally, using his title and family name (next-to-last name).

Expect to spend time establishing a relationship. Don't press toward a business discussion until your counterpart offers an opening.

Maintain formality in dress, posture, and speech until he relaxes the interaction. Your image is important in communicating your own status.

Don't back away if your counterpart chooses to stand close during conversation.

Be prepared to make concessions, but only after appropriate resistance. Do not appear to negotiate these concessions. Latinos like zero-sum games.

Minimize risks in any proposal.

As an American, humble yourself. Do not assume you hold the most power because you are from the United States.

Entertain at the best restaurants.

Eat Continental style.

Once a relationship has been established, your company should not change the U.S. contact person, or else the process will have to begin again. Latinos trust people, not companies.

Local Rules

Be punctual. This is the most punctual of all Latin American countries.

Use a slightly limp handshake.

Women tend to be accepted in business, more than in other tribal countries.

Both machismo and the class system are maintained, but these are tempered by a sense of equality and respect for the individual.

CROATIA

Cultural Data

Culture type: Progressive tribal

Playing field: Central and Eastern Europe

Local influences: Croatia was ruled by the Hapsburg dynasty for centuries. After the fall of the Austro-Hungarian empire after World War I, Croatia, Slovenia, Bosnia, and Serbia were held together in a federation known as Yugoslavia. After the dictator Tito's death and the fall of the USSR, nationalism and ethnicity separated these countries. Strong tribal identity now operates.

Primary motivations: The welfare of the tribal group and the security of the larger ethnic group.

Game Plan

Approach with a personal reference or through a local agent.

First meeting should be at your host's offices.

Trust must be established before you will be accepted.

Participate in Croatia's brand of conformity and modesty. Do not flaunt affluence. Do not entertain lavishly.

Negotiate a win-win outcome.

Sharing is important. Gift giving is common and should be reciprocated.

Presentations should stress minimizing risks.

Respect age. Seniority comes with age. However, be aware that the younger generation has become more entrepreneurial since the demise of the communist system.

Local Rules

Croatians are primarily Roman Catholic. Expect both a stronger power hierarchy and centralized decision making.

Croats value kinship bonds, education, and a good career.

European manners are used.

It is acceptable to express emotion and opinions.

CZECH REPUBLIC

Cultural Data

Culture type: Progressive tribal

Playing field: Central and Eastern Europe

Local influences: During the 15th century, Prague was a center of the Protestant Reformation. In the 16th century, the Czech Republic (formerly the Bohemian empire) came under the rule of the Austrian empire, reasserting Roman Catholicism. Today, 40 percent are Roman Catholic, and the majority of the rest are unaffiliated Christians. Czechs believe in a personal relationship with a universal being.

After World War I, Czechoslovakia was a stable and affluent democracy. It was, however, unable to repel Hitler in World War II, and in 1948 came under Soviet control. Czechoslovakia has always held an independent line against the Soviet Union and openly rebelled against it several times. After the fall of the USSR in 1989, and Czechoslovakia's separation from Slovakia in 1992, the country became the Czech Republic.

Primary motivations: The welfare of the tribal group and the security of the ethnic group.

Game Plan

Approach with a personal reference or through a local agent.

First meeting should be at your host's offices.

Trust must be established before you will be accepted.

Participate in the Czech brand of conformity and modesty. Do not flaunt affluence.

Do not entertain lavishly.

Negotiate a win-win outcome.

Sharing is important. Gift giving is common and should be reciprocated.

Presentations should stress minimizing risks.

Respect age. Seniority comes with age. However, be aware that the younger generation has become more entrepreneurial since the demise of the communist system.

Local Rules

Independent thought has always been encouraged, but Czechs are truly tribal people. Cooperation and contribution are valued over individual accomplishments. The family unit is considered in all decision making.

Hierarchies tend to be formed. Leadership is valued.

Most important values: education, social standing, modesty, and cleverness.

European manners are followed.

Translation of material into Czech will impress them, but English is acceptable.

Czechs are detail oriented and will study all aspects of an agreement. Expect negotiations to move slowly.

Present information clearly, highlighting major points and using visual aids when possible.

Don't get down to business too abruptly. Relationship is important and slow to form.

Dinner entertainment is more common than lunches. Do not discuss business during a meal.

Greet people with a firm but brief handshake. Use the last name, which is the family name. Use professional titles when they are known. Wait to be introduced if there are more than two people present.

Avoid using your index finger, waving, or beckoning.

Keep your feet on the floor.

Business gifts should be inexpensive but of good quality.

Dress conservatively.

DENMARK

Cultural Data

Culture type: Pluralist

Playing field: Western Europe

Local influences: Denmark once ruled Scandinavia, but now is an equal neighbor. Still, ancient animosities remain among its former colonies. Danes recognize that theirs is a small country, and they accept the value of international trade.

Primary motivations: An ordered life, cooperation among people, and individual destiny are guiding forces.

Game Plan

Third-party introductions are not necessary, but they are always helpful.

Use English in all business dealings.

Be sure to treat Danes as equals. Do not compare Danish and American standards of living. Danes do not care. They accept their place in the world and do not strive anxiously to get ahead. They are not impressed by your wealth, possessions, or status.

Do not refer to a Dane as a Scandinavian.

Your proposal should emphasize efficiency, simplicity, and cost savings.

Danes are not rigidly formal, but polite formality should be maintained. Do not be stiff, and don't present a severe or overly elegant image.

Management is not elitist. Socializing among ranks is accepted.

During conversation, avoid personal questions. Privacy is important.

Local Rules

A handshake is as good as a contract. If you agree on something and shake hands, you had better perform.

Shake hands on meeting and leaving. Use a firm grip.

Don't comment on someone's clothes, even with a compliment. It is too personal and considered odd.

Feel free to introduce yourself in a group.

Don't drink until your host makes the first toast. Before drinking, raise your glass and look around at everyone present. Do the same after drinking.

American businesswomen will have no trouble in Denmark.

Appropriate gifts are liquor, products from your area, and coffee-table books. Gifts are not expected in business.

Eat Continental style.

When invited to someone's house, never go empty-handed. Bring flowers or candy.

ECUADOR

Cultural Data

Culture type: Tribal

Playing field: Latin America

Local influences: The population is 65 percent mestizo, and 25 percent Indian. There are few pure Europeans, but they constitute the power elite.

Primary motivations: Family status, power, and welfare are paramount.

Game Plan

Establish contact through a well-regarded local agent.

The first meeting should be on your host's turf.

Send the seniormost person from your company, along with one or two subordinates.

Plan on using an interpreter. Translate materials into Latin American Spanish.

Always address a Latino formally, using his title and family name (next-to-last name).

Expect to spend time establishing a relationship. Don't press toward a business discussion until your counterpart offers an opening.

Maintain formality in dress, posture, and speech until he relaxes the interaction.

Your image is important in communicating your own status.

Don't back away if your counterpart chooses to stand close during conversation.

Be prepared to make concessions, but only after appropriate resistance. Do not appear to negotiate these concessions. Latinos like zero-sum games.

Minimize risks in any proposal.

As an American, humble yourself. Do not assume you hold the most power because you are from the United States.

Entertain at the best restaurants.

Eat Continental style.

Once a relationship has been established, your company should not change the U.S. contact person, or else the process will have to begin again. Latinos trust people, not companies.

Local Rules

Business is somewhat less formal here, especially along the coast.

Ecuador's is a more self-centered form of tribalism. Ecuadorans show more personal interest.

There is a strong work ethic, but they are not goal oriented.

Women do not drink hard liquor.

Don't use head motions to indicate yes or no. Use words.

EGYPT

Cultural Data

Culture type: Tribal

Playing field: Arab world

Local influences: Egyptians are proud of their ancient civilization, but Islam is so dominant over the present culture that ancient influences do not prevail.

Primary motivations: The welfare of the tribe, along with maintaining and increasing its power and status while upholding the laws of Islam and the security of the nation, guides all action.

Game Plan

Be cognizant of the nature of Islamic law and morality. They dictate behavior.

Make your first approach through a well-connected local representative.

You must be present to be of consequence. Meetings should be at your host's offices.

Relationships and trust come before business.

Business associates must stay in constant communication for the relationship to continue.

Expect endless delays in appointments. Time is not linear. Be patient and expect to take a long time completing a transaction.

Humility is highly regarded, especially in a powerful person.

Arabs love to bargain, but do not inflate your price too much. Your first offer must be good enough to attract his attention.

Minimize risks and uncertainty in your proposals. Praise and appreciation for your counterpart must be verbalized often.

Maintain formality in behavior, appearance, and address.

Project a successful image.

Never refuse Arab hospitality. Always reciprocate.

Never reprimand or criticize directly. Failure is not directly acknowledged. Honor is very important. Deal with negatives euphemistically.

Never admit that you are a "self-made man." Lineage is important to Arabs. You are a reflection of your entire family.

Proposals, plans, and negotiations should focus on the people issues. People are most important to Arabs.

Local Rules

Do not use first names immediately. Wait for your host to offer.

Don't take any criticism of the U.S. government personally. Egyptians like Americans, but often criticize U.S. government policies.

Do not discuss bad news on a social occasion.

The U.S. gesture for waving good-bye means *come here.*

Women should avoid direct eye contact with men and avoid crowds, where men may try to touch.

Finishing everything on your plate is considered rude. Leaving food indicates the abundance of the host.

Law requires that a company doing business in Egypt must have an Egyptian agent. Get separate agents for Cairo and Alexandria.

Political contacts do not have the same influence in Egypt as they do in other Arab countries.

In the cities, businesswomen do not have difficulty doing business. Entertain at hotel restaurants that are European style.

ENGLAND

Cultural Data
Culture type: Tribal/pluralist
Playing field: Western Europe
Local influences: Great Britain comprises England, Scotland, and Wales. The United Kingdom comprises Great Britain and Northern Ireland. England is tribal; Scotland and Wales are pluralistic.
Primary motivations: Maintenance of both status and the status quo.

Game Plan
Form first, deference second, competence last—these are what the English expect, in that order.

The English derive their identity from their family and its place in society.

A prestigious third-party introduction will open doors and speed the process.

England is a nation of managers. Form a "coalition" with your counterpart as well as with subordinates.

Formal manners and attention to every detail are necessary.

Be punctual.

Image is everything, but don't play the game of one-upsmanship.

Avoid comments about one's stature, power, or financial status. This would be rude. Personal comments should be avoided in general.

Privacy is important. Do not repeat conversations or distribute information unless your English counterpart is informed in advance.

In presentations, appeal to the rational side of the English and to their desire to maintain tradition.

Local Rules
Shake hands only when meeting. Always wait for a woman to extend her hand first. Say "how do you do," rather than "hello," and expect the same reply. No answer is expected.

If you say something is "quite good," you have not given a compliment. In general, remember that British English and American English are not the same. There are many words that have different meanings. It is best to consult a book on British usage before spending a lot of time there.

To get a waiter's attention, use eye contact. Don't wave.

Businesswomen might find men condescending, depending on their age and the type of business they're in.

If, in the course of working together, you and your English counterpart agree on action items for each side, don't make changes to the plans unless you get together again. He will feel that you are usurping his power if you do anything not agreed on.

Wait for a British businessperson to offer the first invitation to lunch. You should reciprocate when possible.

Don't offer business gifts.

Eat Continental style.

ESTONIA

Cultural Data

Culture type: Pluralist

Playing field: Central and Eastern Europe

Local influences: Although Estonia has been in the Russian sphere of influence, historically its existence was closely tied with the Scandinavian countries, especially Sweden. This produced a strong individual orientation, which is unusual for Central and Eastern Europe.

Primary motivations: Personal achievement and progress.

Game Plan

Third-party introductions are not necessary, but always useful.

Many people you will be doing business with speak English. However, do not take this for granted. Check to see if you should have information translated and use an interpreter.

Greet people with a firm handshake.

Wait until you are invited to use someone's first name.

Remain formal in your manners and posture, even though you are using first names.

Contracts can be verbal. If you assent to an agreement verbally, expect to be held to your word.

Keep your presentation precise, logical, and straightforward.

Eat Continental style.

FINLAND

Cultural Data

Culture type: Pluralist

Playing field: Western Europe

Local influences: Finland is a Scandinavian country that has been ruled at times by both Russia and Sweden. It has retained more of the Swedish influence, and many customs are shared.

Primary motivations: Logic and self-interest are important to success. Finns also wish to preserve their unique national identity.

Game Plan

Third-party introductions are not necessary, but always useful.

Most Finns you will be doing business with speak English. However, do not take this for granted. Check to see if you should have information translated and use an interpreter.

Greet people with a firm handshake.

Finns commonly use first names, but wait until you are invited to use a person's first name.

Remain formal in your manners and posture, even though you are using first names.

Contracts can be verbal. If you assent to an agreement verbally, expect to be held to your word.

Be warned that Finns are very straightforward with their opinions and will aggressively assert their position.

Keep your presentation precise, logical, and straightforward.

Local Rules

Shake hands when introduced and when leaving.

Don't stand with your arms folded. It is a sign of arrogance.

At a meal, the host and hostess toast their guests. They never receive toasts from their guests.

Don't leave food on your plate.

An invitation to a sauna is the equivalent of an invitation to an American golf course. An invitation is unlikely if you are a woman dealing with men.

Foreign businesswomen are accepted.

An agreement is usually celebrated by a long lunch.

FRANCE

Cultural Data

Culture type: Pluralist/tribal

Playing field: Western Europe

Local influences: France is caught between two cultures and so has blended both: tribal in the south and pluralistic in the north.

Primary motivations: Personal freedom, not personal achievement.

Game Plan

Use a prestigious third-party for an introduction. The French are status conscious.

Go to your host's offices.

Translate everything into French. Use an interpreter. It is helpful if you yourself can speak French.

A handshake may not be offered. If it is, use a moderate grip.

Show some sophistication. Be knowledgeable about French culture and history.

Do not attempt to find common ground in a social sense. The French do not want to relate to you personally.

Your appearance should be impeccable and elegant, and a bit on the formal side.

Your proposal must be compelling. The French do not like to deal with foreigners.

Do not trust words. Get it in writing. Get a contract signed.

Appeal to their self-interest.

Time is not money; it is power and is used as a manipulative device.

Use formal etiquette, last names, and titles.

Do not try a hard sell. The French disdain selling.

Use the Continental dining style, or you will be thought of as a barbarian.

Local Rules

Shake hands with a quick, light grip when meeting and leaving. No pumping.

When entering a room, greet everyone in it.

Be careful not to speak or laugh loudly. The French speak more quietly than Americans.

Don't drink until your host proposes a toast, after which everyone will say *santé* (\sahn-TAY\) and drink. Your host will continue pouring you wine if your glass is empty. If you don't want to drink much, take small sips.

Place your bread on the table next to your plate. There are no bread plates.

Finish everything on your plate.

Businesswomen will be more accepted in the north than in the south of France. Businessmen may treat a woman flirtatiously, but not condescendingly. Businesswomen should give special attention to their dress. They must be fashionable and elegant.

Contracts are written in precise detail, but they tend to be advisory. The French may not honor all contract points. As a method of updating their concurrence from time to time, stress often the points that are most important to you.

Business lunches are more popular than dinners. Don't expect to talk business. Lunch could last two hours.

If you are hosting a meal at a restaurant, be sure you get a menu that has prices. Some restaurants give the prices only to the host. If as a guest you are given a menu without prices, either let your host order or ask what he recommends.

The best gifts are those with some intellectual or aesthetic appeal instead of logo gifts. Don't give a gift until you have met someone several times.

It would be wise to know something about California wine. The subject will probably come up over a meal. The French love to discuss wine. Don't expect to know as much as they do on the subject, but be able to offer some opinion.

GERMANY

Cultural Data

Culture type: Pluralist

Playing field: Western Europe

Local influences: Germany varies from strong pluralism in the north to tribal tendencies in the Catholic south. Reunification has revealed the strong communist cultural influence on a generation of East German people. It may take another generation to reawaken their pluralist nature. When dealing with former East Germans, a study of the Central and East European game would be wise.

Primary motivations: Personal achievement and power.

Game Plan

Germans prefer the power position of meeting on their own turf.

Research your targeted company thoroughly. Your hosts will be impressed by preparation and offended by ignorance.

A third-party introduction is imperative. Germans are highly secretive and closed. Bankers and lawyers represent appropriate references. Alternatively, German trade fairs are good sources for establishing contacts.

Do not assume that meetings will be conducted in English. Translate all material and use an interpreter.

All documents should look polished and professional.

Maintain formality at all times. Self-control is very important.

Dress very conservatively and formally.

Be prepared to back up all of your figures. Allow some room for negotiation.

Germans value intelligence. They are impressed by thoughtful questions.

Don't compliment a German. Germans offer compliments only if something is outstanding.

Your presentation should highlight how their performance will be enhanced. You must prove all your claims.

Privacy is important. Don't ask personal questions.

Eat Continental style.

Local Rules

When introduced, use a firm handshake with one distinct shake, and state your last name.

Shake hands when meeting and leaving. Be sure to include the secretary.

Relationship building comes after business for the Germans. At the end of business discussions, a German may ask you to stay and share a brandy with him. Do not refuse.

At a party or business meeting, wait to be introduced by a third person.

Never say anything negative about soccer or the local team. Germans take the sport very seriously.

It is not customary for a woman to thank a man when receiving a compliment.

Men should allow people of higher status to walk through a door first, and in social situations, women also. But when entering a restaurant, a man should walk in front of a woman. During business a woman should let one of higher status enter first, but in social situations proceed first.

Never eat with your fingers—not even a sandwich.

Never use your knife to cut potatoes, pancakes, or dumplings. It implies the food isn't cooked right.

Finish everything on your plate—even in restaurants—or make an excuse.

The guest makes the first move to go. If when you are visiting someone your host does not refill your glass, it is an indication that you should go.

Don't ask for coffee with a meal. It is served afterward.

A businesswoman will be perceived as not having authority to make decisions. Make it clear what your corporate authority is. Have your CEO send a letter introducing you as the company representative and delineating the decision-making authority you have.

Any gift should be small and simple. Large, expensive gifts are considered tasteless. If you are sending flowers to a hostess, never send red roses. They mean love. Avoid chrysanthemums, also. Send an odd number, but not 13.

GREECE

Cultural Data

Culture type: Progressive tribal

Playing field: Greece

Local influences: The present-day Greek's attachment to his ancient Greek ancestors separates him from a Western Europe ruled historically by Rome. The Greek looks eastward, but is strongly democratic and capitalistic.

Primary motivations: Tribal welfare and advancement.

Game Plan

It is wise to use a local intermediary to establish contacts.

Relationship building is important, and friendship comes with obligation.

Be punctual, even though your Greek counterpart will not be.

Shake hands with a firm grip, and don't break away too quickly.

Use last names and titles when introduced, showing special respect for older people.

Business cards should be printed in both Greek and English. Hand the card Greek side up, being sure that the writing is right side up.

Dress conservatively.

Presentations should include a variety of presentation techniques, many visual.

Treat the senior member in a group with respect. Authority usually rests with him, although there is a need for consensus in decision-making groups.

Expect to bargain and make quick decisions.

Patience is important in negotiations, but be prepared to move quickly on a moment's notice.

Language is often exaggerated and emotional.

Local Rules

Business is often conducted over a cup of coffee. Informal meetings may be held in a coffeehouse.

Lunch is the main meal of the day. Dinner is small and served late.

In some restaurants, the communal approach is followed whereby diners share several dishes.

The head-nodding gestures indicating yes and no can be confusing because they are traditionally reversed in Greece. Unfortunately, many people have taken to the American method, and so it is hard to know what is meant. Don't assume that you do.

A smile can mean anger as well as pleasure.

Don't give business gifts at the first meeting. Don't give token gifts merely to display your company logo.

HONG KONG

Cultural Data

Culture type: Collective

Playing field: Pacific Rim

Local influences: Hong Kong is a British Crown Colony until 1997, when it will revert to Chinese rule. It will be allowed to keep its capitalist system for 50 years after 1997, but many Hong Kong Chinese are fleeing the country, not trusting the mainland Chinese.

Primary motivations: Self-determination and collective prosperity.

Game Plan

Approach through a local representative.

Personal relationships must be established before business is done. Do not assume this means you are a personal friend.

Top management should be present at the first meeting. Your company should be represented by a group of specialists at this first meeting. Do not include a lawyer.

Negotiations will be time-consuming. Expect to make many trips. Be patient.

Study *Bing Fa* strategy.

One who is powerful and successful shows his humility.

Harmony must be maintained. Do not confront or question anyone in a negative way. Never say no. Expect your hosts to always say yes, which might mean no.

Allow them to win something in negotiations.

Recognize and respect the social position of all you encounter. Do not expect them to require equality.

Never compliment a person directly. Never praise someone in front of his superiors. Praise the group.

Negotiations may appear cyclical rather than linear. Be prepared to discuss any subject out of sequence at any time.

Local Rules

Greet everyone when you arrive, beginning with the seniormost person. Use a light handshake. Address people with their surname and title.

Be punctual.

Never refuse an invitation to lunch or dinner. If you must, offer an alternative date.

Accept tea if it is offered. Wait for your host to drink first.

A banquet is appropriate at the end of negotiations. Always reciprocate if you are given one.

Refuse hospitality three times before accepting, so you don't look greedy.

Decorum is important in both the Chinese and British cultures in Hong Kong.

Men should not cross their legs, but keep them on the floor.

Do not wear blue or white. These colors are reserved for mourning.

Do not open a gift in the presence of the giver.

HUNGARY

Cultural Data

Culture type: Progressive tribal

Playing field: Central and Eastern Europe

Local influences: Hungary developed a high level of culture during the Renaissance. It came under the influence of the Hapsburg dynasty in the 16th century, and in 1867 a dual monarchy was declared, beginning the Austro-Hungarian empire. This was a union of Germanic and Slavic people that lasted until the end of World War I. In 1949, Hungary became a communist socialist state. It is now a democracy and is one of the most prosperous East European nations.

Primary motivations: Tribal welfare and national identity.

Game Plan

Approach with a personal reference or through a local agent.

First meeting should be at your host's offices.

Trust must be established before you will be accepted.

Participate in the Hungarian brand of conformity and modesty. Do not flaunt affluence.

Do not entertain lavishly.

Negotiate a win-win outcome.

Sharing is important. Gift giving is common and should be reciprocated.

Presentations should stress minimizing risks.

Respect age. Seniority comes with age. However, be aware that the younger generation has become more entrepreneurial since the demise of the communist system.

Local Rules

The country is two-thirds Roman Catholic (a result of the Austrian association) and one-quarter Protestant. Religion is not a big part of Hungarian life.

Vertical hierarchy is preferred, but consensus decision making may prevail until greater confidence in business has been achieved.

Hungarians value family, education, job security, private property, and travel.

They admire professionals and intellectuals over the merely wealthy.

Intentions, feelings, and opinions may be directly expressed. Deviousness is not respected.

Once you have a local representative, do not change to another, or else you may have to start over in your agreements.

Your host will probably entertain you. Hospitality is important to Hungarians. At the end of negotiations, you should host a cocktail party or dinner at a good hotel.

A firm handshake is used when meeting and leaving. Use family names until invited to use first names. In Hungary, the family name precedes the given name.

When visiting a company, bring many small gifts to distribute to everyone you meet.

Hungarians love horses. You may be invited to go riding. If you know how to ride, this is a good topic of conversation.

INDIA

Cultural Data

Culture type: Tribal/collective
Playing field: India
Local influences: India must be understood in context with its religious beliefs. Hinduism, followed by 88 percent of the population, is central to Indian life.
Primary motivations: The welfare of the family group.

Game Plan

A medium-firm handshake is the proper greeting for business. You may see people greeting each other with the *namaste* (\nah-mah-STAY\), which one does by placing the hands together as if in prayer, fingers pointing up, and bowing the head slightly.

Use your host's last name, along with "Mr." It is not appropriate for a foreigner to use the term *sahib*.

Don't shake a woman's hand unless she offers it. Men generally do not touch women in public. It is polite to refer to women as ladies.

A business card printed in English should be provided. Your card should include your title, academic degrees, and professional affiliations. This will help the Indian position you in his universe.

Be punctual. Your host may not be.

Relationship is important, but an Indian will get down to business fairly quickly.

Accept any hospitality offered.

Social distance may be close, but touching is not common during conversation.

British manners prevail. Be subdued. Self-control is favored over impulsiveness. A quietly self-confident aura breeds trust and respect. However, one should be friendly and communicative.

Indians are tolerant of others. Be cautious in giving criticism. They take offense easily.

Use the right hand when passing papers and objects and when eating.

Keep shoes and feet on the floor.

Whistling is considered rude.

Request meetings via fax or telex. The mail is unreliable. Use courier service if necessary.

Your first meeting should include the head of the company, who will probably make the final decision on your proposal. Always try to match the status of meeting participants. If you send your chief technical person, make your appointment with a technical person. Speak to the secretary of your targeted person to be sure you are contacting the right person at the appropriate level.

A business lunch is appropriate after an interest in your business has been established. It is acceptable to talk business over the meal.

Dinner invitations should be offered only after some sort of relationship has been established.

Local Rules

Entertaining is usually done in private clubs or in restaurants.

The guest of honor should be seated to the right of the host. There are no other seating formalities.

There is no toasting ritual. Your host may offer a toast in the British manner, if he has spent time in England.

The Continental style of eating is used in most Westernized restaurants. The traditional manner of eating is by using the right hand and no utensils.

Hindus do not eat beef.

Gifts are a sign of friendship. They should be modest and reserved for later meetings.

There is a significant Moslem population, especially in the northern section of the country. Study the Arab world game for proper interaction with a Moslem. Be sure to use only your right hand, be considerate of Moslems who will be fasting during the month of Ramadan, and remember that they don't eat pork or drink alcohol.

INDONESIA

Cultural Data

Culture type: Collective/tribal

Playing field: Pacific Rim

Local influences: Indonesia has the largest Moslem population in the world. See the Arab world game for much of the protocol that is appropriate here. However, Indonesia has naturally a collective culture base with Islamic culture overlaid. Hierarchies tend to be more authoritarian. A majority of Indonesian businesspeople are ethnic Chinese, so it is important to know the Pacific Rim game as well.

Primary motivations: The welfare, status, and security of the family tribe and collective group.

Game Plan

Because most Indonesian businesspeople are ethnic Chinese, the game plan for collective culture should apply. Try to determine the background of the person you are meeting. His name should give a reliable indication of his ethnic background.

Approach through a local representative.

Personal relationships must be established before business is done. Do not assume this means you are a personal friend.

Top management should be present at the first meeting. Your company should be represented by a group of specialists at this first meeting. Do not include a lawyer.

Negotiations will be time-consuming. Expect to make many trips. Be patient.

Study *Bing Fa* strategy.

One who is powerful and successful shows his humility.

Harmony must be maintained. Do not confront or question anyone in a negative way. Never say no. Expect Indonesians to always say yes, which might mean no.

Allow them to win something in negotiations.

Recognize and respect the social position of all you encounter. Do not expect them to require equality.

Never compliment a person directly. Never praise someone in front of his superiors. Praise the group.

Negotiations may appear cyclical rather than linear. Be prepared to discuss any subject out of sequence at any time.

Local Rules

In the Bahasa Indonesia language, it is difficult to converse with a person until you know his status relative to yourself. Pronouns depend on relative status.

At social gatherings, those of lesser status should arrive first. An invitation may tell you when to arrive. If you are asked to arrive early, you can be sure you are not the most important guest.

The Arab concept of time is followed by Indonesians as well. It is called rubber time. Chinese expect punctuality.

The response, "Yes, but . . . ," means no.

Facts are "degrees of probability." Compromise and accommodation are always in order.

Decisions require consensus.

Agents' fees and such may crop up. The foreigner should stay out of this type of negotiation and allow the Indonesians to attack the issue.

Although Moslem, Indonesians do not like to be singled out in a group, true to their collective nature. Do not compliment an individual, but compliment the group.

Like Arabs, Indonesians are accustomed to physical touching within the same sex. This is often part of a close relationship, unlike in other parts of Asia.

Shake hands only upon initial introduction and before and after a long separation. Use a weak hand clasp. Do not rush the greeting.

Naming conventions are not standardized. Some people have one name; some have several. Ask how to address a person. If he is Chinese, use the first name.

Gifts are given often. Any small occasion is appropriate, even when someone comes to tour the factory. Gifts need not be expensive. Do not open gifts in the presence of the giver. Refuse a gift three times before accepting.

A dinner guest should wait to begin eating or drinking until asked to do so. If you are the guest of honor, refuse the honor several times before accepting.

Be careful not to invite a Moslem to lunch during the month of Ramadan. He will be fasting.

IRAQ

Cultural Data

Culture type: Tribal

Playing field: Arab world

Local influences: Iraq is one of the more progressive and powerful of all Arab countries.

Primary motivations: Tribal power, status, and prosperity, as well as national security and the rule of religious law.

Game Plan

Be cognizant of the nature of Islamic law and morality. It dictates behavior.

Make your first approach through a well-connected local representative.

You must be present to be of consequence. Meetings should be at your host's offices.

Relationships and trust come before business.

Business associates must stay in constant communication for the relationship to continue.

Expect endless delays in appointments. Time is not linear. Be patient and expect to take a long time completing a transaction.

Humility is highly regarded, especially in a powerful person.

Iraqis love to bargain, but do not inflate your price too much. Your first offer must be good enough to attract an Iraqi's attention.

Minimize risks and uncertainty in your proposals. Praise and appreciation for your counterpart must be verbalized often.

Maintain formality in behavior, appearance, and address.

Project a successful image.

Never refuse Iraqi hospitality. Always reciprocate.

Never reprimand or criticize directly. Failure is not directly acknowledged. Honor is very important. Deal with negatives euphemistically.

Never admit that you are a "self-made man." Lineage is important to Iraqis. You are a reflection of your entire family.

Proposals, plans, and negotiations should focus on the people issues. People are most important to Iraqis.

Local Rules

Use first names as soon as you are introduced.

When offered food or drink, refuse the first time, then accept.

Iraq is much less formal than other Arab countries.

Almost all business goes through the Iraqi government.

Iraqis don't like the excessive praise and flowery language used in other Arab nations.

Women have had equal rights for 20 years.

Never try to bribe anyone.

The best business gift is a book.

IRELAND

Cultural Data

Culture type: Tribal

Playing field: Western Europe

Local influences: Ireland is not a part of the United Kingdom, but it shares heavily in the cultural history that formed the British Isles. The Roman Catholic Church has maintained its dominant position in Ireland since the fifth century and even today shapes the life of the Irish. Northern Ireland is not part of Ireland. It is predominantly Protestant and is under British rule. When we speak of Ireland, we are not including Northern Ireland.

Primary motivations: Family or clan welfare and enjoyment of life.

Game Plan

Third-party introductions are not necessary, but are helpful.

The attitude toward business is more relaxed than in other northern European nations.

Punctuality is not required, but you should be on time for meetings.

Use more formal manners in Ireland than you would in the United States.

Relationship building is important. Don't hurry into business discussions.

Dress conservatively, but do not be overly formal.

Shake hands upon greeting and leaving. Use last names until invited to use first names.

The Irish are very tolerant of foreigners. They do not take offense easily.

Business cards are not commonly used in Ireland. Bring them with you to leave with a secretary if the person you want to see is out.

Local Rules

Keep gestures to a minimum.

Wear tailored clothing, even for casual wear. Dress warmly.

Gift giving in business is not done. If you are invited to someone's home, don't go empty-handed. Flowers (not roses, not red or white, not an even number, not 13, and not wrapped), candy, cheeses, and wine all make good hostess gifts. If someone gives you a gift, open it immediately.

When shaking hands, wait for a woman to extend her hand first.

At a large party, introduce yourself. In a small group, wait to be introduced.

When the Irish describe someone as plain, it's a compliment.

When offered a drink, raise your glass before drinking and say cheers.

At dinner, the small plate next to your dinner plate is not for bread. It is for the peelings that you are supposed to remove from boiled potatoes. Bread is rarely served at dinner.

When ordering beer at a pub, a woman is expected to order a half pint, but a man ordering less than a full pint will have his masculinity questioned.

There are few businesswomen in Ireland, but American businesswomen are taken seriously.

ISRAEL

Cultural Data

Culture type: Tribal/pluralist

Playing field: Israel

Local influences: Modern Israel was created in 1948 when Israel claimed itself independent from British control. Although held together by a shared religion, Israel's inhabitants came from many cultural backgrounds. Only 60 percent of the population is native to Israel. Business practices may be North American, Russian, European, or Mediterranean style. The game must be played keeping in mind exactly who the other players are.

Primary motivations: Family and personal gain as well as the security, and the security of Israel. Protocol and etiquette support the needs of the family over the needs of the individual.

Game Plan

Jews are divided into two ethnic heritages. Sephardic Jews come from the Mediterranean area, northern Africa, and the Middle East. Ashkenazic Jews come from Europe. Ashkenazic Jews are dominant in politics and religion, and Sephardic Jews are dominant in government and business.

Ashkenazic Jews tend to show strong pluralist tendencies; Sephardic Jews are tribal. The Jewish religion promotes, or rather, reflects, a tribal perception. Even though some Ashkenazic Jews come from strong pluralist countries such as Germany and the Netherlands, their culture has always maintained the tribal hierarchy.

About 50 percent of the Jews in Israel are Orthodox Jews. It is interesting to note that they share many customs with Moslems.

The approach to Israel is to study general tribal culture, the Arab world game, the Central and East European game, and the West European game.

The game plan to use with a Sephardic contact is similar to that of the Arab game plan. Things happen slowly, and there is not much regard for time. People and their problems and concerns are more important than striking a deal. It will take many meetings to complete a deal.

Spatial attitude is similar to the Arab attitude. People stand close together and touch to emphasize a point.

Israelis put a high regard on hosting, as do Arabs. Coffee is served at the end of a business meeting, as in Moslem countries.

Control of the body in posture and gestures is similar to that in the Arab game plan.

The game plan to be used with Ashkenazic contacts is more European in style. Punctuality is important.

Formality and reserve are noted.

People tend to get down to business faster.

Don't disregard the tribal tendencies of this group. Your hosts must come to trust a person before doing business.

Local Rules

Israel has a democratic and egalitarian culture that values competition.

The Israeli negotiating style is much more confrontational. Israelis love to argue and debate.

Women are legally equal in status and even serve in the military. Men still dominate, however, as in all tribal societies.

The security of the state is taken into consideration when making major decisions.

The holy days are Friday and Saturday each week. Judaism and Islam both use a lunar calendar. Israelis are used to thinking in 28-day months.

Use engraved business cards. Print them in both English and Hebrew (Arabic, if you are visiting an Israeli Arab).

Businesswomen should not extend their hand to greet an Orthodox Jewish man. His religion has laws against touching women. Women should also never hand something directly to an Orthodox man, but put it next to him so he can pick it up. Orthodox Jews can usually be identified by their yarmulke, or skullcap. Half of Israel's Jews are considered secular and do not observe these rituals.

The common greeting is to shake hands and address the person using Mr., etc., plus the surname. *Shalom*, which means *peace*, is said when greeting and leaving.

Conservative business suits are appropriate, and, in general, modest dress is required.

The Continental style of eating is most widely used.

Pointing at someone with the index finger is rude, as in most of the world beyond America.

ITALY

Cultural Data

Culture type: Tribal/pluralist

Playing field: Western Europe

Local influences: There are two Italys: the north, dominated by Milan, and the south, dominated by Rome. Most business is done in the north. Government is attended to in Rome.

Primary motivations: In the pluralist north: personal achievement. In the tribal south: the welfare of the family.

Game Plan

Shake hands when meeting and leaving. Exchange business cards with anyone you haven't already met.

An introduction from a mutual business associate is very useful.

First meeting should take place at your host's offices.

Business takes precedence over relationship building.

Use formal manners, but do not be overly stiff.

Use last names unless asked to do otherwise.

Do not gesture with your hands in the north. Northern Italians value self-control.

Dress should be conservative, yet fashionable.

Sincerity is important.

Local Rules

In the south you may encounter more physical touching during greetings, like the touch of a hand on the shoulder.

Don't drink until your host does. Take small sips, or else your glass will be refilled. Women should not pour wine.

When eating spaghetti, don't cut it or twirl it against a spoon. Twirl it against the side of the dish.

Even though you are the one who has invited people to a restaurant, there will be fighting over the check. You must insist on paying. A businesswoman has almost no chance of picking up the bill unless payment is arranged ahead and she explains that the company has paid.

Women are taken seriously in business, but if a woman is traveling with a man, she will be taken for his secretary. Women must dress very formally and expensively to give the signal that they are a person of some authority. Always place academic degrees and titles on your business card.

When arriving in Italy, send a fax to confirm your appointment. The phones are not reliable.

Don't discuss business or hand out business cards in a social setting.

When you invite an Italian businessperson to a meal, ask which colleagues should be included in the invitation.

JAPAN

Cultural Data

Culture type: Collective

Playing field: Pacific Rim

Local influences: Although Japan is related to other Asian countries through its inheritance of Chinese Confucian philosophy, it has been isolated from other cultures during past centuries, and so has developed a unique culture and a homogeneous society.

Primary motivations: The welfare and honor of the collective group.

Game Plan

Approach through a local representative.

Personal relationships must be established before business is done. Do not assume this means you are a personal friend.

Top management should be present at the first meeting. Your company should be represented by a group of specialists at this first meeting. Do not include a lawyer.

Negotiations will be time-consuming. Expect to make many trips. Be patient.

Study *Bing Fa* strategy.

One who is powerful and successful shows his humility.

Harmony must be maintained. Do not confront or question anyone in a negative way. Never say no. Expect Japanese to always say yes, which might mean no.

Allow them to win something in negotiations.

Recognize and respect the social position of all you encounter. Do not expect them to require equality.

Never compliment a person directly. Never praise someone in front of his superiors. Praise the group.

Negotiations may appear cyclical rather than linear. Be prepared to discuss any subject out of sequence at any time.

Local Rules

The Japanese language is very subtle. There is much left unspoken, but to a Japanese, all is understood.

Use of an interpreter is recommended, even if the Japanese say they speak English. Provide your own interpreter. The two languages require completely different thought processes, and your hosts will probably understand only half of what you are saying. When they respond to your remarks with a big smile, they have not understood.

Numbers should always be written down on paper for clarity.

A negatively phrased question will be answered with yes if the listener agrees. This is one way to elicit negative feedback. Allow the Japanese to say yes to a negative question.

Letters will not be answered if the sender is not known.

Foreign companies do not have to go through trading companies to do business in Japan. However, it is important to have an intermediary or agent to make introductions and set appointments, especially if you are a small company.

Use an intermediary to discuss bad news.

Be punctual for meetings. For social engagements, be somewhat late.

Greet people with a weak handshake and a nod of the head. Don't try the bow. You will never get it right. Cast your eyes down.

Present business cards after shaking hands.

Address the person by his last name. Use *Mr.* and the last name. Foreigners should not use the honor term, *san,* after the name.

The smallest gesture may have great meaning. Keep your hands and face quiet.

Don't blow your nose in public, and never use a cloth handkerchief. Use a disposable one.

Gestures indicating a negative response can be fanning the right hand in front of the face and sucking air.

Maintain greater separation between people when conversing than is normal in the United States.

Gift giving is very important to the Japanese. The ceremony is equally as important as the present itself. Business gifts must be given January 1 and July 15 (year-end and mid-year). Gifts are often exchanged on first meeting. Wait for your host to offer a gift first. Reciprocate with a gift of equal quality. Remember: image is everything. Logo gifts from well-known Western stores are appreciated. Never give an even number of anything, and especially avoid the number four. Avoid giving anything predominantly white, which signifies death. Have gifts wrapped in Japan by a wrapping service or hotel service. The Japanese have their own notions of what is attractive. The wrapping is part of the symbolism. Bows are not used. Consult a local person for color suggestions.

Wear slip-on shoes, because you will be removing them frequently. Slippers are provided for guests on their entering a home and some restaurants. Be aware that special slippers are to be worn in the bathroom. Change your slippers going in, and don't forget to change coming out, or you might be walking around with a pair of slippers that say *toilet* on them.

If you wear a kimono, or kimono-style wrap clothing, always wrap left over right. Only corpses are wrapped right over left.

Use visual aids whenever possible. This does not mean text on an overhead projector, but illustrations and diagrams.

The term *manager* does not mean *the* manager, but more likely means one of many managers in a group. Be careful of Japanese corporate hierarchy and use the Japanese title that best describes your status. Do some company research.

Unless the visitor is selling, your host will make the first invitation for evening entertainment. Entertainment is lavish and should be reciprocated. Keep parity of status in mind when initiating an invitation.

Evening entertainment includes large quantities of alcohol to "aid in the search for inner truth." Dinner is often followed by a trip to several bars, each with decreasing formality. It is not offensive to be drunk, unless you become abusive. Group seating arrangements at a restaurant are important (see Chapter 9).

During meetings, sit opposite the person who matches your rank.

Refuse hospitality three times before accepting, so you don't look greedy.

JORDAN

Cultural Data

Culture type: Tribal

Playing field: Arab world

Local influences: Jordan has allowed Western influence in some aspects of its culture, while remaining an Islamic nation.

Primary motivations: The welfare of the tribal family group, and adherence to Islam.

Game Plan

Be cognizant of the nature of Islamic law and morality. It dictates behavior.

Make your first approach through a well-connected local representative.

You must be present to be of consequence. Meetings should be at your host's offices.

Relationships and trust come before business.

Business associates must stay in constant communication for the relationship to continue.

Expect endless delays in appointments. Time is not linear. Be patient and expect to take a long time completing a transaction.

Humility is highly regarded, especially in a powerful person.

Jordanians love to bargain, but do not inflate your price too much. Your first offer must be good enough to attract your host's attention.

Minimize risks and uncertainty in your proposals. Praise and appreciation for your counterpart must be verbalized often.

Maintain formality in behavior, appearance, and address.

Project a successful image.

Never refuse Jordanian hospitality. Always reciprocate.

Never reprimand or criticize directly. Failure is not directly acknowledged. Honor is very important. Deal with negatives euphemistically.

Never admit that you are a "self-made man." Lineage is important to Jordanians. You are a reflection of your entire family.

Proposals, plans, and negotiations should focus on the people issues. People are most important to Jordanians.

Local Rules

English is Jordan's second language.

Address people you don't know well by the English titles, *Mr.*, *Mrs.*, and *Miss.*

Jordan is much less conservative than other Arab nations. Women may dine out with men.

Private Jordanian businessmen are much more straightforward than other Arabs.

If a woman must do business in Jordan, she is given honorary male status.

KUWAIT

Cultural Data

Culture type: Tribal

Playing field: Arab world

Local influences: Kuwait is a very small, very wealthy independent state.

Primary motivations: The status, power, and wealth of the tribal group.

Game Plan

Be cognizant of the nature of Islamic law and morality. It dictates behavior.

Make your first approach through a well-connected local representative.

You must be present to be of consequence. Meetings should be at your host's offices.

Relationships and trust come before business.

Business associates must stay in constant communication for the relationship to continue.

Expect endless delays in appointments. Time is not linear. Be patient and expect to take a long time completing a transaction.

Humility is highly regarded, especially in a powerful person.

Kuwaitis love to bargain, but do not inflate your price too much. Your first offer must be good enough to attract your host's attention.

Minimize risks and uncertainty in your proposals. Praise and appreciation for your counterpart must be verbalized often.

Maintain formality in behavior, appearance, and address.

Project a successful image.

Never refuse Kuwaiti hospitality. Always reciprocate.

Never reprimand or criticize directly. Failure is not directly acknowledged. Honor is very important. Deal with negatives euphemistically.

Never admit that you are a "self-made man." Lineage is important to Kuwaitis. You are a reflection of your entire family.

Proposals, plans, and negotiations should focus on the people issues. People are most important to Kuwaitis.

Local Rules

When you see someone bowing and kissing someone's hand, do not feel that you must do likewise.

After any meal, leave after you finish coffee.

Send your company's CEO to do all business. Sometimes decisions are made on the spot.

Suggest that instead of meeting at your host's office, you meet at your hotel lobby. There won't be so many interruptions—or so much Turkish coffee. Remember that you are now the host and must be generous in your hospitality.

When meeting with a group from the Kuwaiti company, the Kuwaiti who sits, listens, and says nothing is usually the decision maker.

Your meeting is over when coffee is served again.

Kuwaitis are very punctual. Don't be even 10 minutes late.

Do not send a woman to do business.

Never whistle in public.

LATVIA

Cultural Data

Culture type: Pluralist

Playing field: Central and Eastern Europe

Local influences: Along with Estonia, Latvia has historically been associated with the Scandinavian countries, especially Sweden. Latvians are currently shaking off the communist legacy and returning to their pluralist ways.

Primary motivations: Personal achievement and progress.

Game Plan

Third-party introductions are not necessary, but always useful.

Many people you will be doing business with speak English. However, do not take this for granted. Check to see whether you should have information translated and use an interpreter.

Greet people with a firm handshake.

Wait until you are invited to use someone's first name.

Remain formal in your manners and posture, even though you are using first names.

Contracts can be verbal. If you assent to an agreement verbally, expect to be held to your word.

Keep your presentation precise, logical, and straightforward.

Eat Continental style.

LITHUANIA

Cultural Data

Culture type: Progressive tribal

Playing field: Central and Eastern Europe

Local influences: For centuries, Lithuania and Poland have had close ties, including their Roman Catholic faith. They developed along the same lines until they were partitioned in 1775. Lithuania then came under Russian rule until 1920, when it regained independence briefly. In 1940, it was again annexed by Russia and in 1990 declared independence.

Primary motivations: The welfare and security of the tribal group and ethnic group.

Game Plan

Approach with a personal reference or through a local agent.

First meeting should be at your host's offices.

Trust must be established before you will be accepted.

Participate in the Lithuanian brand of conformity and modesty. Do not flaunt affluence.

Do not entertain lavishly.

Negotiate a win-win outcome.

Sharing is important. Gift giving is common and should be reciprocated.

Presentations should stress minimizing risks.

Respect age. Seniority comes with age. However, be aware that the younger generation has become more entrepreneurial since the demise of the communist system.

Local Rules

Customs and protocol are similar to Poland's.

Lithuania's democratic institutions are not as well developed as Poland's, and much of the Lithuanian focus is on strengthening internal institutions.

MALAYSIA

Cultural Data

Culture type: Collective

Playing field: Pacific Rim

Local influences: According to the constitution, a Malay is someone who speaks the Malay language, professes Islam, and practices Malay customs. Eighty percent of the inhabitants speak Bahasa Malaysia, and many speak English. Islam was brought to the region by Arab traders.

Primary motivations: The welfare of the tribal group.

Game Plan

Approach through a local representative.

Personal relationships must be established before business is done. Do not assume this means you are a personal friend.

Top management should be present at the first meeting. Your company should be represented by a group of specialists at this first meeting. Do not include a lawyer.

Negotiations will be time-consuming. Expect to make many trips. Be patient.

Study *Bing Fa* strategy.

One who is powerful and successful shows his humility.

Harmony must be maintained. Do not confront or question anyone in a negative way. Never say no. Expect Malays to always say yes, which might mean no.

Allow them to win something in negotiations.

Recognize and respect the social position of all you encounter. Do not expect them to require equality.

Never compliment a person directly. Never praise someone in front of his superiors. Praise the group.

Negotiations may appear cyclical rather than linear. Be prepared to discuss any subject out of sequence at any time.

Local Rules

Remember that the holy days of rest are Thursday and Friday (this varies in different parts of Malaysia). The overlay of Islam and Arab culture onto a previously collective culture shows in the necessity for praise and self-esteem, rather than not wanting to stand out. Credit is lavished on the smallest successes. Status and power are not merely organizing principles; they must be demonstrated.

Do not invite a Moslem to lunch during the month of Ramadan. He will be fasting.

Greeting with Westerners is done by a very light hand clasp, which may be held for 10 seconds. Don't rush the greeting. Ethnic Malays used to have no family name. Use their first name. This is also the case for ethnic Chinese. It is all right to ask what is the proper form of address. When you explain how they should address you, match their level of formality.

There is a significant Indian population in Malaysia.

Reciprocity and public recognition facilitate decision making. Cash is not commonly used to speed up decisions.

Economic control lies with the Chinese minority.

Representation in Malaysia is essential. Large trading companies usually control the importing of goods. Personal contacts are important.

A simple, moderate handshake is an appropriate greeting. The family name comes first in sequence. Use titles and first names. The term *manager* does not denote someone very senior in the organization.

Gifts should not be given on the first meeting. Never give trivial or token gifts, such as corporate mementos.

The visitor should never shout, show emotion, or curse.

Never challenge the status, power, or prestige of a Malay.

Early presentations should include a history of your company, mention of leading executives, a listing special awards, and the names of important customers.

Malay executives value problem avoidance and will not easily agree to anything new.

Status is important and is indicated on the business card by titles and degrees.

Dress for hot weather, but know that white long-sleeve shirts are a mark of prestige. A "lounge suit" refers to a dark business suit.

Do not blow your nose in public. Spitting is forbidden.

Do not host a social event until you have been invited as a guest. Let your host make the first invitation.

Avoid giving any gift that might be construed as a bribe.

Although the weather is hot, dress formally until you determine the degree of informality that is accepted by the people you are meeting.

Refuse hospitality three times before accepting, so you don't look greedy.

MEXICO

Cultural Data

Culture type: Tribal

Playing field: Latin America

Local influences: Mexico's proximity to the United States does not necessarily translate into a blend of cultures at the borders. Mexico remains strongly tribal.

Primary motivations: The status, power, and welfare of the family.

Game Plan

Establish contact through a well-regarded local agent.

The first meeting should be on your host's turf.

Send the seniormost person from your company, along with one or two subordinates.

Plan on using an interpreter. Translate materials into Latin American Spanish.

Always address a Latino formally, using his title and family name (next-to-last name).

Expect to spend time establishing a relationship. Don't press toward a business discussion until your counterpart offers an opening.

Maintain formality in dress, posture, and speech until he relaxes the interaction.

Your image is important in communicating your own status.

Don't back away if your counterpart chooses to stand close during conversation.

Be prepared to make concessions, but only after appropriate resistance. Do not appear to negotiate these concessions. Latinos like zero-sum games.

Minimize risks in any proposal.

As an American, humble yourself. Do not assume you hold the most power because you are from the United States.

Entertain at the best restaurants.

Eat Continental style.

Once a relationship has been established, your company should not change the U.S. contact person, or else the process will have to begin again. Latinos trust people, not companies.

Local Rules

The population is 60 percent mestizo, 30 percent Indian, and 9 percent European.

Be careful not to make comparisons with the United States.

In price negotiations, don't start with a very high price, expecting to bargain. This will insult them. Leave a little room for movement, but don't expect them to be ignorant of the marketplace.

MOROCCO

Cultural Data

Culture type: Tribal

Playing field: Arab world

Local influences: French occupation shaped some of the customs and tendencies of this nation. Islam still remains the organizing force.

Primary motivations: The welfare and security of the family group.

Game Plan

Be cognizant of the nature of Islamic law and morality. It dictates behavior.

Make your first approach through a well-connected local representative.

You must be present to be of consequence. Meetings should be at your host's offices.

Relationships and trust come before business.

Business associates must stay in constant communication for the relationship to continue.

Expect endless delays in appointments. Time is not linear. Be patient and expect to take a long time completing a transaction.

Humility is highly regarded, especially in a powerful person.

Moroccans love to bargain, but do not inflate your price too much. Your first offer must be good enough to attract a Moroccan's attention.

Minimize risks and uncertainty in your proposals. Praise and appreciation for your counterpart must be verbalized often.

Maintain formality in behavior, appearance, and address.

Project a successful image.

Never refuse Moroccan hospitality. Always reciprocate.

Never reprimand or criticize directly. Failure is not directly acknowledged. Honor is very important. Deal with negatives euphemistically.

Never admit that you are a "self-made man." Lineage is important to Moroccans. You are a reflection of your entire family.

Proposals, plans and negotiations should focus on the people issues. People are most important to Moroccans.

Local Rules

Women should never make eye contact with men who are strangers. Men will interpret it as an invitation.

Moroccan bureaucracy was patterned after the French. Moroccans conduct business formally, as do the French.

Don't bother to use the telephones. It takes too much time.

Print business cards in both Arabic and English.

French is spoken by many of those in the business class. Use an interpreter.

Business is never done without serving tea first.

You will probably be invited to a home dinner. Men and women eat separately. The women get the leftovers.

THE NETHERLANDS

Cultural Data

Culture type: Pluralist

Playing field: Western Europe

Local influences: The Dutch have always looked beyond their small country to the world beyond. They have an international focus.

Primary motivations: Personal achievement and productivity.

Game Plan

The Dutch have an aversion to chaos and an affinity for self-organizing systems.

Realism and structure are important concepts. Be well organized and realistic.

Punctuality and precise scheduling are important.

Greet with a firm handshake. Begin by using last names. Your hosts may invite you to use first names fairly early on.

Introduce yourself to others in a large group. Self-control is a virtue. Control of the body indicates a disciplined mind.

Privacy is important. Don't ask very personal questions.

Dress in a traditional, understated business suit.

Your presentation material should be in English. A translator will probably not be necessary.

Negotiate a win-win outcome.

Local Rules

Shake hands when meeting and leaving. As you are introduced, repeat your last name. Always stand when being introduced.

If you don't introduce yourself before speaking, the Dutch may be offended by your casual behavior.

Be prepared to discuss world politics with the Dutch.

Don't offer compliments until you know someone well.

Before drinking, all in a group raises their glass simultaneously and says *Proost*.

Don't get up during a meal, even to go to the bathroom. It is considered rude.

When entertaining at a restaurant, the host usually chooses and orders for the whole party.

Women are treated as equals in business.

Business dinners are more popular than business lunches.

Invitations should not be spontaneous.

NEW ZEALAND

Cultural Data

Culture type: Pluralist/tribal

Playing field: Australia

Local influences: New Zealand was originally colonized by Australians. Later, more cultivated settlers arrived from England. New Zealand tends to be more English than Australian, but it is still closer to the pluralists than to the tribal British.

Primary motivations: Personal welfare.

Game Plan

Decrease the New Zealander's sense of isolation by holding the first meeting at your host's offices.

A local agent is not necessary, but a third-party introduction always makes contact easier.

Keep a local representative on staff to keep up on local developments and give you a local presence.

Keep equality in mind at all times—from the structure of your business proposal to opportunities for socializing.

Return their informality, but don't initiate it.

Bargaining is considered to be a waste of time. Take your best shot.

Be sure to communicate the importance to you of your mutual business objectives. Do not defer to him, yet do not project superiority.

Be straightforward.

Local Rules

Greet with a firm handshake and a hello. Begin with last names, but expect that first-name usage will follow almost immediately.

Give your business card at the introduction; your counterpart may not give you one.

Titles and degrees are not impressive. A New Zealander will make his own judgment as to the quality of the person with whom he is speaking.

Business dress is conservative and not overly elegant.

Be friendly, relaxed, modest, and unpretentious. Don't try to impress your host.

Gifts are not given unless you are invited to someone's home.

Don't fill your presentation with hype or glitz. A simple, direct presentation is more effective. Get to the point.

Decision making can occur at lower levels, but things still take longer than in the United States.

You may be invited out for a drink after work. Don't bring up business unless your host does. New Zealanders make a clear distinction between work and play.

NORWAY

Cultural Data

Culture type: Pluralist

Playing field: Western Europe

Local influences: Norway stresses its own independence, having been ruled by Denmark and then Sweden for much of its history. Norwegians are adamant about projecting a national identity.

Primary motivations: Self-interest and national self-determination.

Game Plan

Third-party introductions are not necessary, but they are always helpful.

Use English in all business dealings.

Be sure to treat Norwegians as equals. Do not compare Norwegian and American standards of living. Norwegians do not care. They are fiercely defensive of Norwegian culture.

Do not refer to a Norwegian as a Scandinavian.

Norwegians are not rigidly formal, but polite formality should be maintained. Do not be stiff or present a severe or overly elegant image.

Management is not elitist.

Power is valued over wealth, because the tax system equalizes everyone's wages.

During conversation, avoid personal questions. Privacy is important.

The government officially rigs all contract bidding, favoring Norwegian contractors and suppliers. The only way for you to sell something in Norway is to establish a joint venture with a Norwegian company—if the product has Norwegian content or if you are the sole supplier of something they want. Price is never a determining factor.

Your presentation should be rational and show how your product would benefit Norway.

Local Rules

Never drive a car if you have had *any amount* of alcohol to drink.

Shake hands on meeting and leaving.

Never speak in a loud voice.

Women will not have difficulty being taken seriously in Norway.

Liquor is an excellent gift, for it is so expensive there. Buy it in the duty-free shop.

PAKISTAN

Cultural Data

Culture type: Tribal

Playing field: Arab world

Local influences: Pakistan was established as a separate Moslem state during the British partitioning of India in 1947. The government is a democracy. The country is not Arab, but it conforms to Islamic law. Arab customs, which proceed from Islamic law and tribal culture, largely apply to Pakistan.

Primary motivations: The welfare of the family tribe.

Game Plan

Be cognizant of the nature of Islamic law and morality. It dictates behavior.

Make your first approach through a well-connected local representative.

You must be present to be of consequence. Meetings should be at your host's offices.

Relationships and trust come before business.

Business associates must stay in constant communication for the relationship to continue.

Expect endless delays in appointments. Time is not linear. Be patient and expect to take a long time completing a transaction.

Humility is highly regarded, especially in a powerful person.

Pakistanis love to bargain, but do not inflate your price too much. Your first offer must be good enough to attract a Pakistani's attention.

Minimize risks and uncertainty in your proposals. Praise and appreciation for your counterpart must be verbalized often.

Maintain formality in behavior, appearance and address.

Project a successful image.

Never refuse hospitality. Always reciprocate.

Never reprimand or criticize directly. Failure is not directly acknowledged. Honor is very important. Deal with negatives euphemistically.

Never admit that you are a "self-made man." Lineage is important. You are a reflection of your entire family.

Proposals, plans, and negotiations should focus on the people issues. People are most important in Pakistani culture.

Local Rules

Urdu and English are the official languages. Note that the Urdu words for yesterday and tomorrow are the same.

Forms of address are very complicated, because there are many variations on Pakistani names. Ask how a person should be addressed.

Men should never wear a suit and tie from November through March. The jacket need never be worn except when one visits government officials.

Never gesture with a closed fist.

Women are generally not well received in business, even though the current prime minister is a woman.

PARAGUAY

Cultural Data

Culture type: Tribal

Playing field: Latin America

Local influences: The population is 95 percent mestizo, which seems to indicate a more egalitarian social structure. The European minority still holds economic power.

Primary motivations: Family status and power determine a person's prosperity.

Game Plan

Establish contact through a well-regarded local agent.

The first meeting should be on your host's turf.

Send the seniormost person from your company, along with one or two subordinates.

Plan on using an interpreter. Translate materials into Latin American Spanish.

Always address a Latino formally, using his title and family name (next-to-last name).

Expect to spend time establishing a relationship. Don't press toward a business discussion until your counterpart offers an opening.

Maintain formality in dress, posture, and speech until he relaxes the interaction.

Your image is important in communicating your own status.

Don't back away if your counterpart chooses to stand close during conversation.

Be prepared to make concessions, but only after appropriate resistance. Do not appear to negotiate these concessions. Latinos like zero-sum games.

Minimize risks in any proposal.

As an American, humble yourself. Do not assume you hold the most power because you are from the United States.

Entertain at the best restaurants.

Eat Continental style.

Once a relationship has been established, your company should not change the U.S. contact person, or else the process will have to begin again. Latinos trust people, not companies.

Local Rules

Formal titles are used, but someone with a university degree is referred to as *licenciado* instead of *doctor*, which is reserved for medical doctors and those with a Ph.D.

Don't wink. It has sexual connotations.

PERU

Cultural Data

Culture type: Tribal

Playing field: Latin America

Local influences: Peru was the seat of the Incan civilization, which was overthrown by the Spanish in 1532. The population is 45 percent Indian, 37 percent mestizo (European and Indian mix), and 15 percent European. The business class consists mostly of the European minority. There are also a significant number of Japanese and Chinese businesspeople in Peru. Therefore, you should be familiar with the collective game plan.

Primary motivations: The family status and welfare come first.

Game Plan

Establish contact through a well-regarded local agent.

The first meeting should be on your host's turf.

Send the seniormost person from your company, along with one or two subordinates.

Plan on using an interpreter. Translate materials into Latin American Spanish.

Always address a Latino formally, using his title and family name (next-to-last name).

Expect to spend time establishing a relationship. Don't press toward a business discussion until your counterpart offers an opening.

Maintain formality in dress, posture, and speech until he relaxes the interaction.

Your image is important in communicating your own status.

Don't back away if your counterpart chooses to stand close during conversation.

Be prepared to make concessions, but only after appropriate resistance. Do not appear to negotiate these concessions. Latinos like zero-sum games.

Minimize risks in any proposal.

As an American, humble yourself. Do not assume you hold the most power because you are from the United States.

Entertain at the best restaurants.

Eat Continental style.

Once a relationship has been established, your company should not change the U.S. contact person, or else the process will have to begin again. Latinos trust people, not companies.

Local Rules

Unlike in other South American countries, men should not cross their legs one knee over the other. One ankle on the other knee is all right.

Peruvians use lots of hand gestures when they speak. Be careful of your own.

In Peru, it is best not to discuss ancestry or politics—two sensitive issues. Peru has an extremely strong caste system based on ancestry.

If you are invited to a home, bring the hostess flowers. They must be roses, or you will be considered cheap. Avoid red, which means love.

THE PHILIPPINES

Cultural Data

Culture type: Collective

Playing field: Pacific Rim

Local influences: The Philippines is a predominantly Catholic country. The Christian culture overlies an inherent collective base. The result is an emphasis on power. The public sector is important to all private business transactions. The country operates under a system of guided free enterprise. Power is ultimately held by the government.

Primary motivations: The status, power, and wealth of the family guide behavior.

Game Plan

Approach through a local representative.

Personal relationships must be established before business is done. Do not assume this means you are a personal friend.

Top management should be present at the first meeting. Your company should be represented by a group of specialists at this first meeting. Do not include a lawyer.

Negotiations will be time-consuming. Expect to make many trips. Be patient.

Study *Bing Fa* strategy.

One who is powerful and successful shows his humility.

Harmony must be maintained. Do not confront or question anyone in a negative way. Never say no. Expect Filipinos to always say yes, which might mean no.

Allow them to win something in negotiations.

Recognize and respect the social position of all you encounter. Do not expect them to require equality.

Never compliment a person directly. Never praise someone in front of his superiors. Praise the group.

Negotiations may appear cyclical rather than linear. Be prepared to discuss any subject out of sequence at any time.

Local Rules

Entry into the Philippine market will require a local agent—one who knows the fine line between legal and illegal. Selecting the right agent is important. He must have the proper social connections.

Business is a process, and decisions are not made on factual input. People factors are most important.

Greet a Filipino with a firm handshake, but not with much pumping. The title should be used along with the surname. Many names are Spanish, for the Philippines was colonized by Spain. Therefore the proper surname would be the next-to-the-last name—the name of the father's family.

Philippine culture reveals its tribal bent by the encouragement of praise and the building of self-esteem through compliments, unlike in most of Asia. This is a country that learned machismo from its Spanish ancestors.

Business is not discussed at the first meeting. If the host casually says he would like to hear your proposal sometime, that is the sign to leave, scheduling with the secretary another appointment. The second meeting should include a luncheon invitation from you.

Confrontational style is not appropriate in negotiations. Harmony should prevail. The presenter should plan a multimedia presentation. Local representatives should be present at all negotiations.

Those in upper management do not respond to detail. Rather, they prefer to see the big picture. Control on all issues rests with the CEO, who is a member of the landed oligarchy.

Filipinos run on Latin time. Unlike in the collective cultures of their neighborhood, they are not punctual. They do expect you to be on time though. Waiting is often a status game.

If decisions are delayed, negotiators may require a commission, rebate, or bonus. This is a complex issue for Americans, who cannot, by law, provide kickbacks—all the more reason to have a local agent to counsel you on tactics.

Dinner invitations are the sign of a good relationship. Entertainment will be lavish. Dinners are social affairs and may include wives. Reciprocate invitations.

The visitor should project an air of importance and subtle power. Wealth and social status are important.

Business relationships do not extend to the company. If you are replaced, the new person will have to start all over, unless he is a blood relative.

Filipinos are more relaxed about business cards. You should offer yours first. They may or may not give you theirs.

At the end of a business deal, invite your counterpart and associates to dinner. You may have to ask several times whenever issuing an invitation, because Filipinos believe an invitation may be offered casually simply as a polite gesture.

Social events may end with dancing and singing. Be prepared to sing if asked. Public drunkenness is not acceptable.

At Christmas time, give gifts to everyone you know, in business and socially, especially to secretaries of important clients.

Dress conservatively until you know how casually the people you are meeting with will be dressed.

POLAND

Cultural Data

Culture type: Progressive tribal

Playing field: Central and Eastern Europe

Local influences: Poland has been a Roman Catholic country for over a thousand years. In 1791, Poland adopted a constitution modeled after that of the United States, but it retained its monarchy and nobility. In 1795, Poland was partitioned by Prussia, Austria, and Russia and no longer existed as a nation. Polish identity was maintained through the Roman Catholic Church in Poland. In 1948, Poland came under Soviet control. It is now democratic, with a free-market economy.

Primary motivations: The welfare of the family group and the security of the ethnic group.

Game Plan

Approach with a personal reference or through a local agent.

First meeting should be at your host's offices.

Trust must be established before you will be accepted.

Participate in the Polish brand of conformity and modesty. Do not flaunt affluence.

Do not entertain lavishly.

Negotiate a win-win outcome.

Sharing is important. Gift giving is common and should be reciprocated.

Presentations should stress minimizing risks.

Respect age. Seniority comes with age. However, be aware that the younger generation has become more entrepreneurial since the demise of the communist system.

Local Rules

Poles value punctuality, skill and intelligence, privacy, family, and loyalty to the Polish nation.

They have a strong work ethic.

They are critical of themselves and their institutions.

Direct communication is preferred.

Facts are more important than emotions in decision making, but relationships are more important than laws.

Poland has strong power hierarchies and a male-dominated society.

Translate materials into Polish.

A local representative makes business and social arrangements much easier.

Business lunches and dinners are popular. Expect to stay out late, or you may insult your hosts.

Shake hands to meet, greet, and say good-bye. Use last names.

Avoid loud behavior in public.

Polish men have more traditional views of women. A woman should not talk to a strange man, or it will be considered flirting.

A gift is appropriate at the first meeting.

Dress conservatively.

PORTUGAL

Cultural Data

Culture type: Tribal

Playing field: Western Europe

Local influences: By the 16th century, Portugal had a huge overseas empire. It has a strong national identity—separate from Spain—in spite of its size and proximity. The Portuguese have traditional ties with England and feel comfortable emulating English behavior. The Portuguese are certainly tribal, but without the modifying influence of England's strong Celtic character. Business procedures would be more like the Spanish as far as need for security and relationship building, but more formal and reserved in style.

Primary motivations: The welfare and security of the family group.

Game Plan

Establish contact through a well-regarded local agent.

The first meeting should be on your host's turf.

Send the seniormost person from your company, along with one or two subordinates.

Plan on using an interpreter. Translate materials into Portuguese.

Always address a Portuguese formally, using his title and family name (next-to-last name).

Expect to spend time establishing a relationship. Don't press toward a business discussion until your counterpart offers an opening.

Maintain formality in dress, posture, and speech until he relaxes the interaction.

Your image is important in communicating your own status.

Don't back away if your counterpart chooses to stand close during conversation.

Be prepared to make concessions, but only after appropriate resistance. Do not appear to negotiate these concessions. Tribal players like zero-sum games.

Minimize risks in any proposal.

Entertain at the best restaurants.

Eat Continental style.

Once a relationship has been established, your company should not change the U.S. contact person, or else the process will have to begin again. Tribal players trust people, not companies.

Local Rules

Shake hands when meeting and leaving. Shake hands with everyone present.

Business cards need not be translated, but plan on bringing an interpreter to meetings. Exchange business cards at the beginning of a meeting.

The Portuguese respect professional women. Dress elegantly, but conservatively.

Portuguese tend to be somewhat unreliable in meeting deadlines.

Give gifts after you have begun business dealings. Ask your contact if there is anything he would like from America. He may appreciate access to technical products, like computer programs or to books or CDs.

Dinner is always social. Do business at lunch only.

Finish everything on your plate. Never eat with your hands. Keep your napkin on the table or you will be offered one continually.

ROMANIA

Cultural Data

Culture type: Progressive tribal

Playing field: Central and Eastern Europe

Local influences: The early history of Romania was dominated by the Roman empire, of which Romania was a province. The Romanian language derives from Latin. However, Romania's proximity to the subsequent Byzantine empire along with its progressive tribal nature resulted in a predominantly Orthodox Christian state. After World War II, Romania came under the influence of the USSR. In 1965, Romanians declared themselves an independent communist state. Human rights violations and corruption ensued. Today Romania is a democratic republic and one of the poorest countries in Europe.

Primary motivations: The welfare of the family group.

Game Plan

Approach with a personal reference or through a local agent.

First meeting should be at your host's offices.

Trust must be established before you will be accepted.

Participate in the Romanian brand of conformity and modesty. Do not flaunt affluence.

Do not entertain lavishly.

Negotiate a win-win outcome.

Sharing is important. Gift giving is common and should be reciprocated.

Presentations should stress minimizing risks.

Respect age. Seniority comes with age. However, be aware that the younger generation has become more entrepreneurial since the demise of the communist system.

Local Rules

The Romanian people distrust authority and are reverting to an insular tribal structure.

They have very weak business management skills.

The more educated a person, the more objective he is in decision making, but subjective emotions do play a part.

The current priority for all Romanians is to feed and house their families.

Opinions and emotions are freely expressed.

Send letters in English. Romanians give higher priority to English-language documents. A letter that must be translated is more respected.

Distrust makes it difficult to make contacts. Use local representatives. Once you are accepted, the relationship will be a strong bond.

Romanians are status conscious. Stay in the best hotel. Have your title and degrees printed on business cards.

Small gifts are appreciated at the first meeting.

Shake hands often when coming and going, each time you see someone again during a day, and when being introduced. Use a firm grip. Use last names and professional titles.

Romanians gesticulate a lot with their hands. You should not, for many U.S. gestures can be seriously misunderstood.

Eat Continental style.

Use European manners.

RUSSIA

Cultural Data

Culture type: Progressive tribal

Playing field: Central and Eastern Europe

Local influences: Russians have an affinity for Americans. This may be because both are used to life on a broad canvas. Their nations' territories are extensive, and their political power has been broad ranging. Although they have stood at opposite ideological poles, there is much the two peoples have in common.

Primary motivations: The welfare and security of the family group.

Game Plan

Approach with a personal reference or through a local agent.

First meeting should be at your host's offices.

Trust must be established before you will be accepted.

Participate in the Russian brand of conformity and modesty. Do not flaunt affluence.

Do not entertain lavishly.

Negotiate a win-win outcome.

Sharing is important. Gift giving is common and should be reciprocated.

Presentations should stress minimizing risks.

Respect age. Seniority comes with age. However, be aware that the younger generation has become more entrepreneurial since the demise of the communist system.

Local Rules

Don't hire an expatriate Russian to represent you in Russia.

Russians believe—and those who know Russia agree—that Russia has a soul. Russians feel that they must take their own path and not copy the West.

Russians see themselves as rational and conscious realists. They are also romantic and sentimental.

Private business is based on trust. This makes relationships very important to doing business. Initial contacts should be made through a trusted third party.

European manners are used. Keep your hands out of your pockets, use good posture, don't cross your ankle over the other knee, and remember that whistling indoors brings bad financial luck.

Be punctual. Russians may not be.

Shake hands coming and going and when introduced. Use a firm handshake.

Never shake hands with gloves on, and do not shake hands across a threshold.

Address your host by last name. Do not use the term *comrade*. When you become friendly, he may suggest any variety of nicknames to call him by. A respectful way to refer to someone with whom you are on familiar terms is to use the first name and the second name, which is a patronymic (indicating "son of so-and-so").

Observe age and rank, and adjust your protocol to honor these.

Dress is conservative, and fashion tends to lag behind the West by about 20 years.

Try not to appear too affluent. From a safety standpoint, it would be wise to buy a pair of Russian shoes. Thieves can easily spot Westerners by their good-quality shoes. Save your good shoes for business meetings.

You will probably need an interpreter. But the presence of an interpreter doesn't mean your hosts do not understand English. Avoid making off-the-record comments in English. Translate written materials into Russian, especially sample contracts, to save time in translation.

Bring many business cards. There are few telephone books, so people collect cards. They may not have a goodly supply of their own. Business cards should be printed in English and Russian. Write down a list of meeting participants and their phone numbers.

Token gifts are often exchanged at the first meeting. Go to Russia prepared to give a lot of gifts, and bring an extra bag for the ones they will give to you. Reciprocity of gift giving is very important. Gift giving indicates sharing, respect, interest in a person, and generosity—all the values one would want in a friend.

Business will begin soon after a bit of conversation. Your host may ask you to sign an agreement of cooperation, which is not a contract to work together, but to express mutual interest. It is all right to sign it.

Be clear of your intentions for this first meeting. If it is merely exploratory, say so. Russians may have expectations of you as their savior.

Government permits are not necessary to open an office. If you are hoping for a long-term relationship, establishment of a local office shows commitment. There are local employment agencies that can assist you in staffing the office.

You may save some money and find other advantages to renting an apartment by the week instead of staying in a hotel room. Russians love to talk around a table. After the first meeting, invite the Russians to your apartment for further discussions. Serve them tea and sit around the table.

The Russian negotiating team will usually have specialists with different interests, for example, price specialists or quality specialists. The head of the team will do the most talking, and you should direct most of your remarks to him.

Keep your pricing consistent with that of other European nations. The Russians will have done research. Prepare to make a small price concession.

If you want to make a big impression on them, invite them to come visit you in America. You will be responsible for their expenses in the United States, but they will pay the airfare.

Negotiations may take time. Time is not money. Time is wisdom.

Management skills are often lacking. Don't leave anything unsaid. Don't assume they will fill in the blanks properly.

Presentations should be concrete, visual, and factual, with detailed specifications.

Decisions are often made subjectively, based on emotion. Logic is considered second.

Russians are not afraid to express emotion, and they use it as a tool. Sometimes they storm out of a meeting, only to return later. Don't lose your temper, but it is wise to meet emotion with emotion. It is often necessary to play hardball.

Be creative in offering partnerships, coproduction, training, office equipment, and service.

End all meetings with a summary of the meeting and action items for the next meeting.

Very few people stop for lunch in Russia. Lunch is taken more often in Moscow than elsewhere. There are only a few decent restaurants anyway. At the end of talks, host a dinner at a hotel restaurant. Wives are generally not included.

The Continental style of eating is used.

There will be much toasting, usually with wine or vodka. When a bottle of vodka is opened, it must be finished, not saved. The host starts the toast with a little speech, and the guest replies. Alcohol is served during a meal, not before.

If you are invited to someone's home, which is rare, bring an odd number of flowers; even numbers are for funerals.

Businesswomen are respected in Russia. There is no risk of harassment.

SAUDI ARABIA

Cultural Data

Culture type: Tribal

Playing field: Arab world

Local influences: Saudi Arabia is at the zenith of the Arab world. It maintains the strictest Islamic code of behavior and has no tolerance of transgressions, even by foreigners.

Primary motivations: The welfare and security of the family tribe and upholding Islamic law.

Game Plan

Be cognizant of the nature of Islamic law and morality. It dictates behavior.

Make your first approach through a well-connected local representative.

You must be present to be of consequence. Meetings should be at your host's offices.

Relationships and trust come before business.

Business associates must stay in constant communication for the relationship to continue.

Expect endless delays in appointments. Time is not linear. Be patient and expect to take a long time completing a transaction.

Humility is highly regarded, especially in a powerful person.

Saudis love to bargain, but do not inflate your price too much. Your first offer must be good enough to attract your counterpart's attention.

Minimize risks and uncertainty in your proposals. Praise and appreciation for your counterpart must be verbalized often.

Maintain formality in behavior, appearance, and address.

Project a successful image.

Never refuse Saudi hospitality. Always reciprocate.

Never reprimand or criticize directly. Failure is not directly acknowledged. Honor is very important. Deal with negatives euphemistically.

Never admit that you are a "self-made man." Lineage is important to Saudis. You are a reflection of your entire family.

Proposals, plans, and negotiations should focus on the people issues. People are most important to Saudis.

Local Rules

Saudi Arabia is the most strict of all Islamic countries. Western men will not meet Saudi women.

Whenever someone enters the room, always rise and shake hands.

Never enter the country with Western magazines such as Playboy. The wife of a foreign businessman was deported for carrying a copy of *Cosmopolitan*.

Saudis usually wait to be asked more than once before accepting second helpings of food.

Whenever something is offered, refuse first, then accept.

Never send a woman to do business, even as a member of a team. There are strict legal restrictions on women's activities.

Print business cards in both Arabic and English.

Present a modest gift after meeting someone two or three times.

Immigrants do the paperwork.

SINGAPORE

Cultural Data

Culture type: Collective

Playing field: Pacific Rim

Local influences: Capitalism reigns in Singapore, and the Chinese are in control, representing 76 percent of the population. Singapore is the closest thing to a meritocracy in the Far East. Few people get ahead without long hours and hard work.

Primary motivations: The welfare of the family and ethnic collective group.

Game Plan

Approach through a local representative.

Personal relationships must be established before business is done. Do not assume this means you are a personal friend.

Top management should be present at the first meeting. Your company should be represented by a group of specialists at this first meeting. Do not include a lawyer.

Negotiations will be time-consuming. Expect to make many trips. Be patient.

Study *Bing Fa* strategy.

One who is powerful and successful shows his humility.

Harmony must be maintained. Do not confront or question anyone in a negative way. Never say no. Expect your hosts to always say yes, which might mean no.

Allow them to win something in negotiations.

Recognize and respect the social position of all you encounter. Do not expect them to require equality.

Never compliment a person directly. Never praise someone in front of his superiors. Praise the group.

Negotiations may appear cyclical rather than linear. Be prepared to discuss any subject out of sequence at any time.

Local Rules

Even though Singaporeans appear Western in their work ethic and meritocracy, all other protocol generally follows the Chinese model. Communication and feedback are not direct, saving face is important, and relationships are a must.

Foreigners should use local advisers to understand how to get things done in Singapore.

Sending low-level representatives is a waste of time.

Be punctual.

Singaporeans laugh as a sign of anxiety or embarrassment, not levity.

Use a limp hand clasp as a greeting. Use the person's title and first name—which is usually the family name—or the appropriate given name, if the person is a Moslem Malay.

Singapore prides itself on being the least corrupt state in Asia. Gifts are given only to friends. Decline a gift three times, and do not open it in the presence of the giver.

Business moves fairly quickly—by Asian standards. Communication channels are usually clear.

After an initial meeting of about 45 minutes, the visitor should initiate leaving.

An invitation to one of Singapore's private clubs confers prestige.

Refusing hospitality shows bad manners.

SLOVAKIA

Cultural Data

Culture type: Progressive tribal

Playing field: Central and Eastern Europe

Local influences: Until World War I, Slovakia was under Hungarian rule for about a thousand years. After World War II, it was united with the Czech Republic as Czechoslovakia, a democratic republic. In 1948, Czechoslovakia came under communist domination. In 1989, it became an independent democracy, but nationalism surfaced. In 1992, the Czech Republic and Slovakia became separate nations.

Primary motivations: The welfare of the family tribe and of the national ethnic identity.

Game Plan

Approach with a personal reference or through a local agent.

First meeting should be at your host's offices.

Trust must be established before you will be accepted.

Participate in the Slovak brand of conformity and modesty. Do not flaunt affluence.

Do not entertain lavishly.

Negotiate a win-win outcome.

Sharing is important. Gift giving is common and should be reciprocated.

Presentations should stress minimizing risks.

Respect age. Seniority comes with age. However, be aware that the younger generation has become more entrepreneurial since the demise of the communist system.

Local Rules

Slovaks are proud of their peasant roots and peasant values, which include hard work, generosity, honesty, and modesty.

They view entrepreneurs as greedy.

They do not value aggressiveness and individualistic self-confidence.

Education is valued above wealth.

Use titles when greeting someone.

Print your titles and degrees on your business card.

Many hand gestures are used. Avoid using American gestures, as some of them are considered offensive.

European manners are appropriate.

SOUTH KOREA

Cultural Data
Culture type: Collective
Playing field: Pacific Rim
Local influences: In comparing South Koreans with the Japanese, one Westerner observes that South Koreans are less ethnocentric, less xenophobic, and less chauvinistic. They are strongly capitalistic and are familiar with Western business.
Primary motivations: Collective power, wealth, and security.

Game Plan
Approach through a local representative.

Personal relationships must be established before business is done. Do not assume this means you are a personal friend.

Top management should be present at the first meeting. Your company should be represented by a group of specialists at this first meeting. Do not include a lawyer.

Negotiations will be time-consuming. Expect to make many trips. Be patient.

Study *Bing Fa* strategy.

One who is powerful and successful shows his humility.

Harmony must be maintained. Do not confront or question anyone in a negative way. Never say no. Expect Koreans to always say yes, which might mean no.

Allow them to win something in negotiations.

Recognize and respect the social position of all you encounter. Do not expect them to require equality.

Never compliment a person directly. Never praise someone in front of his superiors. Praise the group.

Negotiations may appear cyclical rather than linear. Be prepared to discuss any subject out of sequence at any time.

Local Rules
Official import-export traders all belong to the Korean Traders Association, a very exclusive organization; this limited group is the foundation of the Korean economy. There are also registered independent agents who belong to the Association of Foreign Trading Agents of Korea; they do not have as much clout as the trading companies.

Be punctual for all appointments.

Shake hands with a moderate grip, and add a slight bow. To indicate added respect, support your right forearm with your left hand.

The junior person should initiate the greeting and be the first to bow. The senior person extends his hand first. Women do not commonly shake hands. A businesswoman has to initiate a handshake with a Korean man.

Do not introduce yourself in a group. Wait to be introduced.

Address a person by his family name—which comes first—along with his title or *Mr.* When writing, use the greeting "To my respected . . ." with the title and *full* name.

Relationships and hospitality are important, but Koreans are most familiar with Western practices.

Although harmony is very important, Koreans are the most likely of all Asians to express emotion and be direct and even somewhat aggressive during negotiations. You, however, should remain calm.

Try to match the rank of individuals who are meeting. Age is an important determining factor in establishing rank.

Koreans often hold one-on-one meetings. This does not contradict their collectivist nature. The person you meet with is acting as an intermediary who must present your proposal to the entire company. It is important to establish a good relationship with this person.

Do not use triangle shapes in your presentation. Triangles have a negative connotation. Remember, this is a culture that uses symbolism.

Silence can be a clue that you were not understood. Do allow some silence for thought, but follow up by rephrasing your last point.

Koreans are more likely than other Asians to say no, but will still avoid it when possible.

If during the meeting the Koreans return to social small talk, it is an indication that they are through discussing business for the day.

Meetings begin and end with a bow. If the ending bow is deeper and longer than the opening bow, it is an indication that the meeting went well.

Never criticize your competition or admit that you do not know the answer to a question. Either will cause you to lose face. You may not care, but Koreans will feel uncomfortable and lose respect for you.

Do not bring gifts from Japan or mention contacts or travel there. Koreans hold great animosity toward the Japanese.

Offer your business card with your right hand. Treat it with dignity. Don't put a person's card in your wallet and then put the wallet in your back pocket.

Do not write a person's name in red ink. It means the person is deceased.

Entertaining is done at night. Do not talk business over a meal unless your host does. If you are a man, you will probably be invited to a *Kinaeng* house or bar where lots of alcohol is served. The alcohol allows them to drop barriers and be more direct. Be aware that you will be held accountable for anything said or promised. These excursions are important for evaluating another person's character and establishing an informal relationship. Wives will not be included in the outing.

At the end of a meal, there may be singing. Singing is very important to Koreans, and you should not refuse when asked. Have a short tune prepared. Singing expresses harmony in a symbolic, extradimensional way. It is a form of controlled emotional release.

At a meal, do not finish everything on your plate. This indicates that the host did not provide enough food and you are still hungry. Always refuse food twice before accepting.

Never blow your nose in public.

Eye contact shows sincerity and attentiveness to the speaker.

Koreans may laugh when embarrassed.

When giving or receiving gifts, use both hands. Do not open a gift in the presence of the giver. Expect a gift you give to be refused at first. This is good manners. Reciprocate gifts and hospitality.

Koreans eat a lot of garlic, which can be detected as odor coming from their skin. They in turn do not like the way red meat eaters smell. Before a trip, you may want to change your diet to be less offensive to them.

SPAIN

Cultural Data

Culture type: Tribal

Playing field: Western Europe

Local influences: Spain's history is dominated by Roman, Islamic, and Catholic rule at various times. Each influence was resident for centuries. These three cultural powers were all tribal in nature, with strong authoritarian power structures. Family structure mirrored early beliefs in the distribution of power. This was carried on by Islamic law, which clearly defines the complete authority of God. Catholicism continued the tradition.

Primary motivations: The power and welfare of the family group.

Game Plan

Establish contact through a well-regarded local agent.

The first meeting should be on your host's turf.

Send the seniormost person from your company, along with one or two subordinates.

Plan on using an interpreter. Translate materials into Spanish.

Always address the Spaniard formally, using his title and family name (next-to-last name).

Expect to spend time establishing a relationship. Don't press toward a business discussion until your counterpart offers an opening.

Maintain formality in dress, posture, and speech until he relaxes the interaction.

Your image is important in communicating your own status.

Don't back away if your counterpart chooses to stand close during conversation.

Be prepared to make concessions, but only after appropriate resistance. Do not appear to negotiate these concessions. The Spanish like zero-sum games.

Minimize risks in any proposal.

Entertain at the best restaurants.

Eat Continental style.

Once a relationship has been established, your company should not change the U.S. contact person, or else the process will have to begin again. Spaniards trust people, not companies.

Local Rules

Shake hands when meeting and leaving.

Older people and people of high rank may address you by your first name. Don't take this as a signal to use theirs. Use their surname until invited to do otherwise. If a person of high rank asks you to use his first name, precede it by *Don* as a sign of respect.

Beware of casual U.S. gestures. Some of them are offensive. Use the whole hand to gesture—and not fingers.

Dressing well at all times gives the impression of accomplishment.

Businesswomen must project a professional air. Dress elegantly, but conservatively. Don't be flirtatious in any way. Men may make comments to women as they walk by. Be sure not to react or acknowledge them in any way. If you return the gaze of a man, he will think you are interested in him.

Correspond with a Spanish company in formal English. Do not have letters translated into Spanish. The translation will probably not be sufficiently formal, flowery, and poetic and might therefore offend.

Be careful in gift giving. Wait until you have formed a relationship. Products or artwork representative of your home state are appropriate gifts.

SWEDEN

Cultural Data

Culture type: Pluralist

Playing field: Western Europe

Local influences: Similar to Denmark and Norway, Sweden has turned its natural sense of independence and equality into a legislated equality by economic conformity. Sweden is strongly capitalistic though, and not as protectionist as Norway. Unlike the Norwegians, the Swedes have a history of strong and adventurous monarchs. Their historical focus looked to the East, whereas Norway looked to the West. Their power hierarchy is stronger than Norway's, but not as strong as Germany's.

Primary motivations: Equality and self-determination.

Game Plan

Third-party introductions are not necessary, but they are always helpful.

Use English in most business dealings.

Be sure to treat Swedes as equals. Do not compare Swedish and American standards of living. Swedes are not impressed by your wealth, possessions, or status.

Do not refer to a Swede as a Scandinavian.

Your proposal should emphasize efficiency, simplicity, and cost savings. It should be rational and linear in its presentation.

Swedes are not rigidly formal, but polite formality should be maintained. Do not be stiff or present a severe or overly elegant image.

During conversation, avoid personal questions. Privacy is important.

Swedes highly value intelligence and education.

Local Rules

Shake hands when meeting and leaving.

Upper-class Swedes address each other in the third person, as in, "How is Mr. Nordstrom today?" instead of, "How are you?"

Businesswomen are taken seriously and can invite men to business lunches without feeling awkward.

SWITZERLAND

Cultural Data

Culture type: Pluralist

Playing field: Western Europe

Local influences: The Swiss are strongly pluralistic and have formed strong power structures, as have the Germans. They are made up of people from France, Germany, and Italy, combining the independent nature in each of these cultures into a contiguous set of provinces called cantons. They are insistent on their own identities and self-determination. The Swiss believe in national unity, but not uniformity.

Primary motivations: Personal accomplishment and self-determination.

Game Plan

The Swiss prefer the power position of meeting on their own turf.

Research your targeted company thoroughly. Your hosts will be impressed by preparation and offended by ignorance.

A third-party introduction is imperative. Bankers and lawyers make appropriate references.

Assume that meetings will be conducted in English. Translate all material, and use an interpreter only if you know the language of the person you will be meeting.

All documents should look polished and professional.

Maintain formality at all times. Self-control is very important.

Dress very conservatively and formally.

Be prepared to back up all of your figures. Allow some room for negotiation.

The Swiss value intelligence. They are impressed by thoughtful questions.

Your presentation should highlight how their business will be enhanced. You must prove all your claims.

Privacy is important. Don't ask personal questions.

Eat Continental style.

Local Rules

When you write to a Swiss company, address the letter to an individual, but address the envelope to the company.

Business cards should include titles in English. If your company is quite old, list the year it was founded.

Be prepared to answer questions about your competition.

Hand your card to the receptionist when you arrive.

Business lunches are more common than dinners. Dinner is purely a social occasion.

Appropriate gifts include whiskey or brandy, food products from your home state, and coffee-table books.

SYRIA

Cultural Data

Culture type: Tribal

Playing field: Arab world
Local influences:

Although Syria is an Arab country and nearly all its citizens profess Islam, it is officially a secular country.

Primary motivations: The welfare and status of the family group.

Game Plan

Be cognizant of the nature of Islamic law and morality.

Make your first approach through a well-connected local representative.

You must be present to be of consequence. Meetings should be at your host's offices.

Relationships and trust come before business.

Business associates must stay in constant communication for the relationship to continue.

Expect endless delays in appointments. Time is not linear. Be patient and expect to take a long time completing a transaction.

Humility is highly regarded, especially in a powerful person.

Syrians love to bargain, but do not inflate your price too much. Your first offer must be good enough to attract a Syrian's attention.

Minimize risks and uncertainty in your proposals. Praise and appreciation for your counterpart must be verbalized often.

Maintain formality in behavior, appearance, and address.

Project a successful image.

Never refuse Syrian hospitality. Always reciprocate.

Never reprimand or criticize directly. Failure is not directly acknowledged. Honor is very important. Deal with negatives euphemistically.

Never admit that you are a "self-made man." Lineage is important to Syrians. You are a reflection of your entire family.

Proposals, plans, and negotiations should focus on the people issues. People are most important to Syrians.

Local Rules

Educated Syrians are cosmopolitan, but conservative.

TAIWAN

Cultural Data

Culture type: Collective
Playing field: Pacific Rim

Local influences: Taiwan consists largely of the Chinese population that fled communist rule in mainland China, which is now called the People's Republic of China. There is deep animosity between the two nations.

Primary motivations: The welfare and progress of the family and collective group.

Game Plan

Approach through a local representative.

Personal relationships must be established before business is done. Do not assume this means you are a personal friend.

Top management should be present at the first meeting. Your company should be represented by a group of specialists at this first meeting. Do not include a lawyer.

Negotiations will be time-consuming. Expect to make many trips. Be patient.

Study *Bing Fa* strategy.

One who is powerful and successful shows his humility.

Harmony must be maintained. Do not confront or question anyone in a negative way. Never say no. Expect Taiwanese to always say yes, which might mean no.

Allow them to win something in negotiations.

Recognize and respect the social position of all you encounter. Do not expect them to require equality.

Never compliment a person directly. Never praise someone in front of his superiors. Praise the group.

Negotiations may appear cyclical rather than linear. Be prepared to discuss any subject out of sequence at any time.

Local Rules

Have written materials translated by a Taiwanese expert. Chinese characters are different in Taiwan and China.

Local contacts are extremely important. The U.S. Department of Commerce or an international bank can help.

In a group, sit according to rank, with the most important member at the center, the next important to his right, third important to his left, and so on.

Greet people with a slight bow and a light handshake. If someone asks of you, "Have you eaten?" the correct response is yes, even if you have not.

Use the person's title or *Mr.* or *Madam*, with the family name, which comes first.

Do not point with the index finger; use your whole hand. Chinese indicate themselves by pointing to their nose instead of their chest, as Americans do.

Gifts may be given on the first trip. If offered a gift, always decline three times before accepting. Avoid giving clocks or anything that cuts, like a letter opener. Avoid the colors white, black, and blue.

Evening business entertainment is very important. Dinner may be followed by entertainment at bars or clubs.

The guest samples the food first. Eat lightly, leaving a small amount of food in the bowl. There may be as many as 20 courses. If your bowl is empty, it will be refilled. Refuse food three times before accepting, so you don't look greedy.

THAILAND

Cultural Data

Culture type: Collective

Playing field: Pacific Rim

Local influences: Thais are very proud that their country has never come under foreign rule, as has much of Southeast Asia. *Thai* means *free.* Ethnic Chinese make up most of the business community. Ethnic Thais are more likely to be found in government positions. Thailand is ruled by a cooperative, yet competitive, triumvirate of bureaucracy, military, and commercial elite.

Primary motivations: The welfare and security of the collective group.

Game Plan

Approach through a local representative.

Personal relationships must be established before business is done. Do not assume this means you are a personal friend.

Top management should be present at the first meeting. Your company should be represented by a group of specialists at this first meeting. Do not include a lawyer.

Negotiations will be time-consuming. Expect to make many trips. Be patient.

Study *Bing Fa* strategy.

One who is powerful and successful shows his humility.

Harmony must be maintained. Do not confront or question anyone in a negative way. Never say no. Expect Thais to always say yes, which might mean no.

Allow them to win something in negotiations.

Recognize and respect the social position of all you encounter. Do not expect them to require equality.

Never compliment a person directly. Never praise someone in front of his superiors. Praise the group.

Negotiations may appear cyclical rather than linear. Be prepared to discuss any subject out of sequence at any time.

Local Rules

Local influence is necessary to accomplish anything. Reputable agents are not always easy to find. The Bangkok Bank and U.S. Department of Commerce can be helpful in locating a good agent. Expect a long-term relationship.

The greeting in Thailand is the *wai*, pronounced *why*. The *wai* is done by pressing the hands together as if in prayer and pointing the fingers outward. Elbows are held close to the body. Lower your head toward your hands. The higher the hands are placed, the greater the respect. Westerners may shake hands, but Thais appreciate the effort.

Titles are very important. Use titles plus a person's first name.

Be punctual.

Entertaining is done in the evening. If you are hosting, you may invite your counterpart's wife to a dinner. Certain evening entertainment is for men only. Don't bring your spouse unless specifically invited to do so.

Thais eat Continental style—almost. They use a fork and spoon instead of a fork and knife. Cut with the spoon. It is an honor to be offered the last bit of food on a serving dish. Refuse several times before accepting.

Dress well as a sign of status, but avoid wearing a black suit, which is reserved for funerals.

A smile could mean yes, hello, thank you, never mind, or excuse me.

The first meeting is to get acquainted, but you should eventually restate your business so the Thais can determine who should be at the next meeting, if there is a next meeting.

Eye contact is desirable.

Thais hesitate to ask questions. It implies that someone is a poor presenter. Public criticism is a form of violence.

If you are selling in Thailand, build in a "brokerage cost" of between 5 and 20 percent. If you are buying, you can expect to be able to negotiate the price down by about 25 percent.

Government is almost always involved in business transactions, and public officials expect "fees" even for a small service.

TUNISIA

Cultural Data

Culture type: Tribal

Playing field: Arab world

Local influences: Tunisia is the most Western of Arab nations because of its long domination by France.

Primary motivations: The status and prosperity of the family tribe.

Game Plan

Be cognizant of the nature of Islamic law and morality. It dictates behavior.

Make your first approach through a well-connected local representative.

You must be present to be of consequence. Meetings should be at your host's offices.

Relationships and trust come before business.

Business associates must stay in constant communication for the relationship to continue.

Expect endless delays in appointments. Time is not linear. Be patient and expect to take a long time completing a transaction.

Humility is highly regarded, especially in a powerful person.

Tunisians love to bargain, but do not inflate your price too much. Your first offer must be good enough to attract a Tunisian's attention.

Minimize risks and uncertainty in your proposals. Praise and appreciation for your counterpart must be verbalized often.

Maintain formality in behavior, appearance, and address.

Project a successful image.

Never refuse Tunisian hospitality. Always reciprocate.

Never reprimand or criticize directly. Failure is not directly acknowledged. Honor is very important. Deal with negatives euphemistically.

Never admit that you are a "self-made man." Lineage is important to Tunisians. You are a reflection of your entire family.

Proposals, plans, and negotiations should focus on the people issues. People are most important to Tunisians.

Local Rules

When greeting someone in business circles for the first time use the French title *Monsieur*.

At a home meal, it is important to wash your hands in front of everyone. The servant will bring a bowl and pitcher.

Hire a French interpreter.

Give your business card to the senior man first and then others.

TURKEY

Cultural Data

Culture type: Tribal

Playing field: Arab world

Local influences: Turkey forms the bridge between Europe and Asia. It is the home of the former Ottoman empire, which came to an end after World War I. It is a democratic, secular state. Turkey is not an Arab nation, but 90 percent of the population is Moslem. Eighty-five percent are ethnic Turks. Turkey is a tribal nation and, because of Islamic law, shares many customs with Arab nations.

Primary motivations: The welfare and security of the family tribe.

Game Plan

Be cognizant of the nature of Islamic law and morality. It dictates behavior.

Make your first approach through a well-connected local representative.

You must be present to be of consequence. Meetings should be at your host's offices.

Relationships and trust come before business.

Business associates must stay in constant communication for the relationship to continue.

Expect endless delays in appointments. Time is not linear. Be patient and expect to take a long time completing a transaction.

Humility is highly regarded, especially in a powerful person.

Turks love to bargain, but do not inflate your price too much. Your first offer must be good enough to attract a Turk's attention.

Minimize risks and uncertainty in your proposals. Praise and appreciation for your counterpart must be verbalized often.

Maintain formality in behavior, appearance, and address.

Project a successful image.

Never refuse hospitality. Always reciprocate.

Never reprimand or criticize directly. Failure is not directly acknowledged. Honor is very important. Deal with negatives euphemistically.

Never admit that you are a "self-made man." Lineage is important. You are a reflection of your entire family.

Proposals, plans, and negotiations should focus on the people issues. People are most important to tribal cultures.

Local Rules

Turks do not shake hands when leave-taking.

The form of address upon introduction is the surname preceded by *Bay* for men and *Bayam* for women.

Most entertaining is done in restaurants.

UKRAINE

Cultural Data

Culture type: Progressive tribal

Playing field: Central and Eastern Europe

Local influences: Until the Mongol invasion in the 13th century, Kiev was the center of the Russian empire. Thereafter, Moscow became the capital. The Cossacks originated in the Ukraine. These peasants banded together to fight the Polish Jesuits who were trying to make Ukraine a Roman Catholic country. Even today there is animosity toward the Jesuits. Ukraine asked Moscow for protection in 1654, and Russia responded by making Ukraine a serfdom. Russia finds it hard to accept losing Ukraine, a region that has been controlled by Russia for centuries and that Russians feel is truly part of Russia. Ukrainians do not.

Primary motivations: The welfare of the family group and national self-determination.

Game Plan

Approach with a personal reference or through a local agent.

First meeting should be at your host's offices.

Trust must be established before you will be accepted.

Participate in the Ukrainian brand of conformity and modesty. Do not flaunt affluence.

Do not entertain lavishly.

Negotiate a win-win outcome.

Sharing is important. Gift giving is common and should be reciprocated.

Presentations should stress minimizing risks.

Respect age. Seniority comes with age. However, be aware that the younger generation has become more entrepreneurial since the demise of the communist system.

Local Rules

Ukrainians are independent thinkers, who are capable of both objective analysis and subjective decision making. Their emotions often take precedence over logic.

They do not have a strong central government at this time, and the Orthodox Church is providing a focal point for the progressive tribal culture.

Beware of both yes and no during decision making. Both are used tactically, either to stall talks until more information has arrived or to keep you talking when you seem to be losing interest. Nothing is certain until a contract is signed.

Negotiations may become emotional. Play hardball.

Avoid compromises. They make you appear weak. Ukrainians are schooled in business the same as Russians are. See the previous notes on Russia.

European manners are used.

Ukrainians are generally more easygoing than Russians. Otherwise, many of the business and social customs are similar.

URUGUAY

Cultural Data

Culture type: Tribal

Playing field: Latin America

Local influences: Uruguay is the most secular of the Latin American countries. The population is 88 percent European, mostly—Spanish and Italian.

Primary motivations: The status, power, and prosperity of the family group.

Game Plan

Establish contact through a well-regarded local agent.

The first meeting should be on your host's turf.

Send the seniormost person from your company, along with one or two subordinates.

Plan on using an interpreter. Translate materials into Latin American Spanish.

Always address a Latino formally, using his title and family name (next-to-last name).

Expect to spend time establishing a relationship. Don't press toward a business discussion until your counterpart offers an opening.

Maintain formality in dress, posture, and speech until he relaxes the interaction.

Your image is important in communicating your own status.

Don't back away if your counterpart chooses to stand close during conversation.

Be prepared to make concessions, but only after appropriate resistance. Do not appear to negotiate these concessions. Latinos like zero-sum games.

Minimize risks in any proposal.

As an American, humble yourself. Do not assume you hold the most power because you are from the United States.

Entertain at the best restaurants.

Eat Continental style.

Once a relationship has been established, your company should not change the U.S. contact person, or else the process will have to begin again. Latinos trust people, not companies.

Local Rules

Uruguayans have a reputation for being pessimistic and opinionated.

There are more professional women than men in Uruguay, yet still men are dominant and women's rights are restricted.

A little known fact: At the time Uruguay was under military rule, the country's economic advisers trained under Milton Friedman at the University of Chicago. In the mind of Uruguayans, this financial procedure was unsuccessful. If you attended the University of Chicago it would be wise not to disclose that fact.

It is common to be invited back to someone's home for coffee after dinner in a restaurant. Don't stay very long.

VENEZUELA

Cultural Data

Culture type: Tribal
Playing field: Latin America
Local influences: The population is 70 percent mestizo, along with Spanish, Italian, Portuguese, Arab, German, African, and Indian making up the balance.
Primary motivations: The power, status, and prosperity of the family group.

Game Plan

Establish contact through a well-regarded local agent.

The first meeting should be on your host's turf.

Send the seniormost person from your company, along with one or two subordinates.

Plan on using an interpreter. Translate materials into Latin American Spanish.

Always address a Latino formally, using his title and family name (next-to-last name).

Expect to spend time establishing a relationship. Don't press toward a business discussion until your counterpart offers an opening.

Maintain formality in dress, posture, and speech until he relaxes the interaction.

Your image is important in communicating your own status.

Don't back away if your counterpart chooses to stand close during conversation.

Be prepared to make concessions, but only after appropriate resistance. Do not appear to negotiate these concessions. Latinos like zero-sum games.

Minimize risks in any proposal.

As an American, humble yourself. Do not assume you hold the most power because you are from the United States.

Entertain at the best restaurants.

Eat Continental style.

Once a relationship has been established, your company should not change the U.S. contact person, or else the process will have to begin again. Latinos trust people, not companies.

Local Rules

A businesswoman going out at night with a businessman will be misconstrued.
Announce your full name when shaking hands.
Businesswomen should not give gifts to their male counterparts.

VIETNAM

Cultural Data

Culture type: Collective
Playing field: Pacific Rim
Local influences: One of the misconceptions about Vietnamese is that they hate Americans. This is not so. Vietnamese are now eager to become players in the international marketplace. They encourage American partnerships.
Primary motivations: The prosperity and security of the collective group.

Game Plan

Approach through a local representative.

Personal relationships must be established before business is done. Do not assume this means you are a personal friend.

Top management should be present at the first meeting. Your company should be represented by a group of specialists at this first meeting. Do not include a lawyer.

Negotiations will be time-consuming. Expect to make many trips. Be patient.

Study *Bing Fa* strategy.

One who is powerful and successful shows his humility.

Harmony must be maintained. Do not confront or question anyone in a negative way. Never say no. Expect Vietnamese to always say yes, which might mean no.

Allow them to win something in negotiations.

Recognize and respect the social position of all you encounter. Do not expect them to require equality.

Never compliment a person directly. Never praise someone in front of his superiors. Praise the group.

Negotiations may appear cyclical rather than linear. Be prepared to discuss any subject out of sequence at any time.

Local Rules

The typical collective pattern is followed: group meetings, greeting every person at the meeting, accepting hospitality, discussing business only when the host is ready, and establishing trust and friendship before business is done.

Unlike in other parts of the world, Vietnamese should be addressed using a given name, which happens to come last in order of appearance. In other words, use the last name, which to us would be the first name.

Establishment of a business in Vietnam requires knowledge of the local ways of doing things. A local representative is very important, for it is important to make the right contacts at the beginning. Your agent can help with this.

Make your business very clear. Start with basics. Do not assume that your counterpart will fill in the blanks.

The government is socialist and very directly involved in private business. Find out who the real decision makers are. The government frequently changes policies, and what you thought was a deal might now have to be renegotiated.

Refuse hospitality three times before accepting, so you don't look greedy.

References

Axtell, R., *Do's and Taboos around the World*, Benjamin Company, Elmsford, New York, 1985.

Chesanow, N., *The World-Class Executive*, Rawson Associates, New York, 1985.

Chu, C., *The Asian Mind Game*, Rawson Associates, New York, 1991.

Copeland, L., and L. Griggs, *Going International*, Random House, New York, 1985.

De Mente, B., *How to Do Business with the Japanese*, NTC Publishing Group, Lincolnwood, IL, 1991.

De Mente, B., *Korean Etiquette and Ethics in Business*, NTC Publishing Group, Lincolnwood, IL, 1990.

Devine, E. and N. Braganti, *The Travelers' Guide to Middle Eastern and North African Customs and Manners*, St. Martin's Press, New York, 1991.

Feig, J., *A Common Core: Thais and Americans*, Intercultural Press, Yarmouth ME, 1988.

Fernandez, J., *The Diversity Advantage*, Macmillan, New York, 1993.

Foster, D., *Bargaining across Borders*, McGraw-Hill, New York, 1992.

Klinkenberg, H., *At Ease . . . Professionally*, Bonus Books, Chicago, 1992.

Kras, E., *Management in Two Cultures*, Intercultural Press, Yarmouth, ME, 1989.

Morris, D., P. Collet, P. Marsh, and M. O'Shaughnessy, *Gestures*, Stein and Day, New York, 1980.

Morrison, T., W. Conaway, and G. Borden, *Kiss, Bow, or Shake Hands*, Bob Adams, Holbrook, MA, 1994.

Nydell, M., *Understanding Arabs: A Guide for Westerners*, Intercultural Press, Yarmouth, ME, 1987.

Shames, G. and G. Glover, *World Class Service*, Intercultural Press, Yarmouth, ME, 1989.

SRI International, *Business Intelligence Program*, Menlo Park, CA, 1987.

Tyler, V. (ed.), *Culturgrams*, Brigham Young University, Provo, UT, 1994.

INDEX

Printed in the United States
35011LVS00007B/1-40